The Greek Code of Private Maritime Law

Law 5030/2023

The Greek Code of Private Maritime Law

Law 5020/2023

Daniel A. Webber & John A. O'Shea
LEX GRAECA

LEX GRAECA

The Greek Code of Private Maritime Law
Law 5020/2023

1 3 5 7 9 10 8 6 4 2

First edition published 2023

Lex Graeca
London

ISBN: 978-1-8384106-3-6

Note to Readers – Disclaimer

This publication is designed to provide an accurate and authoritative translation of the legislation covered. Appropriate diligence has been shown in preparing the translation and the translated legal provisions are as they stand on the date of publication.

It is sold on the understanding that the publisher is not engaged in providing legal or advisory/consultancy or other such professional services in general and in relation to the matters translated in particular. If legal advice or other expert assistance is required, the services of a competent professional person in the jurisdiction concerned should be sought.

Readers should also be aware more recent developments and amendments to the original Greek legislation may have occurred since the time of publication and primary sources in Greek should always be consulted in cooperation with your legal advisors to ensure that they are basing decisions on the most recent version of the legislation.

No responsibility for loss caused to any individual or organization acting on or refraining from action as a result of the translated material in this publication can be accepted by Lex Graeca or the authors.

Acknowledgments

This work would have been impossible without the generous contribution of Panagiota Voutsinou. We must also thank Dr Iliana Christodoulou-Varotsi, Dr Despina Kiltidou and Mr Nigel Ready for their insightful introductions and feedback. We hope this book proves to be a useful, practical resource for readers and another step on the long road towards producing authoritative translations of the main codes of the Greek legal system. Any errors remain our own, and we welcome any comments and feedback regarding our work.

Table of Contents

Introduction

by Dr. Iliana Christodoulou-Varotsi[1], Senior Legal Consultant & Lead Trainer

It is no exaggeration to say that a long-awaited legislative reform is not entirely complete without a translation into the language of international shipping and trade, i.e. English. If a law creates bridges that underpin transactions, translations, including unofficial translations of high quality like the one for which I have the honour to write these introductory words, clearly facilitate and disseminate the outcome. Above all, such a translation is of practical assistance to legal and other practitioners as well as to the international community of learners.

It is in this context that the recent reform of the Greek Code of Private Maritime Law, which has given rise to this translation by Daniel Webber and John O'Shea, should be acknowledged and welcomed. Learned readers may know that 'translation' originates from the Latin verb *'translatio'* which means 'carrying across'; the translation of the Code into English by Webber and O'Shea carries across a highly useful tool and places it at the disposal of English-speaking readers.

A few words about the reform first.

The Code aims to pave the way for new era in maritime law of Greece, the world's leading ship-owning country. The old Greek Code of Private Maritime Law (Law 3816/1958), which was adopted in 1958, had accomplished its mission and from a certain stage onwards was considered by many stakeholders as having fulfilled its potential. As the Code was no longer reflective of key developments in shipping nor its international legal environment, a change was needed. This long-awaited change took place in February 2023 and was the result of a long process. As noted by the Greek Minister of Maritime Affairs and Insular Policy before the Greek Parliament, "more than half of the old Code's provisions were implicitly abolished, had fallen into disuse or were reduced in scope…".

[1] Dr. Iliana Christodoulou-Varotsi is a Senior Legal Consultant & Shipping Industry Trainer with international experience as a consultant, law drafter, author, and educator. Member of the Athens Bar Association since 1995. Law drafting experience with the Republic of Cyprus. Sub-contractor of the European Commission and EMSA in specialised projects pertaining to maritime and EU law. Designing and delivery of training workshops to maritime professionals worldwide through Lloyd's Maritime Academy (Informa Connect) and DNV Maritime Academy Hellas. Visiting lecturer at ALBA Graduate Business School American College of Greece. Honorary Visiting Fellow, Institute of Maritime Law, University of Southampton. Author of five books with international publishers. 'Maîtrise' (Law), 'D.E.A.' (EU Law), and 'Doctorat' (Leventis Foundation grant) with the highest distinction awarded by the Faculty of Laws of Paris I Panthéon-Sorbonne. Post-doctoral research experience, Scandinavian Institute of Maritime Law (Propondis Foundation grant). In her approach, Dr. Christodoulou-Varotsi integrates industry best practice while placing the focus on the human element.

It should be noted that attempts to reform the Code had been made in the past but did not come to fruition. The law drafting committee worked from March 2021 onwards and the reform of the Code was achieved at the beginning of 2023. Law 5020/2023, published in the Government Gazette of the Hellenic Republic on 15 February 2023, came into effect on 1st May 2023. Certain provisions (concerning registration of specified craft) will come into force on 1st November 2023. The reform is a landmark development which deserves the attention of maritime professionals, including those with a connection to Greece or Greek shipping.

This is, after all, an ambitious undertaking. The Code seeks to ensure coherence and enhance legal certainty and transparency in the context where numerous international conventions were adopted by the Greek State and where shipping presents new features which need to be reflected with clarity in the law.

To name but a few, the new Code touches upon a plethora of topics ranging from the digitalisation of the Ship Registry and the redefinition of the concept of 'ship' to the legal position of the purchaser of a ship or the liabilities and claims for wrongful arrest. Electronic bills of lading are now recognized alongside traditional paper bills, the scope of the Hague-Visby Rules is reshaped, and the legal regime governing maritime employment is aligned with the international standard.

The obvious need to have this important text translated into English with supreme skill and dedication cannot be overestimated. The authors of the translation have shared with their readers their approach, methodology and stance on challenging translation aspects.

We should be grateful to Webber and O'Shea, who comprise the Lex Graeca publishing house, for their engagement which has resulted in this demanding output. I have no doubt that the legal community eager to access the Code in English will appreciate this laborious undertaking and will benefit greatly from using it in their day-to-day activities.

Introduction

Introduction by Despina Kiltidou[1]

Attorney at Law, DJur, LL.M., Maritime Training Instructor

As one maritime law jurist put it: "The sea connects what it divides". This phrase, which is the starting point for consolidating and internationalising maritime law, makes it clear that the translation of Greek maritime law into English is vital not only for practical reasons but also out of respect for international maritime law. Consequently, there is great value in a translation of the Greek Code of Private Maritime Law (Law 5020/2023) into English because it communicates Greek legal culture to the international shipping community and also contributes to understanding and implementation of that culture by that community. Daniel Webber and John O'Shea's initiative to translate the Code is commendable, not only because it is timely, coming shortly after the entry into force of Law 5020/2023 on 1 May 2023, but also because it faithfully translates the provisions of the law and reflects Greek maritime legal culture. The most difficult task for a translator of any legal text is to convey the legal culture of the country of origin of the text in a different language. This is a laborious task which requires a broad legal education, and here Daniel Webber and John O'Shea have managed to succinctly express in English legal relationships in the shipping sector from a country like Greece with an immense maritime tradition.

The fully overhauled Code of Private Maritime Law was changed after remaining in force for 65 years; this was an arduous task that had consistently been demanded by the Greek maritime community. In general terms, the new Code bolsters the transparency of key legal transactions relating to the legal status of ships and their operation, such as, for example, the role of shipping agent. It reflects technological developments, such as the keeping of ship registries or ship's articles in electronic format. It regulates modern forms of shipping activity, such as in the container sector, and dispels confusion about charterparties and bills of lading.

---

[1] Despina Kiltidou, attorney with rights of audience before the Court of Appeal, post-doctoral researcher at the University of Macedonia in international shipping policy and EU anti-piracy policies, lecturer at the Aristotle University of Thessaloniki in comparative maritime labour law, LL.M. in international studies at the Aristotle University of Thessaloniki, specialising in private international maritime labour law. Visiting lecturer on comparative law, maritime law and international law at various universities. Visiting lecturer teaching maritime law at the Master's in Shipping and Sea Transports: Economics and Politics programme of the University of Macedonia. Professor at the National Post Training Center for Merchant Shipping Officers (KESEN MAKEDONIAS), run by the Ministry of Shipping & Insular Policy.

A further aspect of the new Code of Private Maritime Law's contribution to maritime labour law is its full harmonisation with the International Maritime Labour Convention 2006 (MLC 2006), as in force following amendments thereto. In fact, certain provisions of the new Greek Code are more detailed than those found in the corresponding international conventions, such as in the case where the employment agreement is terminated or in the case of a seafarer's repatriation, meaning the law provides greater security for seafarers. The new definition of ship and its legislative distinction from stationary floating structure put an end to any previous doubts about the existence or otherwise of a maritime labour relationship. Moreover, the definitions of owner-operator, manager, shipping agent, operator and master clarify issues of liability in the employment relationship. Lastly, clarifications about how an employment agreement is to be entered into, what forms it can take, its mandatory content, the legislative provisions on the preliminary employment agreement already recognised in Greek case-law, and the provisions on termination of the employment agreement, such as termination without notice by the owner-operator or master, are innovative provisions which make the Greek system a safe choice of law to protect seafarers.

In short, the new Code includes innovative provisions which are in line with international law and resolve practical issues via detailed reforms, addressing topics which had remained unregulated under the previous regime. It renders the Greek legislative framework more attractive and friendly to the contracting parties, allowing for Greek law to be chosen more frequently as the applicable law and, thus, helping strengthen the Greek flag. The translation of this legislation into English promotes modern Greek shipping practice, contributes to the legislative development of maritime law in an international environment, and communicates to the international shipping community the intention of the Greek legislator to regulate shipping issues in a truly comprehensive manner.

Introduction

by Nigel Ready, Scrivener Notary, Cheeswrights LLP

The first Greek Code of Private Maritime law was promulgated in the heat of the post-war boom in the Hellenic shipping industry. Greece of course remains at the forefront of maritime nations. By its dynamic nature, the business of shipping is in constant evolution, as are the challenges it must face. The laws which regulate it must therefore adapt accordingly. In recognition of this fact, the Greek legislature has promulgated a new Code which takes into account industry changes over the intervening years, notably by extending many of its provisions to stationary floating structures. The Code also reflects developments in maritime law at an international level. Importantly, the new Code is a work of consolidation, a major example being the inclusion of provisions relating to preferred mortgages – of paramount importance to financing parties – within the Code itself.

Over 40 years ago, I was honoured to be asked by the late Theodoros V. Karatzas – one of the leading maritime and commercial lawyers of his generation – to undertake an English translation of the 1958 Code and associated legislation. The fruit of our joint endeavours was published in The Hague in 1982. That translation has proved a valuable tool of reference for legal practitioners, international maritime bodies and students of maritime law. There is therefore a clear and pressing need for a reliable translation of the new Code into the lingua franca of the shipping community.

Any translation of a legal text is fraught with difficulties; those difficulties are compounded if the source text is in a language as rich and complex as modern Greek. I therefore congratulate Daniel Webber and John O'Shea on their accomplishment in producing an English text of the new Code of Private Maritime Law so soon after its promulgation. Their conscientious and painstaking work will be welcomed by all sectors of the maritime industry worldwide.

London, June 2023

Foreword

Daniel A. Webber & John A. O'Shea

The Greek Code of Private Maritime Law

This book is a stand-alone *Lex Graeca* translation, in the sense that it does not form part of the *Quadricodex*, our series of translations of the four major codes underpinning the Greek legal system, namely the Civil Code, the Penal Code, the Code of Civil Procedure and the Code of Criminal Procedure, yet remains vastly important, given the recent upheaval of the Code of Private Maritime Law after more than 50 years. It is our sincere hope that we will also publish the translation of the Code of Public Maritime Law in the very near future.

Purpose

As is the case with other *Lex Graeca* publications, the translation of the Greek Code of Private Maritime Law aims to serve a dual purpose: to satisfy a clear and present need for English-language versions of Greek codes and legislation, on one hand, and to set a standard in terms of language, quality, accuracy and promptness for such translations, on the other. It is our intention that all further instalments in the *Lex Graeca* series continue to adhere to this standard.

The overarching aim of *Lex Graeca* publications is to clarify Greek law for an international audience. That audience is diverse, consisting of:

- legal practitioners, who might be engaged to provide legal advice to their foreign clients or explain sections of statutes;
- legal translators, who might be called upon to translate sections of the law or need a reference text for terminology and style purposes;
- businesspeople, who have already invested in Greece or are interested in doing so, as well as foreign shareholders in Greek businesses;
- academics, particularly comparative lawyers, who thus far have had little access to information in English about the Greek legal system;
- and the general public, who might be interested in reading about the way Greek laws are structured and the topics touched upon.

The more specific aim of this translation is to make available a thoroughly researched English-language translation of the new Code of Private Maritime Law, exhaustively researched and consistent in the terminology used across our existing translations of Greek codes.

In making this text available in English, another aim is to create momentum for international investors in Greece, facilitating their understanding of Greek law through plain-language translations of the latest business-related laws and the general framework of rules which apply in the country.

Background

In historical terms, the Greek Code of Private Maritime Law was first enacted in 1958 and was translated just once, by Theodoros Karatzas and Nigel P. Ready, in a hard-to-find yet very well written volume published by Martinus Nijhoff in 1982, featuring excellent explanatory introductions prefacing each section of the Code.

Upon learning that the 1958 Code was to be repealed and replaced by a new law, and having obtained a version of the bill brought before Parliament, we began our research into relevant texts and completed our translation.

A painstaking editing process ensued, lasting over a month and consisting of countless hours of back-and-forth between the translators (via video conferencing, by necessity) and consulting sessions with Greek attorneys and experts. This was followed by the translation of the latest amendments to the Code, passed in just April 2023 as part of Law 5039/2023. As will be discussed below, this amendment did not cover any of the issues identified in this Foreword.

Rather than wait for the inevitable next round of amendments, given the propensity of the Greek legislature to amend and supplement laws, the frequency at which such amendments are promulgated, and with a view to remain true to the *Lex Graeca* commitment to publishing timely translations, we decided that this round of amendments would be the last we would translate before going to press. Indeed, our aim, as soon as we learned of the upheaval of the Code, was to publish it as close as possible to the date of promulgation of the Code.

It goes without saying that, should further changes be effected to the Code of Private Maritime Law, we will be prepared to translate them and publish a second edition of this book, having comprehensively addressed the bulk of the Code.

Methodology

The translation and editing were carried out to the highest professional standards and in accordance with current standard practices, so as to ensure consistency and quality throughout the text. The translation process consisted of four stages (**Research and Compilation, Preparation of Source Text, Translation, Review**) which are outlined below:

i) Research and Compilation

The preliminary stage of our process involved three steps:

- familiarising ourselves with the terminology of maritime law in Greece and internationally;
- identifying the texts (historical and recent) on which sections of the Code were based, consisting mainly of relevant EU Regulations and Directives, international Conventions to which Greece is a signatory;
- consulting the explanatory memorandum of Law 5020/2023 amending the Code.

Having identified the relevant texts, we compiled them and leveraged their terminology in order to:

a) identify verbatim sections and, where appropriate, reproduce or at least adhere to the official English-language text;

b) ensure consistency in both the style applied and the terminology used throughout the translation;

c) identify problematic terms in the target text (TT) not only to be discussed and resolved in the context of this publication, but also to be highlighted for research purposes; and

d) identify issues with the source text (ST), examples of which will be discussed below.

As intimated below, the source text presented numerous translational issues to be overcome, given the polysemic nature of Greek legal terminology, so we relied on research into primary sources and consultations with Greek jurists, and on reference texts only on a supplementary basis.

ii) Preparation of Source Text

The second stage of our work, particularly with a view to facilitating the bilingual two-page layout of the book, consisted of identifying the proper version of the source text (i.e. compiling a version that included the very latest amendments to the Code) to use and then editing it for our purposes. This editing was a two-step process:

<u>a) Pagination</u>

This step concerned achieving a logical layout of the book while adhering to an environmentally friendly, space-saving approach. Our conclusion was to insert a page break in the text at every Part rather than every Chapter of the Code.

<u>b) Editing of original text for readability purposes</u>

Where the original text included a list under the subparagraph of an article, we opted to insert a line break in the original so as to have the items on the list one under the other rather than as parts of long, uninterrupted paragraphs, the sole purpose being to enhance readability and ease of reference. An example can be found in Article 124 of the Code, reproduced below as originally appearing in the Greek Government Gazette:

Original:

"Άρθρο 124.

Περιεχόμενο φορτωτικής

1. Η φορτωτική περιέχει: α) την ονομασία «θαλάσσια φορτωτική» ή «φορτωτική» αναφερόμενη στο κείμενο του τίτλου, β) την περιγραφή των παραληφθέντων ή φορτωθέντων πραγμάτων, γ) τον προσδιορισμό του πλοίου, δ) τον λιμένα φόρτωσης, ε) τον λιμένα προορισμού, στ) τον ναύλο και τον τρόπο καταβολής αυτού, ζ) τη χρονολογία και τον τόπο έκδοσης και η) την υπογραφή του εκδότη."

Translation:

"Article 124

Content of bill of lading

1. The bill of lading shall contain:

a) the phase "maritime bill of lading" or "bill of lading" in the text of the title;

b) a description of the goods received or loaded;

c) particulars of the ship;

d) the port of loading;

e) the port of destination;

f) the freight and manner of its payment;

g) the time and date of issue; and

h) the signature of the issuer."

A final minor step was identifying any typographical or grammatical errors in the source text, to be resolved through the use of explicitation, as explained in the Issues section below.

iii) Translation

The translation process was carried out according to the exacting requirements and specifications of modern-day professional translation in terms of style and terminology. In our work, we made use of the following standard translation strategies:

a) Explicitation

A major issue in the field of legal translation is explicitation, i.e. the introduction of additional information to convey meaning inherent in a source-text word or phrase. At first glance, this might seem an obvious strategy when called upon to translate a text. However, the demands of legal translation in terms of conciseness, accuracy and, where possible, one-for-one equivalence, particularly in the case of a comparativist approach, might make explicitation a less likely candidate. Nevertheless, we have opted to employ explicitation where we felt it necessary and have signified such instances with the use of square brackets in order to provide the additional information we felt was necessary for a fuller understanding of the law, particularly by laypeople having to grasp the intricacies of a legal system and language that are foreign to them.

Examples include:

Article 53(3) (emphasis our own)

> *"3. Ο διορισμός, η παραίτηση ή η ανάκληση του διαχειριστή προβάλλονται στους τρίτους μόνον εφόσον σημειωθούν στη* ***μερίδα του πλοίου****."*

Our translation (emphasis our own):

> "3. The appointment, resignation or removal of the manager shall be effective vis-à-vis third parties solely if recorded in the ship's **[ship registry] account**."

Article 58 (emphasis our own):

> *"Για τις διαφορές τις σχετικές με τη συμπλοιοκτησία αρμόδιο είναι και το δικαστήριο του λιμένα νηολόγησης ή* ***καταχώρισης του πλοίου.****"*

Our translation (emphasis our own):

> "The court of the port where the ship was registered or entered **[in the special public register of small ships]** shall also have jurisdiction over disputes concerning the joint ship ownership."

In both the examples above, explicitation was chosen in order to clarify a term in the source text but in a way that would not drastically alter the form and content of the original provision.

Other issues which we considered as part of the overall translation strategy are:

b) Gender-neutral language

Where the Greek text opted for the masculine as the default, we opted for several choices that are available to us and are widely established[1] for translation professionals, with a view to going beyond mere neutrality

1 https://www.europarl.europa.eu/cmsdata/151780/GNL_Guidelines_EN.pdf

and rendering sex and gender irrelevant as a consideration[2]:

- A gender-neutral term, e.g.:

  Ναυτικός

  Seafarer

- A singular noun with plural pronouns, e.g. Article 19(4) (emphasis our own):

  "4. Αν δεν διοριστεί αντίκλητος ή η εξουσία ***του*** *παύσει για οποιαδήποτε αιτία, οι σχετικές με την υποθήκη επιδόσεις μπορούν να γίνουν είτε στον εισαγγελέα πρωτοδικών, στην περιφέρεια του οποίου τηρείται το βιβλίο υποθηκών, είτε στον νηολόγο."*

  "4. If a process agent is not appointed or if **their** powers cease to apply for any reason, service of documents concerning the mortgage may be effected either on the court of first instance public prosecutor in whose district the mortgage register is kept or on the ship registrar."

- A plural noun where the meaning in the ST is intentionally abstract and is not referring to a single specific individual, e.g. Article 165(1) (emphasis our own):

  "1. Η σύμβαση ναυτολόγησης, οι όροι εργασίας και τα δικαιώματα του ***ναυτικού*** *ρυθμίζονται από τις συλλογικές συμβάσεις ναυτικής εργασίας που έχουν εφαρμογή [...]"*

  "1. The employment agreement, the terms of employment and rights of **seafarers** shall be regulated by the maritime labour collective bargaining agreements in effect [...]"

c) Easified language

This aspect of the task we set ourselves was one of the hardest and most time-consuming to address during both the translation and the editing of the Code. Our objective was to publish a comprehensively researched text that offers, to the greatest extent possible, equivalence of terms used in the Greek legal system – belonging to the civil law family – and terms established in the English-speaking legal world – mostly belonging to the common law family. The conundrum facing any translator working in this pair of languages (and legal systems) is immediately apparent.

Nevertheless, in our approach towards using easified language, we opted to minimise the use of Latin legal terms, employing them only where we deemed it necessary, and to use terms more immediately accessible and understandable to a layperson rather than a jurist.

2 Xanthaki, Helen (2020), Gender inclusive legislative drafting in English: A drafter's response to Emily Grabham, *feminists@law*, Vol 10, No 2 (2020), available at: https://journals.kent.ac.uk/index.php/feministsatlaw/article/view/952/1842

The conventions we followed to achieve an easified-language result by and large adhered to common sense, as we understand it, and to the rules prescribed by the European Commission[3], with a view not to simplify or radically reformulate the ST, but to ensure that the TT is clear and comprehensible, reflecting the actual wording and intention of the ST and also being able to be read as a standalone text free from any of the hallmarks of mediocre translations (stunted syntax, excessive adherence to the structure of the original sentence, etc., all of which are hallmarks of the translations of Greek legislation to date).

In more concrete terms, the choices we made concerned:

Syntax:

- Changing word order to reflect what is normal in English-language texts, i.e. Subject-Verb-Object syntax where possible, e.g. Article 235(1):

  > *"[...] Ειδική έκθεση συντάσσεται από τον γραμματέα κάτω από το κείμενο της δήλωσης"*

  Our translation:

  > "[...] The registrar shall prepare a special report at the end of the text of the declaration"

- Changing passive-voice syntax to active-voice where advisable, e.g. in Article 278(1):

  > *"1. Για την καταχώριση στο νηολόγιο κατακυρωτικής έκθεσης ή ισοδύναμου προς αυτή τίτλου μετά από πλειστηριασμό στην αλλοδαπή πλοίου με ελληνική σημαία, υποβάλλονται από τον αποκτώντα ή τον κύριο στην αρμόδια λιμενική αρχή τα παρακάτω έγγραφα:"*

  Our translation:

  > "1. In order to register an award report or title equivalent thereto in the ship registry after a ship flying the Greek flag has been auctioned abroad, the acquirer or owner shall submit the following documents to the competent port authority:"

Given the propensity of Greek legislators to cite specific subparagraphs (or sentences) within Articles of Laws, we have endeavoured not to join or split sentences in our translation, and have faithfully observed and reproduced the paragraph structure of the source text.

3 How to Write Clearly, https://op.europa.eu/en/publication-detail/-/publication/c2dab20c-0414-408d-87b5-dd3c6e5dd9a5

<u>Vocabulary:</u>

When in doubt and presented with a multitude of terminological choices, we opted for the most readily understandable term. An indicative and by no means exhaustive list is presented below, and should be understood as conventions on our part for the sake of consistency across all relevant texts, with a view to easified language and clarity:

- we have rendered the term *"πλοίο"* as "ship" rather than "vessel", in keeping with the latest terminology used in international Conventions and EU legislation;
- given the distinctions drawn between and definitions provided in the source text for the terms *"κύριος", "πλοιοκτήτης"* and *"εφοπλιστής"*, we rendered each term as "owner", "owner-operator" and "operator", respectively;
- given the absence of an established term for *"στατικό ναυπήγημα"*, we decided to use an English term that reflects both the etymology and utility of the Greek term, rendering it as "stationary floating structure";
- the term *"νηολόγιο"* has been rendered as "ship registry", so as to distinguish it from the general registers and books kept by authorities;
- as established in other *Lex Graeca* publications, the terms *"οριστική / τελεσίδικη / αμετάκλητη απόφαση"* have been rendered as "final / *de jure* non-appealable / irrevocable judgment", respectively;
- the term *"θαλάσσιος κίνδυνος"* has been rendered as "peril of the sea" when concerning perils at sea in general (e.g., in Article 211) and as "marine risk" in the context of maritime insurance (e.g., in Article 33);
- the term *"εφοδιασμός"* and *"εφόδια"* have been rendered as "stocking" and "stocks" rather than "victualling", a term we would not consider most laypersons to be familiar with (e.g., in Article 101);
- the term *"ναύλωση-πλαίσιο"* has been rendered as "contract of affreightment", in accordance with the Explanatory Memorandum of Law 5020/2023.

Similar to the Civil Code and other statutes, we are pleased to report that the new Code of Private Maritime Law often provides definitions as words included in brackets at the end of sentences, as seen, for example, in Articles 18(1), 36(1), 51(1), etc.

iv) Review

The final (but by no means shortest) step in our process was to review the translation, discuss and resolve any issues that arose and highlight any problems we considered worthy of inclusion in the **Issues** section of this Foreword.

This stage was particularly time-consuming, consisting of several passes of revisions and corrections, and involved reaching out to experts to explicate terms and clarify legal procedure. Considering the effort involved, we are exceptionally satisfied with the final result and are confident in its quality and utility for readers.

Issues

In previous *Lex Graeca* publications, we categorised the issues we identified into broad categories and provided indicative examples of each problem. Given the number of issues identified in the Code of Private Maritime Law, we decided to highlight characteristic examples of each category of issue that we faced in our efforts, with the hope that they are resolved in future amendments and drive further research into the Greek text. As noted above, Law 5039/2023 only made amendments concerning substantive law to the Code and covered none of the issues we have identified below.

The seven specific categories into which we classified each issue are as follows:

a) **Typographic / Capitalisation / Citation errors - conventions**
b) **Vague / Obscure language**
c) **Problematic syntax / Odd word choices**
d) **Acronyms & official translations and names of entities**
e) **Polysemic terms/ambiguous language**
f) **Elegant variation - Euphemisms**
g) **Discrepancy between text and Article headings**

a) Typographic / Capitalisation / Citation / Other errors - conventions

i) Typographic errors - conventions

One error found in the text of Law 5020/2023 was a missing Greek numeral in the list contained in Article 254:

> *"[...] (ζ) τις τυχόν εξαιρέσεις κάλυψης,*
>
> *(η) το ασφάλιστρο,*
>
> *(ι) το όνομα, την εθνικότητα, τον λιμένα νηολόγησης, και τον αριθμό νηολογίου του πλοίου, καθώς και τον αριθμό του Διεθνούς Ναυτιλιακού Οργανισμού που φέρει το πλοίο."*

As every speaker of the Greek language is or ought to be aware, the correct numbering using Greek numerals from 1 to 10 is α - β - γ - δ - ε - στ - ζ - η - θ - ι. However, as evident in the text above, the list skips θ entirely. We have ignored the error in the translation and produced a correctly numbered list:

> "[...] (g) any exclusions from coverage;
>
> (h) the premium;
>
> (i) the name, nationality, port of registry and ship registry number, as well as the ship's IMO number."

ii) Capitalisation errors

Greek legal texts, perhaps under the influence of the German language, are notorious for capitalising the initial letters of certain terms. While it is standard policy to capitalise terms only after having given a definition (as is often the case in contracts, with a list of terms provided at the beginning of the document to be used in capitalised form thereafter for purposes of specification and disambiguation), Greek legislation often employs unnecessary and arbitrary capitalisation.

However, we are pleased to report that, contrary to past laws, we found no capitalisation errors or inconsistencies in the text of Law 5020/2023.

iii) Citation errors - conventions

The Greek legislative citation system is rather unique in the way reference is made to other laws, down to specific *"εδάφια"* (subparagraphs, indents or simply sentences) of articles. While Law 5020/2023 remains true to this system and, on the whole, adheres to it well, we have identified several cases of citation error.

One manifest error identified is in Article 87(2), where reference is made to the National Customs Code. However, the Law cited in the source text is incorrect (emphasis our own):

> *"2. Σε κάθε περίπτωση τηρούνται οι όροι των ισχυουσών διεθνών συμβάσεων σε σχέση με τη μεταφορά επικίνδυνων φορτίων και οι οικείες διατάξεις του Εθνικού Τελωνειακού Κώδικα (ν.* ***2961****/2001, Α' 265)."*

Our translation (emphasis our own):

> "2. In all cases, the terms of international treaties and conventions in force on the carriage of dangerous goods and the relevant provisions of the National Customs Code (Law **[2960]/**2001, Government Gazette, Series I, Issue 265) shall be complied with."

As seen above, we have employed explicitation brackets to provide the correct number of the Law, and hope that this error will be remedied in the future.

Another such error was found in Article 159(1) (emphasis our own):

> *"[...] περιέχονται στο* ***άρθρο 3*** *του ν. 4195/2013 [...]"*

Having consulted the Law in question, which ratified the Protocol to the Athens Convention, it became immediately apparent that it contains no "Article 3", but a "Third Article". While this might, at first blush, seem overly punctilious, the Greek legislative drafting system does distinguish between the two, with articles with ordinal numbers (sole, first, second, etc.) usually being broad articles that contain numbered articles (Article 1, Article 2, etc.). Therefore, we consider this an inconsistency worth highlighting and have accordingly used explicitation brackets to translate this section as follows (emphasis our own):

> "[...] contained in the **[third Article]** of Law 4195/2013 [...]"

Further errors were identified in the way international Conventions and other texts were cited in the text. Normally, the entire title of the Convention is used in the Code, followed by a short title used thereinafter. Indeed, in Article 69(1), we see such an example:

> *"1. Η ευθύνη για ζημίες ρύπανσης από πετρέλαιο διέπεται αποκλειστικά από τη Διεθνή Σύμβαση του 1992 αναφορικά με την αστική ευθύνη για ζημίες ρύπανσης από πετρέλαιο, όπως κυρώθηκε με το π.δ. 197/1995 (Α' 106) και εκάστοτε ισχύει στην Ελλάδα (Διεθνής Σύμβαση ευθύνης για ρύπανση από πετρέλαιο)."*

Our translation reflects this convention:

> "1. Liability for oil pollution damage shall be governed exclusively by the 1992 International Convention on Civil Liability for Oil Pollution Damage, ratified by Presidential Decree 197/1995 (Government Gazette, Series I, Issue 106) and as in force in Greece from time to time (International Convention on Liability for Oil Pollution Damage)."

Curiously, in Article 70(1), where the same convention is employed, the short name given omits any reference to damage (emphasis our own):

> *"1. Η ευθύνη για ζημίες ρύπανσης από πετρέλαιο κίνησης διέπεται αποκλειστικά από τη Διεθνή Σύμβαση του 2001 αναφορικά με την αστική ευθύνη για* ***ζημίες*** *ρύπανσης από πετρέλαιο κίνησης, όπως κυρώθηκε με τον ν. 3393/2005 (Α' 242) και εκάστοτε ισχύει στην Ελλάδα* ***(Διεθνής Σύμβαση ευθύνης για πετρέλαιο κίνησης)****."*

Moreover, the Convention in question, as ratified by the aforesaid Law 3393/2005, is referred to therein as the *"Διεθνής Σύμβαση για την αστική ευθύνη για ζημία ρύπανσης από πετρέλαιο κίνησης"*. While ultimately of lesser importance, the inconsistency between *"ζημία"* in Law 3393/2005 and *"ζημίες"* in Law 5020/2023 at hand is striking.

Another issue encountered several times concerned citation of the Hague-Visby Rules. While their Articles feature Roman numerals (I, II, III, etc.), the Greek text uses Arabic numerals (1, 2, 3, etc.) to refer to the Rules. This inconsistency is compounded by the way subsequently inserted Articles of the Rules are cited in the Code at hand, as is the case in Article 85(1) (emphasis our own):

> *"1. Ο εκναυλωτής ευθύνεται απέναντι στον ναυλωτή ή στον δικαιούχο του φορτίου για κάθε ζημία από απώλεια ή βλάβη στο μεταφερόμενο φορτίο ή σε σχέση με αυτό, κατά τα* ***άρθρα 3, 4, 4β και 6*** *των Κανόνων Χάγης-Βίσμπυ, όπως εκάστοτε ισχύουν."*

Apart from the use of Arabic numerals, the reference to *"[άρθρο] 4β"* is misleading, as, in accordance with the Greek system of numbering articles, one would expect that an article inserted after Article 4 would be Article 4A, and that would be followed by Article 4B. However, upon consulting the Hague-Visby Rules, we see that there is only Article IV, which is followed by Article IV bis. It stands to reason that a Greek reader would expect Article IV bis to be translated as 4A in a Greek text.

The same issue arises in Article 284(3) (emphasis our own):

> *"[...] Κατά τα λοιπά ισχύουν οι παρ. 6 και* ***6β*** του άρθρου 3 των Κανόνων Χάγης-Βίσμπυ, όπως εκάστοτε ισχύουν στην Ελλάδα."

Article III of the Hague-Visby Rules has paragraphs 6 and 6 bis, therefore the citation style used is surprising.

One final citation issue identified was one of citation which was missing altogether, as seen in Article 158(2), where reference is made to IMO Guildelines (emphasis our own):

> *"2. Ειδικώς για τους κινδύνους που αναφέρονται στο άρθρο 2.2. των* ***Κατευθυντήριων Γραμμών*** *του Διεθνούς Ναυτιλιακού Οργανισμού, ισχύουν τα προβλεπόμενα στις ως άνω Κατευθυντήριες Γραμμές όρια ευθύνης [...]"*

There is no indication of which specific guidelines are being referred to. We had to consult the law cited in order to render the above text as follows using explicitation brackets in our translation (emphasis our own):

> "2. With specific regard to the risks referred to in Article 2.2 of the IMO Guidelines **[for the Implementation of the Athens Convention]**, the limits of liability laid down in the aforesaid Guidelines shall apply [...]"

iv) Other errors

This category includes grammatical errors, such as the one seen at the end of Article 240(1) (emphasis our own):

> *"Η παρ. 3 του άρθρου 245* ***εφαρμόζονται*** *αναλόγως."*

The third-person plural is used for a singular noun, whereas the correct verb should have been *"εφαρμόζεται"*. We have translated this sentence as follows:

> "Article 245(3) shall apply *mutatis mutandis*."

Another error was found in Article 288(3), which contains a six-item list. At the end of the third item of this list, the word *"και"* ("and") is used (emphasis our own):

> *"γ) τα μέσα απόδειξης της παράδοσης του αρχείου στον κομιστή και της ιδιότητας του τελευταίου* ***και****"*

This word is normally inserted at the end of the penultimate item of any list in order to indicate that the subsequent item is the final one. We consider this an error and have thus not reproduced the word in our translation:

> "c) the means of proving delivery of the file to the bearer and the capacity of the latter;"

Similarly, the word "και" is missing altogether from the penultimate item of the list contained in Article 292:

> *"(ζ) Η παρ. 2 του άρθρου 16 του ν. 4504/2017 (Α' 184) περί τροποποιήσεων των ορίων αστικής ευθύνης που προβλέπονται στο άρθρο 6 της Διεθνούς Σύμβασης για τον περιορισμό της ευθύνης για ναυτικές απαιτήσεις.*
>
> *(η) Η παρ. 3 του άρθρου 3 του ν. 2844/2000 (Α' 220), περί ενεχύρου χωρίς παράδοση και δημοσιότητας συμβάσεων παροχής ασφάλειας επί κινητών."*

We have included it in explicitation brackets in our translation (emphasis our own):

> "(g) Article 16(2) of Law 4504/2017 (Government Gazette, Series I, Issue 184) amending the limits of civil liability provided for in Article 6 of the International Convention on Limitation of Liability for Maritime Claims; **[and]**
>
> (h) Article 3(3) of Law 2844/2000 (Government Gazette, Series I, Issue 220) on pledges without delivery [of the movable] and the disclosure of agreements for the provision of security concerning movables."

One final issue identified was in Article 289, which amends Law 1665/1986. At the end of the Article, the text makes reference to the *"[Υπουργός] Ναυτιλίας και Αιγαίου"*, which we have rendered as the Minister of Shipping and the Aegean. While it is understood that the titles of Greek ministries (and, therefore, ministers) change frequently, the text curiously employs the old title of the Ministry (emphasis our own):

> *"Με κοινή απόφαση των Υπουργών Οικονομικών, Ανάπτυξης και Ανταγωνιστικότητας και* ***Ναυτιλίας και Αιγαίου*** *καθορίζονται οι ειδικοί όροι που ρυθμίζουν τη χρηματοδοτική μίσθωση ως προς τα ιδιωτικά και επαγγελματικά πλοία αναψυχής"*

We are not aware of any rule under which Greek legislators are bound to use the old titles of Ministries when amending older laws. In fact, the opposite is frequently the case, with older laws containing references to Ministries bearing titles that were established decades after each such law was enacted. Nevertheless, we have decided to translate the text as is, without changing the title to the present-day one used throughout the Code, i.e. "Minister of Maritime Affairs and Insular Policy":

> "A joint decision of the Minister of Finance, Development and Competitiveness and the Minister of Shipping and the Aegean shall lay down the specific conditions regulating financial leasing in respect of private and professional pleasure craft."

b) Vague / Obscure language

The richness of the modern Greek language belies the many pitfalls and shortcomings awaiting the unseasoned translator. The Code of Private Maritime Law features numerous examples of vague language and obscure terminology not encountered elsewhere that required extensive discussions with Greek legal practitioners to help us threefold by explaining the term, helping us understand what the actual situation in a court of law would be, and enabling us to identify the best candidate term for translation. A few examples are given below to highlight such issues:

- In Article 114, we encountered the term *"προσβολές"* in the following context:

  Original text (emphasis our own):

  > *"Ο ναυλωτής γυμνού πλοίου επιδεικνύει κάθε επιμέλεια για την προστασία των δικαιωμάτων του εκναυλωτή από προσβολές τρίτων."*

  Our translation (emphasis our own):

  > *"The bareboat charterer shall exercise all due diligence to protect the rights of the shipowner from being **infringed** by third parties."*

  Upon reading the text and encountering such a vague term, the most reasonable question a reader would have would be what these *"προσβολές"* (a polysemic Greek term with renderings ranging from "insult" to "violation") might entail. We decided to resolve this issue by using a verb rather than a noun and relying on "infringe" as the broadest such verb concerning any violation of rights.

- The heading of Article 281 makes reference to *"ενιαύσια"*, a rather antiquated adjective meaning "with a duration of one year". Indeed, the very first sentence of the Article uses the term most Greek-speakers would be familiar with to denote the same meaning:

  > *"Άρθρο 281*
  >
  > ***Ενιαύσια** παραγραφή*
  >
  > *Σε **ετήσια** παραγραφή υπόκεινται [...]"*

  We have rendered both adjectives as follows:

  > "Article 281
  >
  > One-year time-barring
  >
  > The following shall become time-barred after one year [...]"

- As a final example, Article 169(2) also employs a rather antiquated term, i.e. *"ναυλοχία"* ("anchorage") (emphasis our own):

  > *"2. Ο πλοιοκτήτης υποχρεούται να καταβάλει στον ναυτικό τις δαπάνες μετακίνησής του στον λιμένα* ***ναυλοχίας*** *του πλοίου και παραμονής σε αυτόν, καθώς και τον αναλογούντα πλήρη μισθό για το χρονικό διάστημα από τη σύναψη του προσυμφώνου μέχρι την υπογραφή της σύμβασης ναυτολόγησης."*

  We are confident that our rendering is accurate and are highlighting this odd word choice for the sake of completeness.

c) Problematic syntax / Odd word choices

The Code of Private Maritime Law is no exception to the odd and esoteric language often found in Greek statutes. Certain cases which we had to discuss both among ourselves and with legal practitioners in order to resolve are presented below as an example of our methodology when such issues often arose:

- Article 69 (emphasis our own):

  > *"1. Η ευθύνη για ζημίες ρύπανσης από πετρέλαιο διέπεται αποκλειστικά από τη Διεθνή Σύμβαση του 1992 αναφορικά με την αστική ευθύνη για ζημίες ρύπανσης από πετρέλαιο,* ***όπως κυρώθηκε*** *με το π.δ. 197/1995 (Α' 106)* ***και εκάστοτε ισχύει στην Ελλάδα*** *(Διεθνής Σύμβαση ευθύνης για ρύπανση από πετρέλαιο).*

  While this wording is used in Greek legislation in numerous cases, a more correct version is used with much greater frequency: *"[...] που κυρώθηκε [...] και όπως ισχύει [...]"*, which is the rendering we have used in our translation whenever this issue arose (emphasis our own):

  > "1. Liability for oil pollution damage shall be governed exclusively by the 1992 International Convention on Civil Liability for Oil Pollution Damage, **ratified** by Presidential Decree 197/1995 (Government Gazette, Series I, Issue 106) **and as in force in Greece from time to time** (International Convention on Liability for Oil Pollution Damage)."

- Article 76(3) (emphasis our own):

  > *"3. Σε περίπτωση μη καταβολής του ναύλου από τον ναυλωτή, ο εκναυλωτής ειδοποιεί τον υποναυλωτή για την ύπαρξη και το ύψος της απαίτησής του κατά του ναυλωτή και τον καλεί να καταβάλει σε* ***αυτόν*** *τον υποναύλο. [...]"*

  Our translation (emphasis our own):

  > "3. Where the charterer fails to pay the freight, the shipowner shall notify the sub-charterer of the existence and amount of its claim against the charterer and call upon the sub-charterer to pay the sub-freight **to the shipowner**. [...]"

We considered the use of the pronoun *"αυτόν"* ("him") quite vague, especially considering that there are three parties in the case in question, i.e. the charterer, the sub-charterer, and the shipowner. We therefore chose not to use a pronoun in our translation but to refer to the most likely candidate among the three involved.

- Article 86(4) (emphasis our own):

  *"[...] **Έπειτα** από τη διενέργεια του πλειστηριασμού ακολουθεί διαδικασία αναγγελιών και κατάταξης."*

  However, Article 140(3) (emphasis our own):

  *"[...] **Μετά από** τη διενέργεια του πλειστηριασμού ακολουθεί διαδικασία αναγγελιών και κατάταξης."*

  Similarly, Article 145(3) (emphasis our own):

  *"[...] **Μετά** τη διενέργεια του πλειστηριασμού ακολουθεί διαδικασία αναγγελιών και κατάταξης."*

  While the inconsistency is noteworthy, the meaning obviously remains the same, and has been rendered as such in all cases (emphasis our own):

  "**After** the auction has been completed, the procedure for the lodgement and ranking [of claims] shall take place."

- Similarly, Article 199(2) (emphasis our own):

  *"2. Το παρόν κεφάλαιο εφαρμόζεται πάντοτε όταν όλα τα εμπλεκόμενα πλοία φέρουν την ελληνική σημαία, ανεξαρτήτως αν **τα περιστατικά του άρθρου 201** έλαβαν χώρα στα ελληνικά χωρικά ή στα διεθνή ύδατα."*

  However, Article 200(2)(c) (emphasis our own):

  *"γ) αν **τα γεγονότα του άρθρου 201** συνέβησαν στα ελληνικά χωρικά ύδατα"*

  Again, despite the inconsistency, the meaning remains the same, and has been rendered as such in both cases:

  "[...] the incidents referred to in Article 201 [...]"

- An inconsistency in use of prepositions was identified in Article 239(3) (emphasis our own):

  *"3. Ανακοπή κατά της απόφασης αυτής επιτρέπεται **σε** όποιον έχει έννομο συμφέρον, μέσα σε προθεσμία δεκαπέντε (15) ημερών από την κοινοποίησή της στο πρόσωπο που συνέστησε το κεφάλαιο και στον Υπουργό Ναυτιλίας και Νησιωτικής Πολιτικής αντίστοιχα ή από την ανάρτησή της στον ιστότοπο της παρ. 2, **για** κάθε άλλο πρόσωπο [...]"*

We would have expected to see the same preposition used in both cases, and have rendered this sentence as

such (emphasis our own):

> "3. An opposition may be filed against this judgment **by** any person with a legitimate interest, within a deadline of 15 days from the date the judgment was notified to the person who constituted the fund and to the Minister of Maritime Affairs and Insular Policy, respectively, or **by** any other person from the time the judgment was uploaded to the website referred to in paragraph 2 [...]"

- Article 275(4) employs the hard-to-translate word *"εικοσιτετράωρο"* ("24-hour period") (emphasis our own):

> *"[...] Η απαγόρευση απόπλου αίρεται αυτοδίκαια αν δεν επιβληθεί από τον επισπεύδοντα δανειστή αναγκαστική κατάσχεση του πλοίου και δεν επιδοθεί στον λιμενάρχη έως την παρέλευση του πέμπτου (5ου)* ***εικοσιτετραώρου*** *από την επίδοση της επιταγής."*

While some might argue that common sense dictates that this simply means "day", we believe the Greek legislator wished to be specific (e.g., in cases where detention is imposed in the evening) and chose the words used carefully. Therefore, we decided to reflect this choice in our translation (emphasis our own):

> "[...] The detention shall be automatically lifted if it is not imposed by the creditor expediting compulsory arrest of the ship and [the order for enforcement] is not served on the harbour master by the elapse of the 5th **24-hour period** from the date the order was served."

- One final example identified occurs in Article 284, where reference is made to the time-barring periods provided for in the Civil Code:

> *"1. Αν δεν ορίζεται διαφορετικά στον παρόντα, η παραγραφή των αξιώσεων των άρθρων 281 και 282 αρχίζει μόλις λήξει το έτος, μέσα στο οποίο συμπίπτει η έναρξή της σύμφωνα με τα άρθρα 251 και 252 του Αστικού Κώδικα."*

What we considered missing from the Greek text and chose to render differently is the hypothetical involved, i.e. that year during which time-barring would have commenced in accordance with the Civil Code were it not for the Code at hand:

> "1. Unless otherwise provided for in this Code, the time-barring period for the claims referred to in Articles 281 and 282 shall commence at the end of the year during which it would have commenced in accordance with Articles 251 and 252 of the Civil Code."

d) Acronyms, official translations and names of entities

Whenever we encountered acronyms, e.g., *"ΦΕΚ"* (Government Gazette Issue) etc., we chose not to use existing or create new acronyms in English, but rather to type out the full translation of the term being abbreviated, both in order to save readers from having to consult a table of abbreviations and acronyms and for reasons of clarity. In any event, it should be noted that the number of acronyms used in the Code of Private Maritime Law is rather low.

The only issue we identified in this category arose in Article 166(3) (emphasis our own):

> *"3. Η σύμβαση ναυτολόγησης καταχωρίζεται στο ναυτολόγιο του πλοίου. Η καταχώριση θεωρείται από τη λιμενική ή προξενική αρχή ή από τη* ***Διεύθυνση Ναυτικής Εργασίας*** *του Υπουργείου Ναυτιλίας και Νησιωτικής Πολιτικής."*

We could find no official name for the Directorate in question since, as is frequently and lamentably the case, the English-language version of the Ministry website is extremely sparse and features no organisation chart for us to consult. However, we did find the term "Seafarers' Labour Directorate" in several Hellenic Coast Guard (HCG) documents online, including the HCG website, and chose to use that rendering (emphasis our own):

> "3. The employment agreement shall be recorded in the crew list of the ship. The entry shall be certified by the port or consular authority or the **Seafarers' Labour Directorate** of the Ministry of Maritime Affairs and Insular Policy."

e) Polysemic terms/ambiguous language

Perhaps the most egregious problem facing translators from Greek into English is the plethora of polysemic terms to convey often completely unrelated concepts. There are numerous examples we could cite, but for the purpose of saving space and illustrating the issue, we will note but two:

- *Ναύλος*

  When used in relation to the carriage of goods, we have rendered this noun as "freight". When used in relation to the carriage of persons, we have rendered this noun as "fare".

- *Νομιμοποίηση*

  Depending on the context, this noun can mean "legitimacy", "authorisation", "entitlement", etc. This required in-depth discussions between us in order to fully grasp the intended meaning of each appearance of the term so as to feel confident in the accuracy of our translation.

The problem of polysemic terms, that is, terms having a finite number of possible meanings based on context, is aggravated by the occurrence of ambiguous language, which could have any number of meanings, with context often providing no aid, if there even is context to speak of. Again, for the sake of brevity, we employ a single but highly illustrative example of this issue:

- *Επισπεύδων*

The above adjective, literally translated as "the expediting party" or "he who expedites", is encountered several times in the Code. Considered literally, the meaning appears *prima facie* rather unambiguous, i.e. it denotes one who accelerates or expedites a procedure in question. However, as a mainstay of Greek legislative jargon, its meaning is far more specific, denoting a person who initiates or institutes proceedings or who petitions the court to order that a procedure be set in motion:

Article 42(3) (emphasis our own):

> *"3. Οι απαιτήσεις της παρ. 1 κατατάσσονται στον πίνακα διανομής μετά την αφαίρεση των εξόδων* ***του επισπεύσαντος τον πλειστηριασμό****, που έγιναν προς το κοινό συμφέρον των δανειστών, συμπεριλαμβανομένης της επιβαλλόμενης από τον νόμο δαπάνης φύλαξης του πλοίου.."*

Our translation (emphasis our own):

> "3. The claims referred to in paragraph 1 shall be ranked in the distribution table after deducting the costs of **the person who initiated the auction** incurred in the common interest of the creditors, including the legally required expenditure for custody of the ship."

A further complication arises when the above Greek word is used (in verb form) for an official, e.g.:

Article 245(4):

> *"4. Κατά την κατάθεση των ανακοπών δεν ορίζεται δικάσιμος. Ο εκκαθαριστής υποχρεούται μετά τη λήξη της προθεσμίας της παρ. 1 να* ***επισπεύσει*** *τη συζήτηση των ανακοπών κατά την ίδια υποχρεωτικά δικάσιμο, καλώντας σε αυτή τους διαδίκους τριάντα (30) ημέρες νωρίτερα.."*

Our translation (emphasis our own):

> "4. When oppositions are filed, no hearing date shall be set. After the deadline laid down in paragraph 1 has elapsed, the liquidator shall be obligated to **initiate** the hearing of the oppositions, which must necessarily be heard on the same hearing date, and to summon the parties in the proceedings to that hearing 30 days beforehand."

Again, the intended meaning is not to expedite or accelerate, but rather to initiate.

f) Elegant variation - Euphemisms

The first part of this category stands in contrast to the previous category. Whereas before we were facing a single term having several possible meanings, we now have to consider the problem of several terms being used interchangeably, often within the same article. This might well be an example of elegant variation, as defined by the brothers Fowler in the early 20th century, but in legal texts, in particular, one cannot but wonder if employing this strategy could cause more harm than good. There are several examples to be found in the Code of Private Maritime Law, with two noted below:

- Article 181 (emphasis our own):

  "[...] 2. Εάν ο πλοιοκτήτης κηρυχθεί σε πτώχευση, ο αντιπρόσωπος του πλοιοκτήτη ευθύνεται μόνο για τις ***απαιτήσεις του ναυτικού*** *που δημιουργήθηκαν τους τελευταίους έξι (6) μήνες πριν από την ημέρα της κήρυξης της πτώχευσης.*

  3. Οι ***αξιώσεις του ναυτικού*** *κατά του αντιπροσώπου του πλοιοκτήτη υπόκεινται σε ετήσια παραγραφή, εκτός των αξιώσεων από εργατικό ατύχημα, οι οποίες υπόκεινται σε παραγραφή τριάντα (30) μηνών. Σε κάθε περίπτωση, η παραγραφή αρχίζει από τη λύση της σύμβασης ναυτολόγησης."*

  Both terms have been rendered as "claims" (emphasis our own):

  "2. If the owner-operator is declared bankrupt, the owner-operator's proxy shall be liable only for the **claims of the seafarer** which arose during the six months prior to the date on which bankruptcy was declared.

  3. The **seafarer's claims** against the owner-operator's proxy shall become time-barred after one year, save claims arising from an occupational accident, which shall become time-barred after 30 months. In all events, the time-barring [period] shall commence on the date the employment agreement is dissolved."

  There is a line to be drawn between acceptable and problematic elegant variation. We would consider the above example to fall under the former, given that, pedantically speaking, *"απαιτήσεις"* are not *"αξιώσεις"* until they have been raised before a court of law. Nevertheless, seeking a different English term would be a futile endeavour and we have opted to just consider this acceptable elegant variation in this case. However, in Article 186(3), both terms are used in the same sentence:

  "Ο ναυτικός έχει ευθεία αξίωση κατά του ασφαλιστή για τις απαιτήσεις των παρ. 1 και 2."

  In this case, we had to employ a different term in order to ensure that the meaning was properly conveyed in the target text:

  "The seafarer shall have a direct claim against the insurer for the amounts referred to in paragraphs 1 and 2."

- An example of elegant variation on our part can be found in Article 78(3) (emphasis our own):

  "[...] Σε περίπτωση πταίσματος του εκναυλωτή, δεν αποκλείεται η ***αποκατάσταση*** *ζημίας που υπέστη ο ναυλωτής κατά τις κοινές διατάξεις."*

  Our translation (emphasis our own):

  "In the event of fault by the shipowner, **restitution** of the losses incurred by the charterer in accordance with the ordinary provisions may not be precluded."

  However, in Article 84(3) (emphasis our own):

  "3. Εάν, κατ' εκτέλεση οδηγιών του ναυλωτή, το φορτίο παραδοθεί σε μη νομιμοποιούμενο πρόσωπο, ο ναυλωτής υποχρεούται να ***αποκαταστήσει*** *τη ζημία που προκαλείται στον εκναυλωτή από το γεγονός αυτό."*

  Our translation (emphasis our own):

  "3. Where, in performance of the charterer's instructions, the cargo is delivered to an unauthorised person, the charterer shall be obligated to **make good** the losses incurred by the shipowner due to this fact."

In this case, we have chosen a variant, given that the verb "restitute" would not be a good candidate term in the target text. Therefore, where appropriate, as in the case at hand, we resorted to elegant variation as well.

The second part of this category concerns the use of euphemism. Contrary to our other publications, we are pleased to report that the Code of Private Maritime Law made no use of euphemism.

Finally, a further issue that is compounded by the combination of all the above issues (a meta-issue, perhaps) is the fact that consulting or reproducing our translation of the Code without referring to the introduction for a better understanding, if not resolution, of the translational issues we faced could result in risk.

"A ship in harbor is safe, but that is not what ships are built for."

— John A. Shedd, *Salt from My Attic*, 1928

ΝΟΜΟΣ ΥΠ' ΑΡΙΘΜ. 5020/2023
ΦΕΚ 29/Α/15-2-2023

Κώδικας Ιδιωτικού Ναυτικού Δικαίου και άλλες επείγουσες διατάξεις του Υπουργείου Ναυτιλίας και Νησιωτικής Πολιτικής

Η ΠΡΟΕΔΡΟΣ

ΤΗΣ ΕΛΛΗΝΙΚΗΣ ΔΗΜΟΚΡΑΤΙΑΣ

Εκδίδομε τον ακόλουθο νόμο που ψήφισε η Βουλή:

ΜΕΡΟΣ ΠΡΩΤΟ
ΤΟ ΚΑΘΕΣΤΩΣ ΤΟΥ ΠΛΟΙΟΥ

ΚΕΦΑΛΑΙΟ Α'
ΠΛΟΙΟ - ΣΤΑΤΙΚΟ ΝΑΥΠΗΓΗΜΑ - ΝΗΟΛΟΓΗΣΗ

Άρθρο 1
Έννοια πλοίου - στατικού ναυπηγήματος

1. Κατά την έννοια του παρόντος, πλοίο είναι κάθε πλωτή κατασκευή, ικανή να κινείται αυτοδύναμα στη θάλασσα για εκτέλεση ναυσιπλοΐας.

2. Στατικό ναυπήγημα είναι κάθε κατασκευή που επιπλέει στη θάλασσα και προορίζεται να χρησιμοποιείται για παραγωγή έργου ή παροχή υπηρεσίας συνήθως σε σταθερή θέση.

Άρθρο 2
Εξαιρέσεις από το πεδίο εφαρμογής

1. Τα Κεφάλαια Δ' και Ε' του Μέρους Τρίτου, τα Μέρη Τέταρτο, Πέμπτο, Έκτο, το Κεφάλαιο Γ' του Μέρους Όγδοου και το Κεφάλαιο Γ' του Μέρους Ένατου δεν εφαρμόζονται σε στατικά ναυπηγήματα. Το Έβδομο Κεφάλαιο εφαρμόζεται σε στατικά ναυπηγήματα, εφόσον έχει συναφθεί σύμβαση ναυτολόγησης.

2. Τα Μέρη Πρώτο έως και Έβδομο, το Κεφάλαιο Γ' του Μέρους Όγδοου, το Κεφάλαιο Γ' του Μέρους Ένατου και τα Μέρη Δέκατο και Ενδέκατο δεν εφαρμόζονται στα πλοία και στατικά ναυπηγήματα κρατικής ιδιοκτησίας ή εκμετάλλευσης που χρησιμοποιούνται αποκλειστικά για την άμεση εξυπηρέτηση δημόσιων μη εμπορικών σκοπών.

LAW No 5020/2023
GOVERNMENT GAZETTE, SERIES I, ISSUE 29/15-2-2023

Code of Private Maritime Law, and other emergency provisions relating to Ministry of Maritime Affairs and Insular Policy

THE PRESIDENT

OF THE HELLENIC REPUBLIC

We hereby promulgate the following law passed by Parliament:

PART ONE
SHIP STATUS

CHAPTER I
SHIP - STATIONARY FLOATING STRUCTURE - REGISTRATION

Article 1
Concept of a ship - stationary floating structure

1. For the purposes of this Code, "ship" means any floating construction able to move under its own power at sea for the purpose of performing navigation.

2. A stationary floating structure is any structure floating at sea and intended to be used to produce work or provide services normally in a fixed location.

Article 2
Exemptions from scope

1. Chapters IV and V of Part Three, Parts Four, Five and Six, Chapter III of Part Eight and Chapter III of Part Nine shall not apply to stationary floating structures. Chapter VII shall apply to stationary floating structures, provided an employment agreement has been entered into.

2. Parts One to Seven, Chapter III of Part Eight, Chapter III of Part Nine and Parts Ten and Eleven shall not apply to ships and stationary floating structures which belong to or are operated by the Greek State and which are used exclusively to directly serve public, non-commercial purposes.

Άρθρο 3

Νηολόγηση

1. Πλοίο καθαρής χωρητικότητας ίσης ή ανώτερης των δέκα (10) κόρων, ως προς το οποίο πληρούνται οι ουσιαστικές προϋποθέσεις κτήσης της ελληνικής εθνικότητας, εγγράφεται στο νηολόγιο του κράτους, με αίτηση του κυρίου αυτού. Από και δια της εγγραφής, το νηολογημένο πλοίο αναγνωρίζεται ως ελληνικό.

2. Η πράξη της νηολόγησης αναγράφει το όνομα και την ιθαγένεια του κυρίου του πλοίου, τον τίτλο κτήσης κυριότητας, τον διορισμό αντικλήτου που κατοικεί στην ημεδαπή, το όνομα του πλοίου, το διεθνές διακριτικό σήμα, τον αριθμό του Διεθνούς Ναυτιλιακού Οργανισμού (ΔΝΟ), τα στοιχεία τεχνικής ταυτοποίησης του πλοίου, όπως αυτά προκύπτουν από επίσημο πιστοποιητικό καταμέτρησης, το είδος της κινητήριας δύναμης και, αν πρόκειται για μηχανοκίνητο πλοίο, τη δύναμη μηχανής. Επικυρωμένο αντίγραφο του τίτλου της κυριότητας, νόμιμα θεωρημένο σε περίπτωση που ο τίτλος καταρτίσθηκε στην αλλοδαπή, κατατίθεται από τον κύριο του πλοίου και τηρείται από την αρμόδια λιμενική αρχή.

3. Η πράξη της νηολόγησης χρονολογείται και υπογράφεται από τον νηολόγο. Με βάση την πράξη νηολόγησης, εκδίδεται το έγγραφο εθνικότητας του πλοίου.

4. Εγγράφονται, κατ' εξαίρεση, στο νηολόγιο του κράτους και πλοία καθαρής χωρητικότητας κάτω των δέκα (10) κόρων, εφόσον δρομολογούνται βάσει του Κώδικα θαλασσίων ενδομεταφορών και δικαιωμάτων επιβατών (ν. 4948/2022, Α' 125) ή εφόσον η εκμετάλλευσή τους προϋποθέτει την έκδοση εγγράφου εθνικότητας. Με απόφαση του Υπουργού Ναυτιλίας και Νησιωτικής Πολιτικής ορίζονται και άλλες κατηγορίες πλοίων κάτω των δέκα (10) κόρων που υπόκεινται κατ' εξαίρεση σε νηολόγηση.

5. Με την επιφύλαξη ειδικότερων διατάξεων διμερών διεθνών συνθηκών, ο κύριος νηολογούμενου πλοίου προσκομίζει, εντός προθεσμίας δύο (2) μηνών από τη νηολόγηση, πιστοποιητικό διαγραφής από την αρμόδια αρχή του κράτους στο νηολόγιο του οποίου το πλοίο ήταν προηγουμένως εγγεγραμμένο, εφόσον η έκδοση του πιστοποιητικού διαγραφής προβλέπεται από το δίκαιο του κράτους αυτού. Η ισχύς της πράξης νηολόγησης δεν θίγεται από τη μη προσκόμιση πιστοποιητικού διαγραφής.

Άρθρο 4

Καταχώριση μη νηολογούμενων πλοίων

Με την επιφύλαξη της παρ. 4 του άρθρου 3, τα πλοία καθαρής χωρητικότητας κάτω των δέκα (10) κόρων καταχωρίζονται, κατά κατηγορίες, σε ειδικό δημόσιο βιβλίο μικρών πλοίων.

Άρθρο 5

Νηολόγηση στατικών ναυπηγημάτων

1. Σε νηολόγιο που τηρείται στις αρμόδιες λιμενικές αρχές καταχωρίζονται τα στατικά ναυπηγήματα ανεξαρτήτως ολικής χωρητικότητας ή εκτοπίσματος.

2. Σε ειδικό νηολόγιο που τηρείται στο Κεντρικό Λιμεναρχείο Πειραιά καταχωρίζονται στατικά ναυπηγήματα ανεξαρτήτως χωρητικότητας ή εκτοπίσματος που προορίζονται για εργασίες έρευνας και εκμετάλλευσης υδρογονανθράκων, συμπεριλαμβανομένης της διύλισης και αποθήκευσης αυτών, ή παραλαβής, προσωρινής αποθήκευσης και επαναεριοποίησης φυσικού αερίου.

3. Η παρ. 2 του άρθρου 3 εφαρμόζεται αναλόγως και επί στατικών ναυπηγημάτων. Με βάση την πράξη νηολόγησης, εκδίδεται το έγγραφο εθνικότητας του στατικού ναυπηγήματος.

Article 3
Registration

1. A ship with a net tonnage equal to or greater than 10 tons which meets the substantive requirements for being granted Greek nationality shall be entered in the ship registry of the Greek state, following an application by its owner. From the time of and by means of registration, the registered ship shall be recognised as Greek.

2. The registration decision shall indicate the name and nationality of the owner of the ship, the document of title, the appointment of a process agent domiciled in Greece, the name of the ship, the international call sign, the International Maritime Organisation (IMO) number, the technical identification details of the ship, as these arise from an official tonnage certificate, the means of propulsion and, in cases of a motorised ship, the rated engine power. A certified copy of the document of title, duly certified if prepared abroad, shall be filed by the owner of the ship and kept by the competent port authority.

3. The registration decision shall be dated and signed by the registrar. The ship's certificate of nationality shall be issued on the basis of the registration decision.

4. By way of exception, ships with a net tonnage under 10 tons shall also be registered in the ship registry of the Greek State, provided they operate on the basis of the Code of Maritime Cabotage and Passenger Rights (Law 4948/2022, Government Gazette, Series I, Issue 125) or their operation requires issuance of a certificate of nationality. Other categories of ships under 10 tons which, by way of exception, are subject to registration may also be specified in a decision issued by the Minister of Maritime Affairs and Insular Policy.

5. Without prejudice to more specific provisions of international bilateral treaties and conventions, within a deadline of two months from the date of registration, the owner of a registered ship shall produce a deregistration certificate issued by the competent authority of the state where the ship was previously registered, provided issuance of a deregistration certificate is envisaged by the law of that state. The validity of the registration decision shall not be prejudiced by failure to produce a deregistration certificate.

Article 4
Registration of ships not subject to mandatory registration

Without prejudice to Article 3(4), ships with a net tonnage under 10 tons shall be registered, in categories, in a special public register of small ships.

Article 5
Registration of stationary floating structures

1. Stationary floating structures, irrespective of gross tonnage or displacement, shall be entered in a ship registry kept by the competent port authorities.

2. Stationary floating structures, irrespective of tonnage or displacement, intended for hydrocarbon exploration and exploitation, including the refining and storage of hydrocarbons, or the receipt, temporary storage and regasification of natural gas, shall be entered in a special ship registry kept by the Central Port Authority of Piraeus.

3. Article 3(2) shall also apply *mutatis mutandis* to stationary floating structures. The stationary floating structure's certificate of nationality shall be issued on the basis of the registration decision.

Άρθρο 6
Νηολόγηση ναυπηγούμενου

1. Στο νηολόγιο του κράτους μπορεί να νηολογηθεί πλοίο που ναυπηγείται ή πρόκειται να ναυπηγηθεί.

2. Για τη νηολόγηση πλοίου ως ναυπηγούμενου υποβάλλεται στην τηρούσα το νηολόγιο αρχή σύμβαση ναυπήγησης ή γραπτή δήλωση ναυπηγού ότι πρόκειται να κατασκευάσει ή κατασκευάζει πλοίο για λογαριασμό του.

3. Η πράξη της νηολόγησης αναγράφει το ναυπηγείο και τον τόπο ναυπήγησης, το όνομα και την ιθαγένεια του προσώπου για λογαριασμό του οποίου ναυπηγείται το πλοίο, διορισμό αντικλήτου που κατοικεί στην Ελλάδα, την ύλη από την οποία κατασκευάζεται το πλοίο, το όνομα ή άλλο διακριτικό γνώρισμά του, τα στοιχεία τεχνικής ταυτοποίησής του, το είδος της κινητήριας δύναμης, και αν πρόκειται για μηχανοκίνητο πλοίο, το είδος και τη δύναμη της μηχανής.

4. Τα πλοία του άρθρου 4 δεν εγγράφονται στο ειδικό δημόσιο βιβλίο, όσο τελούν υπό ναυπήγηση.

Άρθρο 7
Τηρούμενα βιβλία

1. Η αρμόδια για το νηολόγιο αρχή τηρεί υποθηκολόγιο και βιβλίο κατασχέσεων για τα πλοία και τα στατικά ναυπηγήματα. Τηρεί, επίσης, χωριστό βιβλίο κατασχέσεων αλλοδαπών πλοίων.

2. Οι διατάξεις που αφορούν στην τήρηση των νηολογίων, υποθηκολογίων και βιβλίων κατασχέσεων ελληνικών πλοίων εφαρμόζονται και στα νηολόγια, υποθηκολόγια και βιβλία κατασχέσεων των στατικών ναυπηγημάτων.

Άρθρο 8
Δημοσιότητα

1. Σε δημοσιότητα με καταχώριση στα οικεία βιβλία υποβάλλονται οι εξής πράξεις και στοιχεία:

(α) τίτλοι κτήσης κυριότητας πλοίου και στατικού ναυπηγήματος,

(β) οι δικαιοπραξίες και δικαστικές αποφάσεις που προβλέπονται στα άρθρα 14 και 15,

(γ) ναυτικές υποθήκες επί πλοίων και στατικών ναυπηγημάτων και εξαλείψεις αυτών,

(δ) συντηρητική κατάσχεση, δικαστική μεσεγγύηση και λοιπά συντηρητικά μέτρα, προσωρινές απαγορεύσεις απόπλου και λοιπές προσωρινές διαταγές, καθώς και η άρση αυτών,

(ε) αναγκαστικές κατασχέσεις επί πλοίων και στατικών ναυπηγημάτων,

(στ) διεκδικητικές αγωγές επί πλοίων και στατικών ναυπηγημάτων, οι οποίες καταχωρίζονται στη μερίδα του πλοίου ή στατικού ναυπηγήματος στο νηολόγιο,

(ζ) δηλώσεις εφοπλισμού και δηλώσεις ανάληψης εκμετάλλευσης από προτιμώμενο ενυπόθηκο δανειστή,

(η) πράξεις σύστασης συμπλοιοκτησίας και διορισμού, παραίτησης και ανάκλησης διαχειριστή αυτής,

(θ) δήλωση εγκατάλειψης πλοίου από τον πλοιοκτήτη, δήλωση αμφισβήτησης της εγκατάλειψης από τον ασφαλιστή και η τελεσίδικη δικαστική απόφαση που εκδίδεται επ' αυτών,

(ι) απορριπτικές εκθέσεις επί αιτούμενων πράξεων ή εγγράφων,

(ια) έναρξη διαδικασίας αφερεγγυότητας του πλοιοκτήτη ή εφοπλιστή σε άλλο κράτος μέλος της Ευρωπαϊκής Ένωσης, τα στοιχεία του διορισθέντος διαχειριστή αφερεγγυότητας και δήλωση για το αν πρόκειται για κύρια ή δευτερεύουσα διαδικασία.

2. Οι υποθήκες, οι διεκδικητικές αγωγές, καθώς και οι συντηρητικές και αναγκαστικές κατασχέσεις επί πλοίων που εμπίπτουν στο πεδίο εφαρμογής του άρθρου 4 καταχωρίζονται στο ειδικό δημόσιο βιβλίο του εν λόγω άρθρου.

Article 6
Registration of a ship under construction

1. A ship which is or will be under construction may be entered in the ship registry of the Greek State.

2. In order for a ship to be registered as being under construction, a shipbuilding contract or declaration in writing from the shipbuilder that it is constructing or intends to construct a ship on its own account shall be submitted to the authority keeping the ship registry.

3. The registration decision shall indicate the shipyard and place of construction, the name and nationality of the person on whose account the ship is being constructed, the appointment of a process agent domiciled in Greece, the material used to manufacture the ship, its name or other distinguishing feature, its technical identification details, the means of propulsion and, in cases of a motorised ship, the rated engine power.

4. While they remain under construction, the ships referred to in Article 4 shall not be entered in the special public register.

Article 7
Registers kept

1. The authority responsible for keeping the ship registry shall keep a mortgage register and an arrest register for ships and stationary floating structures. That authority shall also keep a separate register on the arrest of foreign ships.

2. The provisions concerning the keeping of registries, mortgage registers and arrest registers for Greek ships shall also apply to the registries, mortgage registers and arrest registers for stationary floating structures.

Article 8
Disclosure

1. The following [documents] and information shall be disclosed by entering them in the relevant registers:

(a) documents of title for ships and stationary floating structures;

(b) the legal transactions and court judgments provided for in Articles 14 and 15;

(c) mortgages on ships and stationary floating structures and the extinction thereof;

(d) preventive arrest, judicial sequestration and other preventive measures, temporary detention and other temporary orders, as well as the lifting thereof;

(e) compulsory arrest of ships and stationary floating structures;

(f) revendication actions concerning ships and stationary floating structures in the [ship registry] account of the ship or stationary floating structure;

(g) declarations of ship operation and declarations of undertaking of operation by a preferred mortgagee;

(h) deeds establishing joint ship ownership and concerning the appointment, resignation and removal of the manager of such ownership;

(i) a declaration of abandonment of ship by the owner-operator, a declaration challenging the abandonment by the insurer, and the *de jure* non-appealable court judgment handed down thereon;

(j) reports on the rejection of requested decisions or documents;

(k) opening of insolvency proceedings against the owner-operator or operator in a different Member State of the European Union, the particulars of the insolvency practitioner appointed, and a declaration on whether these are main or secondary proceedings.

2. Mortgages, revendication actions, as well as preventive and compulsory arrests of ships falling within the scope of Article 4 shall be entered in the special public register referred to in that Article.

Άρθρο 9

Ηλεκτρονική τήρηση βιβλίων νηολογίου και υποβολή εγγράφων με ηλεκτρονικά μέσα

1. Η τήρηση των βιβλίων, σύμφωνα με τα άρθρα 3 έως 8, καθώς και κάθε πράξη ή εγγραφή σε αυτά, μπορεί να γίνεται, εν όλω ή εν μέρει, με ηλεκτρονικά μέσα.

2. Τα υποβαλλόμενα στην τηρούσα το νηολόγιο και τα λοιπά βιβλία αρχή έγγραφα κάθε φύσης είναι δυνατόν να υποβάλλονται και με ηλεκτρονικά μέσα, εφόσον φέρουν εγκεκριμένη ηλεκτρονική υπογραφή. Το έγγραφο που έχει υποβληθεί με ηλεκτρονικά μέσα θεωρείται ότι κατατέθηκε, εφόσον επιστραφεί στον αποστολέα του εγγράφου από την αρμόδια αρχή ηλεκτρονική απόδειξη, που φέρει προηγμένη ή εγκεκριμένη ηλεκτρονική υπογραφή.

3. Η ανωτέρω αρχή μπορεί να χορηγεί σε ψηφιακή μορφή, στην ελληνική και στην αγγλική γλώσσα, κάθε είδους πιστοποιητικά, βεβαιώσεις ή άλλα έγγραφα σχετικά με τις καταχωρίσεις στα οικεία βιβλία. Τα ηλεκτρονικά έγγραφα και πιστοποιητικά έχουν την ισχύ που προβλέπεται στο άρθρο 14 του ν. 4727/2020 (Α' 184).

4. Τα έγγραφα εθνικότητας πλοίου και στατικού ναυπηγήματος μπορούν επίσης να εκδίδονται με τη μορφή ηλεκτρονικού αρχείου.

Άρθρο 10

Τήρηση ηλεκτρονικού αρχείου

1. Η αρμόδια για το νηολόγιο και τα λοιπά βιβλία αρχή μπορεί να τηρεί ηλεκτρονικό αρχείο σχετικών εγγράφων που κατατίθενται, των εκθέσεων κατάθεσης και κάθε άλλου συναφούς ηλεκτρονικού εγγράφου που σχετίζεται με συγκεκριμένη πράξη ή εγγραφή.

2. Τα τηρούμενα ηλεκτρονικά αρχεία πρέπει να πληρούν τους όρους και τις προϋποθέσεις ασφαλείας και να εγγυώνται ιδίως την ακεραιότητα, αυθεντικότητα, εμπιστευτικότητα και την ποιότητα των εγγράφων, καθώς και των δεδομένων και πληροφοριών που περιέχονται σε αυτά.

ΚΕΦΑΛΑΙΟ Β'

ΚΥΡΙΟΤΗΤΑ ΕΠΙ ΠΛΟΙΟΥ

Άρθρο 11

Κυριότητα ναυπηγούμενου πλοίου

1. Η σύμβαση ναυπήγησης καταρτίζεται εγγράφως. Σε αυτήν εφαρμόζονται αναλόγως οι διατάξεις του Αστικού Κώδικα (π.δ. 456/1984, Α' 164) για τη μίσθωση έργου, εκτός από τα άρθρα 683, 693 και 695 αυτού.

2. Κύριος του ναυπηγούμενου πλοίου είναι ο ναυπηγός, εκτός αν συμφωνήθηκε διαφορετικά.

3. Αν ο κύριος του ναυπηγούμενου πλοίου καθορίζεται στη σύμβαση ναυπήγησης, η νηολόγηση του πλοίου, σύμφωνα με το άρθρο 6, γίνεται στο όνομά του.

Article 9

Electronic keeping of registers at the ship registry and submission of documents

1. The keeping of registers in accordance with Articles 3 to 8 and the registration of any document or entry in such registers may be effected, whether in whole or in part, using electronic means.

2. All manner of documents submitted to the authority keeping the ship registry and other registers may also be submitted using electronic means, provided they bear an approved electronic signature. Documents submitted using electronic means shall be deemed to have been filed if the competent authority sends an electronic receipt to the sender of the document bearing an advanced or approved electronic signature.

3. The aforesaid authority may issue all manner of certificates, attestations or other documents concerning entries in the relevant registers in digital form, in the Greek and English languages. Electronic documents and certificates shall have the effect provided for in Article 14 of Law 4727/2020 (Government Gazette, Series I, Issue 184).

4. The certificates of nationality of ships and stationary floating structures may also be issued in the form of an electronic file.

Article 10

Keeping of electronic files

1. The authority competent to keep the ship registry and other registers may keep an electronic file of the relevant documents submitted to it, the filing reports and all other relevant electronic documents concerning the specific decisions or entry.

2. The electronic files kept must meet the security requirements and conditions and, in particular, guarantee the integrity, authenticity, confidentiality and quality of the documents and the data and information they contain.

CHAPTER II

SHIP OWNERSHIP

Article 11

Ownership of ships under construction

1. Shipbuilding contracts shall be drawn up in writing. The provisions of the Civil Code (Presidential Decree 456/1984, Government Gazette, Series I, Issue 164) on works contracts, save Articles 683, 693 and 695 of the Civil Code, shall apply to shipbuilding contracts.

2. Unless otherwise agreed upon, the shipbuilder is the owner of the ship under construction.

3. If the owner of the ship under construction is specified in the shipbuilding contract, the ship shall be registered in the owner's name, in accordance with Article 6.

Άρθρο 12
Μεταβίβαση κυριότητας πλοίου

1. Για τη μεταβίβαση της κυριότητας πλοίου απαιτείται συμφωνία μεταξύ του κυρίου και εκείνου που την αποκτά ότι μετατίθεται σε αυτόν η κυριότητα για νόμιμη αιτία. Καλόπιστη κτήση κυριότητας πλοίου από μεταβιβάζοντα μη κύριο δεν είναι δυνατή.

2. Η συμφωνία γίνεται εγγράφως και υποβάλλεται σε καταχώριση στο νηολόγιο. Η αποδοχή της πρότασης μπορεί να γίνει και με χωριστό έγγραφο. Αν το έγγραφο της συμφωνίας, της πρότασης ή της αποδοχής της πρότασης για τη μεταβίβαση της κυριότητας πλοίου καταρτίζεται στην αλλοδαπή, απαιτείται νόμιμη θεώρηση.

3. Χωρίς την καταχώριση στο νηολόγιο σύμφωνα με την παρ. 2, δεν επέρχεται η μεταβίβαση της κυριότητας του πλοίου.

4. Η παρ. 3 εφαρμόζεται και για τη μεταβίβαση της κυριότητας πλοίου που εγγράφεται στο ειδικό βιβλίο του άρθρου 4.

5. Επί πλειστηριασμού πλοίου, ο υπερθεματιστής δεν αποκτά την κυριότητα αυτού, αν ο καθ' ου η εκτέλεση οφειλέτης δεν είναι κύριος του πλοίου.

Άρθρο 13
Μεταβίβαση κυριότητας ναυπηγούμενου πλοίου

Το άρθρο 12 εφαρμόζεται και επί ναυπηγούμενου πλοίου, εφόσον αυτό έχει νηολογηθεί.

Άρθρο 14
Κτήση κυριότητας πλοίου με χρησικτησία

1. Όποιος νέμεται πλοίο για μία τριετία, με καλή πίστη και νόμιμο τίτλο προσηκόντως εγγεγραμμένο στο νηολόγιο, γίνεται κύριος αυτού.

2. Όποιος νέμεται πλοίο για μία δεκαετία γίνεται κύριος αυτού, από και δια της καταχώρισης τελεσίδικης δικαστικής απόφασης στο νηολόγιο.

Άρθρο 15
Δικαιοπραξίες αιτία θανάτου και δικαστικές αποφάσεις

Οι περ. 1 έως 4 του άρθρου 1192 και τα άρθρα 1193 έως 1195, 1197 και 1199 έως 1204 του Αστικού Κώδικα εφαρμόζονται αναλόγως και για τη μεταβίβαση της κυριότητας επί πλοίου.

Άρθρο 16
Εφαρμοστέο δίκαιο επί της κυριότητας στο πλοίο

1. Το δίκαιο της πολιτείας, της οποίας τη σημαία φέρει το πλοίο, διέπει τις προϋποθέσεις κτήσης κυριότητας και τις εξουσίες του κυρίου.

2. Σε περίπτωση αλλαγής σημαίας, εφαρμοστέο είναι το δίκαιο της πολιτείας της οποίας τη σημαία φέρει το πλοίο κατά τον χρόνο της μεταβίβασης ή της επιβολής της αναγκαστικής κατάσχεσης.

3. Ως προς τα πλοία που δεν υπόκεινται σε νηολόγηση, εφαρμοστέο είναι το δίκαιο του τόπου καταχώρισής τους.

Article 12
Transfer of ship ownership

1. Transfers of ship ownership shall require an agreement between the owner and the person acquiring ownership whereby ownership is transferred to the latter for a legitimate purpose. Acquisition in good faith of ship ownership from a transferor who is not the owner is not possible.

2. The agreement shall be drawn up in writing and entered in the ship registry. The offer may also be accepted by means of a separate document. If the document containing the agreement, offer or acceptance of the offer for transfer of ship ownership is drawn up abroad, certification in accordance with legal form shall be required.

3. Ship ownership shall not be transferred without an entry in the ship registry in accordance with paragraph 2.

4. Paragraph 3 shall also apply to the transfer of ship ownership entered in the special register referred to in Article 4.

5. Where a ship is auctioned, the highest bidder shall not acquire ship ownership if the debtor against whom enforcement is taking place is not the owner of the ship.

Article 13
Transfer of ownership of a ship under construction

Article 12 shall also apply to a ship under construction, provided it has been registered.

Article 14
Acquisition of ship ownership by means of adverse possession

1. Any person who possesses a ship for three years, in good faith and holds a lawful document of title duly entered in the ship registry shall become its owner.

2. Any person who possesses a ship for ten years shall become its owner from the date and by means of the entry of a *de jure* non-appealable court judgment in the ship registry.

Article 15
Legal transactions *mortis causa* and court judgments

Points 1 to 4 of Article 1192 and Articles 1193 to 1195, 1197 and 1199 to 1204 of the Civil Code shall also apply *mutatis mutandis* to the transfer of ship ownership.

Article 16
Law applicable to ship ownership

1. The law of the state whose flag the ship flies shall govern the conditions for acquisition of ownership and the powers of the owner.

2. In the event of transfer of flag, the law of the state whose flag the ship flies at the time of transfer or compulsory arrest shall be the applicable law.

3. With regard to ships not subject to mandatory registration, the law of the place of their registration shall be applicable.

ΜΕΡΟΣ ΔΕΥΤΕΡΟ
ΕΜΠΡΑΓΜΑΤΗ ΑΣΦΑΛΕΙΑ ΕΠΙ ΠΛΟΙΟΥ

ΚΕΦΑΛΑΙΟ Α'
ΝΑΥΤΙΚΕΣ ΥΠΟΘΗΚΕΣ

Άρθρο 17
Εμπράγματη ασφάλεια σε πλοίο

Η ναυτική υποθήκη (απλή και προτιμώμενη) και τα ναυτικά προνόμια εξασφαλίζουν τις ναυτικές απαιτήσεις.

Άρθρο 18
Απλή και προτιμώμενη ναυτική υποθήκη

1. Για την εξασφάλιση απαίτησης με προνομιακή ικανοποίηση του δανειστή μπορεί να συσταθεί εμπράγματο δικαίωμα υποθήκης σε ξένο πλοίο (απλή ναυτική υποθήκη).

2. Έγκυρη είναι και η συμφωνία για τη σύσταση ναυτικής υποθήκης κατά την έννοια του άρθρου 26, προς μείζονα εξασφάλιση της απαίτησης του δανειστή, εφόσον το πλοίο έχει ολική χωρητικότητα πεντακοσίων (500) κόρων και άνω ή το στατικό ναυπήγημα έχει ολική χωρητικότητα πεντακοσίων (500) κόρων και άνω ή εκτόπισμα χιλίων (1000) τόνων και άνω (προτιμώμενη ναυτική υποθήκη).

3. Η εξασφαλιζόμενη με ναυτική υποθήκη απαίτηση περιλαμβάνει το κεφάλαιο, τους δεδουλευμένους τόκους και, εφόσον συμφωνηθεί, τις δαπάνες.

4. Το δικαίωμα μπορεί να συσταθεί και σε ναυπηγούμενο πλοίο, εφόσον αυτό είναι νηολογημένο.

5. Ενέχυρο με βάση την ιδιωτική βούληση δεν μπορεί να συσταθεί σε πλοίο.

Άρθρο 19
Υποθήκη σε ιδανικό μέρος και σε επικαρπία - Υποθήκευση επί συμπλοιοκτησίας

1. Απλή ναυτική υποθήκη μπορεί να συσταθεί και σε ιδανικό μέρος πλοίου.

2. Αν το ιδανικό ποσοστό ανήκει σε συμπλοιοκτήτη, για την έγκυρη σύσταση απαιτείται συναίνεση τουλάχιστον των δύο τρίτων (2/3) των μερίδων της συμπλοιοκτησίας. Η συναίνεση παρέχεται με έγγραφο που έχει βέβαιη χρονολογία.

3. Με απόφαση των τεσσάρων πέμπτων (4/5) των μερίδων συμπλοιοκτησίας ή των δύο τρίτων (2/3) των μερίδων και δικαστική απόφαση μπορεί να εγγραφεί απλή ναυτική υποθήκη σε ολόκληρο το πλοίο.

4. Προτιμώμενη ναυτική υποθήκη συστήνεται μόνο σε ολόκληρο το πλοίο. Αν πρόκειται για πλοίο που ανήκει σε συμπλοιοκτησία, απαιτείται ομόφωνη απόφαση των μελών της συμπλοιοκτησίας.

5. Στην επικαρπία πλοίου μόνο απλή ναυτική υποθήκη μπορεί να παραχωρηθεί.

PART TWO
SECURITY INTEREST IN SHIPS

CHAPTER I
MARITIME MORTGAGES

Article 17
Security interest in a ship

Maritime claims are secured by mortgages (simple and preferred) and maritime liens.

Article 18
Simple and preferred mortgage

1. In order to secure preferential satisfaction of a creditor's claim, a right *in rem* of mortgage may be established on a ship belonging to another (simple mortgage).
2. An agreement to establish a mortgage within the meaning of Article 26 for the preferred satisfaction of the creditor's claim shall also be valid, provided the ship has a gross tonnage equal to or greater than 500 tons or the stationary floating structure has a gross tonnage equal to or greater than 500 tons or a displacement equal to or greater than 1,000 tons (preferred mortgage).
3. A claim secured by a mortgage shall include the principal, accrued interest and, if agreed upon, costs.
4. The right may also be established on a ship under construction, provided it has been registered.
5. A ship may not be pledged on the basis of the private will of the parties.

Article 19
Mortgage of an ideal share and usufruct - Mortgaging in cases of joint ship ownership

1. A simple mortgage may also be established on an ideal share in a ship.
2. If the ideal share belongs to a joint owner-operator, the valid establishment of a mortgage shall require the consent of at least 2/3 of the shares in the joint ship ownership. This consent shall be provided in a time-stamped document.
3. A simple mortgage may be registered on the entire ship pursuant to a decision of 4/5 of the shares in the joint ship ownership or 2/3 of the shares and a court judgment.
4. A preferred mortgage may only be established on the entire ship. Where the ship is under joint ship ownership, a unanimous decision of the members of the joint ship ownership shall be required.
5. In cases of usufruct of a ship, only a simple mortgage may be granted.

Άρθρο 20
Τίτλος κτήσης

Τίτλο για την απόκτηση υποθήκης σε πλοίο αποτελεί μόνο η ιδιωτική βούληση.

Άρθρο 21
Τίτλος απλής ναυτικής υποθήκης

1. Το δικαίωμα για απόκτηση απλής ναυτικής υποθήκης παρέχεται με δήλωση του κυρίου του πλοίου ή του επικαρπωτή ενώπιον συμβολαιογράφου.

2. Η δήλωση πρέπει να περιέχει, εκτός από τα απαιτούμενα σύμφωνα με το κοινό δίκαιο στοιχεία, την περιγραφή του πλοίου σύμφωνα με το άρθρο 3, τον αριθμό νηολογίου καθώς και τον διορισμό αντίκλητου με κατοικία στον τόπο όπου τηρείται το βιβλίο υποθηκών.

3. Για ναυπηγούμενο πλοίο απαιτούνται και τα στοιχεία που αναφέρονται στην παρ. 3 του άρθρου 6.

4. Αν δεν διοριστεί αντίκλητος ή η εξουσία του παύσει για οποιαδήποτε αιτία, οι σχετικές με την υποθήκη επιδόσεις μπορούν να γίνουν είτε στον εισαγγελέα πρωτοδικών, στην περιφέρεια του οποίου τηρείται το βιβλίο υποθηκών, είτε στον νηολόγο.

Άρθρο 22
Τίτλος προτιμώμενης ναυτικής υποθήκης

1. Το δικαίωμα για απόκτηση προτιμώμενης ναυτικής υποθήκης παρέχεται μόνο με σύμβαση μεταξύ του δανειστή και του κυρίου του πλοίου, που περιβάλλεται τον συμβολαιογραφικό τύπο στην ημεδαπή ή τον απαιτούμενο τύπο του τόπου κατάρτισης στην αλλοδαπή.

2. Στη σύμβαση περιέχονται τα στοιχεία της παρ. 2 του άρθρου 21.

Άρθρο 23
Χρόνος σύστασης ναυτικής υποθήκης

1. Η ναυτική υποθήκη συστήνεται από την εγγραφή της στο υποθηκολόγιο της περιφέρειας όπου είναι νηολογημένο το πλοίο ή, για τα πλοία που εμπίπτουν στο πεδίο εφαρμογής του άρθρου 4, στο ειδικό δημόσιο βιβλίο του εν λόγω άρθρου.

2. Αντίγραφο της υποθηκικής δήλωσης ή σύμβασης τηρείται από τον πλοίαρχο επί του πλοίου.

Άρθρο 24
Υποθηκική τάξη

1. Η χρονολογική τάξη εγγραφής της υποθήκης στο υποθηκολόγιο κατά το άρθρο 23, καθορίζει την προτεραιότητα οποιουδήποτε απλού ή προτιμώμενου ενυπόθηκου δανειστή.

2. Ναυτικές υποθήκες που εγγράφονται την ίδια ημέρα έχουν προτεραιότητα που αντιστοιχεί στη σειρά εγγραφής τους, η οποία είναι η ίδια με τη σειρά κατάθεσης της σχετικής αίτησης στην αρμόδια λιμενική αρχή.

Άρθρο 25
Χρήση ενυπόθηκου πλοίου

Ο εκμεταλλευόμενος ενυπόθηκο πλοίο έχει την υποχρέωση να χρησιμοποιεί αυτό με επιμέλεια και σύμφωνα με τους κανόνες τακτικής εκμετάλλευσης.

Article 20
Mortgage deed

A ship may only be mortgaged pursuant to a deed drawn up on the basis of the private will of the parties.

Article 21
Simple mortgage deed

1. The right to acquire a simple mortgage shall be provided by means of a declaration made by the owner of the ship or the usufructuary in the presence of a notary public.
2. In addition to the information required under the ordinary provisions, the declaration must contain a description of the ship, in accordance with Article 3, the ship registry number and the appointment of a process agent domiciled in the place where the mortgage register is kept.
3. In cases of ships under construction, the information referred to in Article 6(3) shall also be required.
4. If a process agent is not appointed or if their powers cease to apply for any reason, documents concerning the mortgage may be served either on the court of first instance public prosecutor in whose district the mortgage register is kept or on the ship registrar.

Article 22
Preferred mortgage deed

1. The right to acquire a preferred mortgage shall be conferred solely by means of an agreement entered into by the creditor and the owner of the ship, in the form of a notarial deed if drawn up in Greece or in the prescribed form of the place where it is drawn up abroad.
2. The agreement shall contain the information referred to in Article 21(2).

Article 23
Time of establishment of a mortgage

1. A mortgage shall be established from the time it is entered in the mortgage register of the district where the ship is registered or, in cases of ships falling within the scope of Article 4, in the special public register referred to in that Article.
2. A copy of the mortgage declaration or agreement shall be kept by the master aboard the ship.

Article 24
Ranking of mortgages

1. The timing of entry of mortgages in the mortgage register in accordance with Article 23 determines the priority of any simple or preferred mortgagee.
2. Mortgages entered on the same day shall have priority based on the timing of their entries, which shall be identical to the timing of the filing of the applications in question with the competent port authority.

Article 25
Use of a mortgaged ship

A person operating a mortgaged ship shall be obligated to use the ship diligently and in accordance with rules of sound management.

Άρθρο 26
Δικαιώματα προτιμώμενου ενυπόθηκου δανειστή

1. Στην προτιμώμενη ναυτική υποθήκη ο ενυπόθηκος δανειστής έχει το δικαίωμα να αναλάβει την εκμετάλλευση του πλοίου μόλις το χρέος καταστεί ληξιπρόθεσμο ή σε άλλες συμφωνηθείσες περιπτώσεις.
2. Στην προτιμώμενη ναυτική υποθήκη είναι έγκυρη η συμφωνία με την οποία παρέχονται στον ενυπόθηκο δανειστή και άλλα δικαιώματα εξασφάλισης της απαίτησής του, όπως είναι η εκποίηση του πλοίου χωρίς πλειστηριασμό.
3. Με την επιφύλαξη των διατάξεων περί δημοσίων εγγράφων και δικαστικών συμβιβασμών του Κανονισμού (ΕΕ) 1215/2012 του Ευρωπαϊκού Κοινοβουλίου και του Συμβουλίου της 12ης Δεκεμβρίου 2012 «για τη διεθνή δικαιοδοσία, την αναγνώριση και την εκτέλεση αποφάσεων σε αστικές και εμπορικές υποθέσεις» (L 351/1), οι συμβάσεις δανείων, εκχωρήσεων, υποθηκών και οι δικαστικές αποφάσεις αποτελούν τίτλους εκτελεστούς στην Ελλάδα, χωρίς να περιαφθούν τον τύπο της εκτέλεσης.

Άρθρο 27
Ανάληψη και παύση εκμετάλλευσης

1. Η δήλωση ανάληψης της εκμετάλλευσης είναι έγγραφη και επιδίδεται στον οφειλέτη και τον πλοίαρχο. Επίσης γνωστοποιείται χωρίς υπαίτια βραδύτητα από τον προτιμώμενο ενυπόθηκο δανειστή στην αρμόδια λιμενική αρχή, η οποία τη σημειώνει στο νηολόγιο και στο υποθηκολόγιο.
2. Επιτρέπεται η ανάληψη της εκμετάλλευσης κατά τη διάρκεια εκτελούμενου πλου και ο πλους ολοκληρώνεται υποχρεωτικά από τον προτιμώμενο ενυπόθηκο δανειστή.
3. Στο νηολόγιο και το υποθηκολόγιο σημειώνεται και η δήλωση του προτιμώμενου ενυπόθηκου δανειστή για την παύση της εκμετάλλευσης ή η δικαστική απόφαση που αναγνωρίζει την παύση. Η δήλωση αυτή επιδίδεται στον οφειλέτη και στον πλοίαρχο.
4. Οι έννομες συνέπειες έναντι τρίτων επέρχονται με την εγγραφή της σχετικής δήλωσης στα οικεία βιβλία.
5. Σε περίπτωση μη εκούσιας παράδοσης του πλοίου, ο ενυπόθηκος δανειστής αναλαμβάνει την εκμετάλλευση αυτού κατά τις διατάξεις περί αναγκαστικής εκτέλεσης. Ο ίδιος μπορεί να ζητήσει από το δικαστήριο του τόπου νηολόγησης του πλοίου την προσωρινή ρύθμιση κατάστασης ως προς τη χρήση του πλοίου.

Άρθρο 28
Έκταση εκμετάλλευσης

1. Με την ανάληψη της εκμετάλλευσης η κατοχή του πλοίου περιέρχεται στον προτιμώμενο ενυπόθηκο δανειστή, ο οποίος εκμεταλλεύεται εφεξής αυτό για λογαριασμό του και προς τον σκοπό ικανοποίησης της απαίτησής του.
2. Η ανάληψη της εκμετάλλευσης παρέχει στον ενυπόθηκο δανειστή την εξουσία για κάθε ενέργεια και δικαιοπραξία συμφυή με την εκμετάλλευση πλοίου.

Άρθρο 29
Καταλογισμός προσόδων - Υποχρέωση λογοδοσίας

1. Οι πρόσοδοι που εισπράττονται από τον προτιμώμενο ενυπόθηκο δανειστή κατά τη διάρκεια της εκμετάλλευσης του πλοίου καταλογίζονται στην εξόφληση της απαίτησης μετά από την αφαίρεση κάθε σχετικής δαπάνης.
2. Ο ανωτέρω δανειστής υπέχει υποχρέωση λογοδοσίας.

Article 26

Rights of preferred mortgagees

1. In cases of preferred mortgage, preferred mortgagees shall have the right to undertake operation of the ship when the debt becomes overdue or in other circumstances agreed upon.

2. In cases of preferred mortgage, an agreement which also confers on the mortgagee other rights to secure their claim, such as sale of the ship without an auction, shall be valid.

3. Without prejudice to the provisions on authentic instruments and court settlements of Regulation (EU) No 1215/2012 of the European Parliament and of the Council of 12 December 2012 on jurisdiction and the recognition and enforcement of judgments in civil and commercial matters (OJ L 351/1), agreements on loans, assignments and mortgages, as well as court judgments shall constitute enforceable titles in Greece without being endorsed as enforcement orders.

Article 27

Undertaking and cessation of operation

1. A declaration of undertaking of operation shall be drawn up in writing and served on the debtor and on the master. Additionally, such declaration shall be notified without undue delay by the preferred mortgagee to the competent port authority, which shall make note of such declarations in the ship registry and the mortgage register.

2. Operation may be undertaken during a voyage in progress, and the preferred mortgagee shall be obligated to complete the voyage.

3. A declaration by the preferred mortgagee on the cessation of operation or a court judgment acknowledging such cessation shall also be noted in the ship registry and the mortgage register. This declaration shall be served on the debtor and on the master.

4. Entry of the declaration in question in the relevant registers shall generate legal effects for third parties.

5. In cases of forced handover of the ship, the mortgagee shall undertake its operation in accordance with the provisions on compulsory enforcement. The mortgagee may petition the court of the ship's place of registration for provisional regulation of the situation concerning use of the ship.

Article 28

Extent of operation

1. Upon undertaking operation, the preferred mortgagee shall acquire detentorship of the ship and shall, from that moment onwards, operate it on its own behalf and for the purpose of satisfying its claim.

2. Upon undertaking operation, the mortgagee shall be empowered to take any steps and enter into any legal transaction concerning operation of the ship.

Article 29

Allocation of revenues - Obligation to render account

1. The revenues collected by the preferred mortgagee during operation of the ship shall be allocated to repay the claim, after all the relevant costs have been deducted.

2. The aforesaid creditor shall be obligated to render account.

Άρθρο 30
Εξόφληση απαίτησης

Η εξόφληση της απαίτησης που επέρχεται με οποιονδήποτε τρόπον επιφέρει την παύση της εκμετάλλευσης του πλοίου. Σε περίπτωση αμφισβήτησης της εξόφλησης, ο προτιμώμενος ενυπόθηκος δανειστής υποχρεούται να παράσχει στον οφειλέτη κάθε στοιχείο σχετικό με την εκμετάλλευση.

Άρθρο 31
Δικαίωμα αναγκαστικής εκτέλεσης

Η ανάληψη της εκμετάλλευσης δεν εμποδίζει τον προτιμώμενο ενυπόθηκο δανειστή να επιδιώξει την εξόφληση του χρέους με επίσπευση αναγκαστικής εκτέλεσης στο πλοίο.

Άρθρο 32
Δικαιώματα προηγούμενων κατά τάξη δανειστών

Σε περίπτωση ανάληψης της εκμετάλλευσης από προτιμώμενο ενυπόθηκο δανειστή, κάθε άλλος ενυπόθηκος δανειστής που προηγείται κατά την υποθηκική τάξη δικαιούται να απαιτήσει την άμεση εξόφληση του χρέους.

Άρθρο 33
Ασφάλιση ενυπόθηκου πλοίου από δανειστή

1. Εφόσον δεν υπάρχει ήδη αντίστοιχη ασφαλιστική κάλυψη, ο ενυπόθηκος δανειστής δικαιούται να ασφαλίζει με δαπάνη του οφειλέτη το πλοίο κατά θαλάσσιων κινδύνων και κινδύνων πολέμου μέχρι αξίας ίσης με το ποσό του δανείου, προσαυξημένου κατά ποσοστό τριάντα τοις εκατό (30%).

2. Το ίδιο δικαίωμα υπάρχει και σε ναυπηγούμενο πλοίο για κινδύνους συναφείς με την κατασκευή του.

3. Αν ο οφειλέτης δεν αποδίδει στον ενυπόθηκο δανειστή τα καταβληθέντα από τον τελευταίο ασφάλιστρα, ο δανειστής δικαιούται να απαιτήσει την άμεση εξόφληση του χρέους. Το ίδιο ισχύει, αν το πλοίο καταστράφηκε ή υπέστη βλάβες που έχουν απομειώσει ουσιωδώς την αξία του, εκτός εάν οι βλάβες δεν οφείλονται σε πταίσμα του οφειλέτη και ο τελευταίος προσφέρει επαρκή ασφάλεια.

4. Το δικαίωμα της υποθήκης ασκείται και στο ασφάλισμα. Το άρθρο 1287 του Αστικού Κώδικα δεν εφαρμόζεται.

5. Ο ενυπόθηκος δανειστής μπορεί να ασφαλίσει οποτεδήποτε το ίδιο συμφέρον που έχει επί του ενυπόθηκου πλοίου.

Άρθρο 34
Ακυρότητα εγγραφής υποθήκης

Μετά την εγγραφή αναγκαστικής κατάσχεσης στο νηολόγιο, η εγγραφή υποθήκης είναι άκυρη υπέρ εκείνου που επέβαλε την κατάσχεση και υπέρ των δανειστών που αναγγέλθηκαν. Το ίδιο ισχύει υπέρ αυτού που επέβαλε συντηρητική κατάσχεση.

Άρθρο 35
Υποχρεωτική ανάκληση υποθήκης σε πτώχευση

Η περ. δ' του άρθρου 117 του ν. 4738/2020 (Α' 207), περί υποχρεωτικής ανάκλησης, εφαρμόζεται και στις ναυτικές υποθήκες.

Article 30

Payment of claims in full

Once the claim has been paid in full in any manner, operation of the ship [by the preferred mortgagee] shall cease. If payment in full is disputed, the preferred mortgagee shall be obligated to provide the debtor with all information concerning operation of the ship.

Article 31

Right to compulsory enforcement

Undertaking operation of the ship shall not hinder a preferred mortgagee from seeking payment of the debt in full by instituting compulsory enforcement on the ship.

Article 32

Rights of higher-ranking creditors

Where operation of the ship is undertaken by a preferred mortgagee, any other mortgagee with a higher mortgage ranking shall be entitled to seek immediate payment of the debt in full.

Article 33

Insurance of a mortgaged ship by a creditor

1. Where such insurance coverage does not already exist, the mortgagee shall be entitled to insure the ship against marine risks and war risks, at the expense of the debtor, up to a value equal to the loan amount, augmented by 30%.

2. The same right shall also apply to a ship under construction for construction-related risks.

3. If the debtor does not pay the mortgagee the insurance premiums paid by the latter, the mortgagee shall be entitled to seek immediate payment of the debt in full. This shall also apply if the ship was destroyed or suffered damage that materially impaired its value, unless the damage is not due to a fault by the debtor and the latter offers sufficient security.

4. Rights under the mortgage shall also attach to the indemnity. Article 1287 of the Civil Code does not apply.

5. A mortgagee may, at any time, insure their interest in the mortgaged ship.

Article 34

Nullity of mortgage registration

Following the entry of a compulsory arrest in the ship registry, the entry of a mortgage shall be null and void vis-à-vis the person who obtained an arrest order and any creditors who lodged a claim. This shall also apply vis-à-vis the person who obtained a preventive arrest order.

Article 35

Compulsory revocation of a mortgage in cases of bankruptcy

Article 117(d) of Law 4738/2020 (Government Gazette, Series I, Issue 207) on compulsory revocation shall also apply to mortgages.

Άρθρο 36

Μετανηολόγηση - Μετονομασία ενυπόθηκου πλοίου

1. Απαγορεύεται η αλλαγή του λιμένα νηολόγησης (μετανηολόγηση) ή η μετονομασία ενυπόθηκου πλοίου χωρίς την έγγραφη συναίνεση των ενυπόθηκων δανειστών.

2. Το νέο όνομα, ο νέος λιμένας νηολόγησης και η έγγραφη συναίνεση των ενυπόθηκων δανειστών καταχωρίζονται στο νηολόγιο και το υποθηκολόγιο με μέριμνα της αρμόδιας λιμενικής αρχής.

Άρθρο 37

Ακυρότητα εκποίησης πλοίου

Εκποιητική δικαιοπραξία ενυπόθηκου πλοίου που επιφέρει απώλεια της ελληνικής εθνικότητας, εφόσον έγινε χωρίς την έγγραφη συναίνεση των ενυπόθηκων δανειστών, είναι άκυρη.

Άρθρο 38

Διατήρηση υποθήκης

1. Απλή ή προτιμώμενη υποθήκη που έχει καταχωρισθεί σε δημόσιο βιβλίο σύμφωνα με το δίκαιο της προηγούμενης σημαίας του πλοίου, εξακολουθεί να διατηρεί την ισχύ της κατά τον χρόνο κτήσης της ελληνικής εθνικότητας, εφόσον εγγραφεί στο ελληνικό υποθηκολόγιο εντός εξήντα (60) ημερών από τη νηολόγηση.

2. Η κατά τα ως άνω εγγραφή της υποθήκης διασφαλίζει την τάξη που είχε κατά τον χρόνο εγγραφής στο προηγούμενο νηολόγιο.

Άρθρο 39

Επιφύλαξη ειδικότερων διατάξεων

Η παραχώρηση προτιμώμενης ναυτικής υποθήκης σε πλοίο ολικής χωρητικότητας τουλάχιστον χιλίων πεντακοσίων (1.500) κόρων, σύμφωνα με το ν.δ. 2687/1953 (Α' 317) δεν θίγεται από τις διατάξεις του παρόντος.

Άρθρο 40

Ανάλογη εφαρμογή

Οι σχετικές με την υποθήκη διατάξεις του Αστικού Κώδικα εφαρμόζονται αναλόγως για τα μη ρυθμιζόμενα με τον παρόντα θέματα.

Άρθρο 41

Περαιτέρω σύσταση προτιμώμενης υποθήκης

Με προεδρικό διάταγμα, μετά από πρόταση των Υπουργών Ναυτιλίας και Νησιωτικής Πολιτικής και Δικαιοσύνης, μπορεί να προβλέπεται η σύσταση προτιμώμενης υποθήκης και σε πλοία ολικής χωρητικότητας μικρότερης των πεντακοσίων (500) κόρων.

Article 36

Transfer of register - Re-naming of a mortgaged ship

1. It shall be prohibited to change the port of registry (transfer of register) or to re-name a mortgaged ship without the written consent of the mortgagees.

2. The competent port authority shall enter the new name, the new port of registry and the written consent of the mortgagees in the ship registry and the mortgage register.

Article 37

Nullity of sale of a ship

Any legal transaction concerning sale of a mortgaged ship and resulting in loss of Greek nationality shall be null and void if done without the written consent of the mortgagees.

Article 38

Continued effect of mortgages

1. A simple or preferred mortgage entered in a public register in accordance with the law of the state of the flag previously flown by the ship shall remain effective when the ship acquires Greek nationality, provided it is entered in the Greek mortgage register within 60 days of the date of registration.

2. The entry of the mortgage in accordance with the foregoing shall retain the same class it had when it was entered in the previous register.

Article 39

Operation of more specific provisions

The provisions of this Code are without prejudice to the granting of a preferred mortgage on a ship with a gross tonnage of at least 1,500 tons, in accordance with Legislative Decree 2687/1953 (Government Gazette, Series I, Issue 317).

Article 40

Mutatis mutandis application

The provisions of the Civil Code on mortgages apply *mutatis mutandis* to issues not regulated by this Code.

Article 41

Further establishment of a preferred mortgage

A Presidential Decree, issued on a proposal from the Minister of Maritime Affairs and Insular Policy and the Minister of Justice, may also provide for the establishment of preferred mortgages on ships with a gross tonnage under 500 tons.

ΚΕΦΑΛΑΙΟ Β'

ΝΑΥΤΙΚΑ ΠΡΟΝΟΜΙΑ

Άρθρο 42

Προνομιούχες απαιτήσεις

1. Από τις απαιτήσεις κατά προσώπου που εκμεταλλεύεται πλοίο για δικό του λογαριασμό, εξοπλίζονται με προνόμιο επί του πλοίου από τη γέννησή τους μόνο:

α) οι συναφείς προς τη ναυσιπλοΐα φόροι, τα βαρύνοντα το πλοίο τέλη και δικαιώματα, κατά το τελευταίο, πριν την αναγκαστική κατάσχεση, εξάμηνο, και τα έξοδα συντήρησης του πλοίου από τον κατάπλου του στον λιμένα όπου κατασχέθηκε (πρώτη τάξη),

β) οι απαιτήσεις του πλοιάρχου και του πληρώματος που πηγάζουν από τη σύμβαση της ναυτικής εργασίας τους και οι απαιτήσεις των φορέων της κοινωνικής ασφάλισής τους, στην έκταση που προσδιορίζεται από τις εκάστοτε ισχύουσες ειδικές διατάξεις (δεύτερη τάξη),

γ) τα έξοδα και οι αμοιβές λόγω επιθαλάσσιας αρωγής (τρίτη τάξη) και

δ) οι οφειλόμενες στα πλοία, τους επιβάτες και τα φορτία αποζημιώσεις λόγω σύγκρουσης ή πρόσκρουσης πλοίων (τέταρτη τάξη).

2. Τα προνόμια προηγούνται κάθε υποθήκης.

3. Οι απαιτήσεις της παρ. 1 κατατάσσονται στον πίνακα διανομής μετά την αφαίρεση των εξόδων του επισπεύσαντος τον πλειστηριασμό, που έγιναν προς το κοινό συμφέρον των δανειστών, συμπεριλαμβανομένης της επιβαλλόμενης από τον νόμο δαπάνης φύλαξης του πλοίου.

Άρθρο 43

Κατάταξη προνομιούχων απαιτήσεων

1. Οι προνομιούχες απαιτήσεις της ίδιας τάξης κατατάσσονται συμμέτρως.

2. Στις απαιτήσεις της τρίτης τάξης οι μεταγενέστερες προηγούνται των προγενέστερων. Κατ' εξαίρεση, προνόμια που εξασφαλίζουν απαιτήσεις από την τελευταία πριν από τον πλειστηριασμό αρωγή ή διάσωση του πλοίου προηγούνται όλων των προνομίων που επιβάρυναν το πλοίο πριν τη διενέργεια των αντίστοιχων πράξεων αρωγής ή διάσωσης. Απαιτήσεις της τρίτης τάξης που αφορούν στο ίδιο συμβάν κατατάσσονται συμμέτρως.

Άρθρο 44

Απόσβεση προνομίου λόγω συμβατικής εκποίησης πλοίου

1. Αν το πλοίο εκποιηθεί συμβατικά, το προνόμιο εξακολουθεί να υφίσταται, εφόσον με δικαστική απόφαση αναγνωριστεί έναντι αυτού που το απέκτησε, κατόπιν άσκησης σχετικής αγωγής μέσα σε αποσβεστική προθεσμία τριών (3) μηνών από την εγγραφή της εκποιητικής σύμβασης στο νηολόγιο.

2. Προκειμένου περί προνομιούχων απαιτήσεων από τη σύμβαση εργασίας του πλοιάρχου και του πληρώματος, η προθεσμία της παρ. 1 είναι ένα (1) έτος από την εγγραφή της εκποιητικής σύμβασης στο νηολόγιο.

CHAPTER II
MARITIME LIENS

Article 42
Preferential claims

1. The following claims against a person operating a ship on own account shall enjoy a lien on the ship from the time they arise alone:

a) navigation-related taxes, fees and charges concerning the ship during the six months prior to compulsory arrest, as well as ship maintenance costs from the time the ship calls at the port where it was arrested (first-class liens);

b) the claims of the master and the crew arising from their seafarers' employment agreement, as well as claims of their social security organisations, to the extent specified by the specific provisions in force at any given time (second-class liens);

c) costs and fees due to salvage (third-class liens); and

d) compensation concerning ships, passengers and cargo due to collision or impact of ships (fourth-class liens).

2. Liens have priority over all mortgages.

3. The claims referred to in paragraph 1 shall be ranked in the distribution table after deducting the costs of the person who initiated the auction incurred in the common interest of the creditors, including the legally required expenditure for custody of the ship.

Article 43
Ranking of preferential claims

1. Preferential claims belonging to the same class shall be ranked *pari passu*.

2. In claims secured by third-class liens, later claims shall outrank earlier claims. By way of exception, liens securing claims from the last salvage of the ship prior to auction shall outrank all liens encumbering the ship before the corresponding salvage or rescue operations were carried out. Claims secured by third-class liens concerning the same incident shall be ranked *pari passu*.

Article 44
Extinction of liens due to contractual sale of a ship

1. If a ship is sold by means of a contract, the lien shall continue to exist, provided it is acknowledged in a court judgment handed down against the person who acquired the ship, following a relevant action filed within a fixed deadline of three months from the entry of the sale contract in the ship registry.

2. In cases of preferential claims arising from the master's and crew's employment agreements, the deadline

Άρθρο 45

Απόσβεση προνομίου με τον πλειστηριασμό πλοίου

1. Εκτός των γενικών λόγων, το προνόμιο αποσβέννυται και με την εκποίηση του πλοίου σε δημόσιο πλειστηριασμό.

2. Στην περίπτωση της παρ. 1 οι απαιτήσεις που αναγγέλθηκαν, ανεξαρτήτως της κατάταξής τους ή μη, παύουν να βαρύνουν το πλοίο.

Άρθρο 46

Προνόμιο επί του ασφαλίσματος

Το προνόμιο δεν ασκείται επί του ασφαλίσματος.

Άρθρο 47

Εφαρμοστέο δίκαιο

1. Τα ναυτικά προνόμια, οι ναυτικές υποθήκες και τα λοιπά εμπράγματα δικαιώματα επί του πλοίου διέπονται από το δίκαιο που καθορίζεται στο άρθρο 16.

2. Ως προς την κατάταξη των προνομιούχων απαιτήσεων εφαρμόζεται το δίκαιο του τόπου εκτέλεσης.

referred to in paragraph 1 shall be one year from the entry of the sale contract in the ship registry.

Article 45

Extinction of liens following auctioning of the ship

1. In addition to the general grounds [for extinction], liens shall also be extinguished by sale of the ship at public auction.

2. In the case referred to in paragraph 1, any lodged claims, irrespective of whether or not they are ranked, shall cease to encumber the ship.

Article 46

Lien on indemnity

Liens may not attach to indemnity.

Article 47

Applicable law

1. Maritime liens, mortgages and other rights *in rem* on ships shall be governed by the law specified in Article 16.

2. The law of the place of enforcement shall apply to the ranking of preferential claims.

ΜΕΡΟΣ ΤΡΙΤΟ
ΕΚΜΕΤΑΛΛΕΥΣΗ ΤΟΥ ΠΛΟΙΟΥ

ΚΕΦΑΛΑΙΟ Α'
ΠΛΟΙΟΚΤΗΣΙΑ

Άρθρο 48
Έννοια πλοιοκτήτη

Με την επιφύλαξη ειδικότερων ορισμών που περιέχονται σε κυρωθείσες διεθνείς συμβάσεις, πλοιοκτήτης είναι το φυσικό ή νομικό πρόσωπο που εκμεταλλεύεται δικό του πλοίο, στο όνομα και για λογαριασμό του.

Άρθρο 49
Ευθύνη πλοιοκτήτη

1. Ο πλοιοκτήτης ευθύνεται από τις δικαιοπραξίες τις οποίες επιχείρησε ο πλοίαρχος κατά την εκτέλεση των καθηκόντων που ανατέθηκαν σε αυτόν.

2. Επίσης ευθύνεται από τις αδικοπραξίες, τις οποίες διέπραξε ο πλοίαρχος, το πλήρωμα ή ο πλοηγός κατά την εκτέλεση των καθηκόντων που τους ανατέθηκαν, με την επιφύλαξη του ναυτικού πταίσματος στη σύμβαση θαλάσσιας μεταφοράς πραγμάτων.

3. Ο πλοιοκτήτης δικαιούται να περιορίσει την ευθύνη του σύμφωνα με τη Διεθνή Σύμβαση του Λονδίνου του 1976/1996 για τον περιορισμό της ευθύνης για ναυτικές απαιτήσεις, (Διεθνής Σύμβαση Περιορισμού), η οποία κυρώθηκε με τον ν. 1923/1991 (Α' 13), όπως εκάστοτε ισχύει, και το Κεφάλαιο Β' του Ένατου Μέρους του παρόντος.

Άρθρο 50
Ευθύνη επί μεταβίβασης κυριότητας πλοίου από τον πλοιοκτήτη

Σε περίπτωση μεταβίβασης κυριότητας πλοίου από τον πλοιοκτήτη, το άρθρο 479 του Αστικού Κώδικα δεν εφαρμόζεται.

PART THREE
OPERATION OF SHIPS

CHAPTER I
SHIP OWNERSHIP-OPERATION

Article 48
Concept of an owner-operator of a ship

Without prejudice to more specific definitions contained in ratified international treaties and conventions, an owner-operator is a natural or legal person operating its own ship, in its own name and on its own account.

Article 49
Liability of owners-operators

1. The owner-operator shall be liable for the legal transactions entered into by the master in the performance of the duties assigned to him or her.

2. Moreover, the owner-operator shall be liable for torts committed by the master, the crew or the pilot in the performance of the duties assigned to them, without prejudice to nautical fault in the contract of carriage of goods by sea.

3. The owner-operator shall be entitled to limitation of liability in accordance with the Convention on Limitation of Liability for Maritime Claims (London, 1976/1996), which was ratified by Law 1923/1991 (Government Gazette, Series I, Issue 13), as in force from time to time, and in accordance with Chapter II of Part Nine of this Code.

Article 50
Liability in cases of transfer of ownership of a ship by the owner-operator

In cases of transfer of ship ownership by the owner-operator, Article 479 of the Civil Code shall not apply.

ΚΕΦΑΛΑΙΟ Β'

ΣΥΜΠΛΟΙΟΚΤΗΣΙΑ

Άρθρο 51

Έννοια και χαρακτηριστικά συμπλοιοκτησίας

1. Όταν συγκύριοι πλοίου εκμεταλλεύονται αυτό από κοινού (συμπλοιοκτησία), εφαρμόζεται το παρόν Κεφάλαιο και συμπληρωματικά οι διατάξεις περί ομόρρυθμης εταιρείας.

2. Αν δεν συνάγεται κάτι άλλο από τη μερίδα του πλοίου, τεκμαίρεται ότι οι συγκύριοι του πλοίου συνεκμεταλλεύονται αυτό.

3. Η συμπλοιοκτησία έχει ικανότητα δικαίου και πτωχευτική ικανότητα.

4. Συμφωνίες μεταξύ συμπλοιοκτητών με περιεχόμενο διαφορετικό από τις διατάξεις του παρόντος Κεφαλαίου, εφόσον επιτρέπονται, καταρτίζονται εγγράφως.

5. Συμπλοιοκτησία μπορεί να υπάρξει και επί ναυπηγούμενου πλοίου που έχει νηολογηθεί.

Άρθρο 52

Σχέσεις των συμπλοιοκτητών - Συμμετοχή στις δαπάνες

1. Εκτός αν συμφωνείται διαφορετικά, οι αποφάσεις σε ζητήματα που αφορούν στη συμπλοιοκτησία λαμβάνονται κατά πλειοψηφία του συνόλου των μερίδων.

2. Αν η εκμετάλλευση του πλοίου δυσχεραίνεται ουσιωδώς, διότι δεν είναι εφικτή η επίτευξη πλειοψηφίας, το δικαστήριο μπορεί, δικάζοντας κατά τη διαδικασία της εκούσιας δικαιοδοσίας, ύστερα από αίτηση οποιουδήποτε συμπλοιοκτήτη, και με κλήση των λοιπών συμπλοιοκτητών, εκτός αν αυτό είναι δυσχερές, να διατάξει τον διορισμό προσωρινού διαχειριστή ή την εκποίηση του πλοίου σε δημόσιο πλειστηριασμό.

3. Εκτός αν συμφωνείται διαφορετικά, οι συμπλοιοκτήτες συμμετέχουν στα κέρδη, τις ζημίες και τις δαπάνες της συμπλοιοκτησίας κατά τον λόγο της μερίδας τους.

Άρθρο 53

Διαχείριση και εκπροσώπηση της συμπλοιοκτησίας - Υποχρέωση λογοδοσίας

1. Η παρ. 1 του άρθρου 52 ισχύει και ως προς τις σχέσεις της συμπλοιοκτησίας με τους τρίτους.

2. Η διαχείριση και εκπροσώπηση της συμπλοιοκτησίας μπορεί να ανατεθεί σε ένα ή περισσότερα πρόσωπα, συμπλοιοκτήτες ή μη, είτε με την εταιρική σύμβαση, είτε με απόφαση των συμπλοιοκτητών. Σε περίπτωση ορισμού περισσότερων διαχειριστών, αυτοί ενεργούν ομόφωνα.

3. Ο διορισμός, η παραίτηση ή η ανάκληση του διαχειριστή προβάλλονται στους τρίτους μόνον εφόσον σημειωθούν στη μερίδα του πλοίου.

4. Ο πλοίαρχος ακολουθεί τις οδηγίες μόνον του διαχειριστή.

5. Ο διαχειριστής έχει υποχρέωση να τηρεί ίδια βιβλία για τη διαχείριση της συμπλοιοκτησίας και να φυλάσσει τα δικαιολογητικά έγγραφα της διαχείρισης. Λογοδοτεί σε κάθε συμπλοιοκτήτη, εφόσον του ζητηθεί.

CHAPTER II

JOINT SHIP OWNERSHIP

Article 51

Concept and characteristics of joint ship ownership

1. Where joint owners of a ship jointly operate it (joint ship ownership), this Chapter shall apply and the provisions on general partnerships shall apply on a supplementary basis.

2. Unless the contrary can be inferred from the shares in the ship, it shall be presumed that the joint owners of the ship are jointly operating it.

3. [As a corporate form,] the joint ship ownership has legal capacity and bankruptcy capacity.

4. Where the contents of agreements between joint shipowners of a ship differ from the provisions of this Chapter, provided that is permissible, such agreement shall be drawn up in writing.

5. A registered ship under construction may also be subject to joint ship ownership.

Article 52

Relationships between joint shipowners - Participation in costs

1. Unless otherwise agreed upon, decisions on matters concerning the joint ship ownership shall be made by majority of the total number of shares.

2. If operation of the ship is materially hindered due to inability to achieve a majority, the court may, trying the matter under non-contentious proceedings following an application filed by any joint ship owner and after the other joint shipowners have been summoned, unless this is difficult, order that a temporary manager be appointed or that the ship be sold at public auction.

3. Unless otherwise agreed upon, the joint ship owners shall participate in the profits, losses and costs of the joint ship ownership pro rata to their share.

Article 53

Management and representation of the joint ship ownership - Obligation to render account

1. Article 52(1) shall also apply to relationships between the joint ship ownership and third parties.

2. The management and representation of the joint ship ownership may be assigned to one or more persons, whether or not joint shipowners, either in the partnership agreement or in a decision made by the joint shipowners. Where several managers are appointed, they shall act unanimously.

3. The appointment, resignation or removal of the manager shall be effective vis-à-vis third parties solely if recorded in the ship's [ship registry] account.

4. The master shall follow the instructions of the manager alone.

5. The manager shall be obligated to keep special ledgers concerning management of the joint ship ownership and to safekeep the documentation concerning management. Where requested to do so, the manager shall render account to any joint shipowner.

Άρθρο 54
Ευθύνη συμπλοιοκτητών

1. Οι συμπλοιοκτήτες ευθύνονται έναντι των τρίτων κατά τον λόγο της μερίδας τους.

2. Συμφωνίες για περιορισμό ή αποκλεισμό της ευθύνης, όπως αυτή ορίζεται στην παρ. 1, δεν ισχύουν έναντι των τρίτων.

Άρθρο 55
Μεταβίβαση πλοίου ή μερίδας - Αποτελέσματα

1. Για τη μεταβίβαση της κυριότητας του πλοίου απαιτείται απόφαση των συμπλοιοκτητών που συγκεντρώνει πλειοψηφία τουλάχιστον τεσσάρων πέμπτων (4/5) του συνόλου των μερίδων. Κατά τα λοιπά εφαρμόζεται το άρθρο 12.

2. Κάθε ένας από τους συμπλοιοκτήτες μπορεί να εκποιήσει ελεύθερα τη μερίδα του επί του πλοίου, σύμφωνα με το άρθρο 12. Αντίθετη συμφωνία ενεργεί μόνο ενοχικώς. Ο αποκτών υπεισέρχεται αυτοδίκαια στη σύμβαση για τη συμπλοιοκτησία.

3. Συμβατική εκποίηση μερίδας επί του πλοίου που επιφέρει απώλεια της ελληνικής εθνικότητας είναι άκυρη, αν γίνεται χωρίς την έγγραφη συναίνεση των συμπλοιοκτητών που συγκεντρώνουν τουλάχιστον τα τέσσερα πέμπτα (4/5) των μερίδων. Μνεία της δήλωσης συναίνεσης περιλαμβάνεται στην πράξη της διαγραφής.

4. Ο μεταβιβάσας και ο αποκτών ευθύνονται σε ολόκληρο, κατά τον λόγο της μεταβιβασθείσας μερίδας, για αξιώσεις κατά της συμπλοιοκτησίας που γεννήθηκαν μέχρι την καταχώριση της μεταβίβασης στη μερίδα του πλοίου.

Άρθρο 56
Εκποίηση πλοίου με άδεια του δικαστηρίου

1. Κάθε συμπλοιοκτήτης μπορεί να ζητήσει από το δικαστήριο να επιτρέψει την εκποίηση του πλοίου σε δημόσιο πλειστηριασμό, εάν τούτο κατέστη ανίκανο προς πλου ή αν συντρέχει άλλος σπουδαίος λόγος.

2. Ο πλειστηριασμός ενεργείται εντός έξι (6) μηνών από την τελεσιδικία της απόφασης, σύμφωνα με τις διατάξεις για την αναγκαστική εκποίηση πλοίων.

Άρθρο 57
Έξοδος συμπλοιοκτήτη

1. Αν ληφθεί απόφαση για την επισκευή ή μετασκευή του πλοίου σε μεγάλη έκταση ή για σύσταση κεφαλαίου περιορισμού ευθύνης σύμφωνα με το Κεφάλαιο Β' του Ενάτου Μέρους, κάθε συμπλοιοκτήτης που δεν συναίνεσε, μπορεί να απαλλαγεί από την υποχρέωσή του προς εκτέλεση της απόφασης, διαθέτοντας, χωρίς αποζημίωση, τη μερίδα του υπέρ των λοιπών συμπλοιοκτητών, κατά τον λόγο των μερίδων τους. Το δικαίωμα παραχώρησης ασκείται, εντός τριάντα (30) ημερών από την κοινοποίηση της απόφασης, με δήλωση που επιδίδεται στους λοιπούς συμπλοιοκτήτες και καταχωρίζεται στο νηολόγιο.

2. Συμπλοιοκτήτης ο οποίος είναι και μέλος του πληρώματος, αν απολυθεί, έχει δικαίωμα να ζητήσει την εξαγορά της μερίδας του από τους λοιπούς συμπλοιοκτήτες. Το τίμημα καθορίζεται από το δικαστήριο με τη διαδικασία της εκούσιας δικαιοδοσίας μετά από τη διενέργεια πραγματογνωμοσύνης. Η κυριότητα μεταβιβάζεται, εφόσον το τίμημα καταβληθεί στον δικαιούχο ή γίνει δημόσια κατάθεσή του.

Article 54

Liability of joint shipowners

1. Joint shipowners shall be liable vis-à-vis third parties pro rata to their share [in the ship].

2. Agreements on limitation or exclusion of the liability provided for in paragraph 1 are not effective vis-à-vis third parties.

Article 55

Transfer of a ship or share - Effects

1. Transferring ownership of a ship shall require a decision of the joint shipowners with a majority of at least 4/5 of the total number of shares. In all other respects, Article 12 shall apply.

2. Any joint shipowner may freely sell their share in the ship, in accordance with Article 12. Any agreement to the contrary shall only entail a personal obligation. The transferee shall automatically become a party to the joint ship ownership agreement.

3. A contractual sale of a share in a ship resulting in loss of Greek nationality shall be null and void if effected without the written consent of joint shipowners holding at least 4/5 of the shares. The deregistration decision shall make reference to the declaration of consent.

4. The transferor and the transferee shall be severally liable, pro rata to the transferred share, for claims against the joint ship ownership which arose up to the date the transfer was entered into the ship's [ship registry] account.

Article 56

Sale of a ship with permission of the court

1. If the ship becomes unseaworthy or if there is other good cause, any joint shipowner may petition the court for permission to sell the ship at public auction.

2. The auction shall be held within six months from the date the judgment becomes *de jure* non-appealable, in accordance with the provisions on forced sale of ships.

Article 57

Withdrawal from the joint ship ownership

1. If it is decided to extensively repair or retrofit the ship or establish a liability limitation fund in accordance with Chapter II of Part Nine, any non-consenting joint shipowner may be exempted from the obligation to carry out the decision, and shall offer their share, without compensation, to the other joint ship owners, pro rata to their shares. The right of concession shall be exercised within 30 days from notification of the decision by means of a declaration served on the other joint shipowners and entered in the ship registry.

2. If a joint shipowner who is also a crew member is dismissed, they shall have the right to request that their share be bought out by the other joint shipowners. The price shall be set by the court under non-contentious proceedings, following preparation of expert evidence. Ownership shall be transferred if the price is paid to the beneficiary or deposited with the state.

Άρθρο 58

Συντρέχουσα δικαιοδοσία

Για τις διαφορές τις σχετικές με τη συμπλοιοκτησία αρμόδιο είναι και το δικαστήριο του λιμένα νηολόγησης ή καταχώρισης του πλοίου.

ΚΕΦΑΛΑΙΟ Γ'

ΕΦΟΠΛΙΣΜΟΣ

Άρθρο 59

Έννοια εφοπλιστή

Εφοπλιστής είναι το φυσικό ή νομικό πρόσωπο που εκμεταλλεύεται για δικό του λογαριασμό πλοίο που ανήκει σε άλλον.

Άρθρο 60

Δημοσιότητα εφοπλισμού

1. Ο εφοπλιστής δηλώνει τη σχέση εφοπλισμού από κοινού με τον κύριο του πλοίου στη λιμενική αρχή του τόπου νηολόγησης, εγγράφως ή με ηλεκτρονικά μέσα. Η υποβολή χωριστών δηλώσεων είναι δυνατή.

2. Η δήλωση που περιλαμβάνει το όνομα, την ιθαγένεια και την κατοικία του εφοπλιστή, τη διάρκεια της εκμετάλλευσης, καθώς και τα χαρακτηριστικά του πλοίου, καταχωρίζεται στο νηολόγιο και σημειώνεται στο έγγραφο εθνικότητας του πλοίου.

3. Εάν δεν γίνει καταχώριση της δήλωσης, ο κύριος του πλοίου τεκμαίρεται ότι εκμεταλλεύεται τούτο για λογαριασμό του.

4. Η διαγραφή της σχέσης εφοπλισμού από το νηολόγιο γίνεται είτε με κοινή δήλωση των μερών, είτε με δικαστική απόφαση.

5. Η σχέση εφοπλισμού που καταχωρίσθηκε στο νηολόγιο ισχύει, μεταξύ του αποκτώντος και του εφοπλιστή, και μετά τη μεταβίβαση της κυριότητας του πλοίου, εκτός εάν έχει συμφωνηθεί διαφορετικά στη σύμβαση εφοπλισμού.

6. Οι ανωτέρω καταχωρίσεις γίνονται στο ειδικό δημόσιο βιβλίο του άρθρου 4 για τα πλοία που εμπίπτουν στο πεδίο εφαρμογής του.

Άρθρο 61

Διορισμός πλοιάρχου

Ο εφοπλιστής, αν δεν υπάρχει αντίθετη συμφωνία, διορίζει τον πλοίαρχο.

Άρθρο 62

Ευθύνη εφοπλιστή

Ο εφοπλιστής ευθύνεται σύμφωνα με το άρθρο 49.

Article 58

Concurrent jurisdiction

The court of the port where the ship was registered or entered [in the special public register of small ships] shall also have jurisdiction over disputes concerning the joint ship ownership.

CHAPTER III

OPERATION

Article 59

Concept of operator

An operator is a natural or legal person operating on its own account a ship belonging to another.

Article 60

Disclosure of operation

1. The operator and the owner of the ship shall jointly declare the operation relationship to the port authority of the place of registration, whether in writing or using electronic means. Separate declarations may be filed.

2. The declaration containing the name, nationality and domicile of the operator, the duration of operation and the particulars of the ship shall be entered in the ship registry and noted in the ship's certificate of nationality.

3. If no declaration is registered, the owner of the ship shall be presumed to be operating the ship on own account.

4. The operation relationship may be deregistered either by means of a joint declaration made by the parties or pursuant to a court judgment.

5. Unless otherwise agreed upon in the operation agreement, the operation relationship entered in the ship registry shall remain effective between the transferee and the operator even after ownership of the ship has been transferred.

6. The above entries shall be made in the special public register referred to in Article 4 concerning ships falling within its scope.

Article 61

Appointment of a master

Unless otherwise agreed upon, the operator shall appoint the master.

Article 62

Liability of the operator

The operator shall be liable in accordance with Article 49.

Άρθρο 63

Ευθύνη του κυρίου του πλοίου

1. Οι απαιτήσεις που απορρέουν από τον εφοπλισμό πλοίου, με εξαίρεση τις απαιτήσεις από σύμβαση μεταφοράς πραγμάτων, ασκούνται και κατά του κυρίου αυτού, υπό τους όρους των παρ. 2 και 3 του παρόντος.

2. Εφόσον οι απαιτήσεις που απορρέουν από τον εφοπλισμό υπόκεινται σε περιορισμό κατά την έννοια της Διεθνούς Σύμβασης Περιορισμού, όπως εκάστοτε ισχύει, ο κύριος ευθύνεται μέχρι των ορίων που προβλέπονται στη Σύμβαση.

3. Εφόσον οι απαιτήσεις που απορρέουν από τον εφοπλισμό δεν υπόκεινται σε περιορισμό κατά την έννοια της Διεθνούς Σύμβασης της παρ. 2, ο κύριος ευθύνεται δια του πλοίου και μέχρι την αξία αυτού. Σε περίπτωση πλειστηριασμού, ο κύριος ευθύνεται μέχρι την αξία του εκπλειστηριάσματος, εφόσον ήταν κύριος κατά τον χρόνο της γένεσης των απαιτήσεων και επιβολής της αναγκαστικής κατάσχεσης στο πλοίο.

4. Η ευθύνη του κυρίου του πλοίου για τις ανωτέρω απαιτήσεις διέπεται από το δίκαιο που αρμόζει στη σχέση από το σύνολο των ειδικών συνθηκών.

ΚΕΦΑΛΑΙΟ Δ'

ΔΙΑΧΕΙΡΙΣΗ ΚΑΙ ΝΑΥΤΙΚΗ ΠΡΑΚΤΟΡΕΙΑ

Άρθρο 64

Έννοια διαχείρισης πλοίου

1. Ο πλοιοκτήτης ή ο εφοπλιστής μπορεί να αναθέτει σε τρίτο (διαχειριστή) την ολική ή μερική διαχείριση του πλοίου, έναντι αμοιβής. Η διαχείριση του πλοίου μπορεί να είναι τεχνική, εμπορική ή και τα δύο.

2. Η σχέση που συνδέει τον διαχειριστή πλοίου με τον πλοιοκτήτη ή τον εφοπλιστή είναι μίσθωση ανεξαρτήτων υπηρεσιών.

Άρθρο 65

Ευθύνη διαχειριστή πλοίου

1. Έναντι των τρίτων, ο διαχειριστής πλοίου ενεργεί ως άμεσος αντιπρόσωπος του πλοιοκτήτη ή του εφοπλιστή σύμφωνα με τις διατάξεις περί αντιπροσώπευσης του Αστικού Κώδικα, εκτός εάν διεθνής σύμβαση ή ειδικός νόμος ορίζουν διαφορετικά.

2. Ο διαχειριστής πλοίου έχει προσωπική ευθύνη, όταν δεν δηλώνει ρητά σε τρίτους ότι ενεργεί για τον πλοιοκτήτη ή τον εφοπλιστή και δεν συνάγεται τούτο από τις περιστάσεις, καθώς και όταν η δικαιοπραξία υπερβαίνει τα όρια της εξουσίας του.

3. Ο διαχειριστής δικαιούται να περιορίσει την ευθύνη του με βάση τη Διεθνή Σύμβαση Περιορισμού όπως εκάστοτε ισχύει και το Κεφάλαιο Β' του Ένατου Μέρους του παρόντος.

Article 63

Liability of the owner of the ship

1. Save claims arising from contracts for the carriage of goods, claims arising from the operation of a ship shall also be brought against its owner, subject to the conditions laid down in paragraphs 2 and 3 of this Article.

2. Where the claims arising from operation are subject to limitation, within the meaning of the International Convention on Limitation of Liability, as in force from time to time, the owner shall be liable up to the limits laid down in the Convention.

3. Where the claims arising from operation are not subject to limitation, within the meaning of the International Convention referred to in paragraph 2, the owner shall be liable for the ship and up to its value. In the event of an auction, the owner shall be liable up to the value of the auction price, provided they were the owner when the claims arose and when the ship was placed under compulsory arrest.

4. The owner's liability for the aforesaid claims shall be governed by the law applicable to the relationship in light of all the specific circumstances.

CHAPTER IV

MANAGEMENT AND SHIPPING AGENCY

Article 64

Concept of ship management

1. The owner-operator or the operator may assign management of the ship, in whole or in part, to a third party (manager) for a fee. Management of the ship may be technical, commercial or both.

2. The relationship between the ship manager and the owner-operator or operator shall be one of hire of independent services.

Article 65

Liability of the ship manager

1. Unless otherwise provided for in an international convention or treaty or a specific law, the ship manager shall act towards third parties as the direct agent of the owner-operator or of the operator, in accordance with the provisions of the Civil Code on agency.

2. The ship manager shall be personally liable where they do not expressly declare to third parties that they are acting on behalf of the owner-operator or the operator and this cannot be inferred from the circumstances, and where the legal transaction is *ultra vires*.

3. The manager shall be entitled to limit their liability on the basis of the International Convention on Limitation of Liability, as in force from time to time, and Chapter II of Part Nine of this Code.

Άρθρο 66

Έννοια ναυτικού πράκτορα - Σύμβαση ναυτικής πρακτορείας

1. Ναυτικός πράκτορας είναι το φυσικό ή νομικό πρόσωπο που παρέχει υπηρεσίες πρακτορείας στο πλοίο ή και στο φορτίο.

2. Για την κατάρτιση σύμβασης ναυτικής πρακτορείας δεν απαιτείται η τήρηση έγγραφου τύπου. Κάθε συμβαλλόμενο μέρος έχει το δικαίωμα να ζητήσει την έγγραφη κατάρτιση της σύμβασης.

3. Με την επιφύλαξη ειδικότερων διατάξεων, στη σύμβαση ναυτικής πρακτορείας εφαρμόζεται αναλόγως το π.δ. 219/1991 (Α' 81), περί εμπορικής αντιπροσωπείας.

Άρθρο 67

Αξιώσεις ναυτικού πράκτορα - Ευθύνη

1. Ο ναυτικός πράκτορας δικαιούται αμοιβής για τις υπηρεσίες του και απόδοσης των σχετικών δαπανών του.

2. Ο ναυτικός πράκτορας ευθύνεται κατά την εκτέλεση των εργασιών του για κάθε πταίσμα.

Άρθρο 68

Αντιπροσωπευτική εξουσία ναυτικού πράκτορα

1. Ο ναυτικός πράκτορας ενεργεί στο όνομα και για λογαριασμό του εντολέα του.

2. Περιορισμοί της αντιπροσωπευτικής εξουσίας του ναυτικού πράκτορα αντιτάσσονται στους τρίτους, εφόσον οι τρίτοι τους γνώριζαν ή, λαμβανομένων υπόψη των περιστάσεων, όφειλαν να τους γνωρίζουν.

3. Αναφορικά με τις υποθέσεις που του ανατίθενται, ο ναυτικός πράκτορας είναι αντίκλητος του εντολέα του.

ΚΕΦΑΛΑΙΟ Ε'

ΕΙΔΙΚΑ ΚΑΘΕΣΤΩΤΑ ΕΥΘΥΝΗΣ

Άρθρο 69

Ευθύνη για ζημίες ρύπανσης από πετρέλαιο

1. Η ευθύνη για ζημίες ρύπανσης από πετρέλαιο διέπεται αποκλειστικά από τη Διεθνή Σύμβαση του 1992 αναφορικά με την αστική ευθύνη για ζημίες ρύπανσης από πετρέλαιο, όπως κυρώθηκε με το π.δ. 197/1995 (Α' 106) και εκάστοτε ισχύει στην Ελλάδα (Διεθνής Σύμβαση ευθύνης για ρύπανση από πετρέλαιο).

2. Με την επιφύλαξη ειδικότερων ρυθμίσεων, για ζημίες ρύπανσης που δεν εμπίπτουν στο πεδίο εφαρμογής της διεθνούς σύμβασης της παρ. 1, εφαρμόζονται τα άρθρα 49 και 62 του παρόντος.

3. Η διαδικασία περιορισμού της ευθύνης και σύστασης κεφαλαίου, δυνάμει του άρθρου VI της Διεθνούς Σύμβασης ευθύνης για ρύπανση από πετρέλαιο, διέπεται από το Κεφάλαιο Β' του Ένατου Μέρους του παρόντος.

Article 66

Concept of shipping agent - Shipping agency agreements

1. A shipping agent is a natural or legal person providing agency services concerning the ship and/or cargo.

2. Shipping agency agreements need not be drawn up in writing. Each contracting party shall have the right to request that the agreement be drawn up in writing.

3. Without prejudice to more specific provisions, Presidential Decree 219/1991 (Government Gazette, Series I, Issue 81) on commercial agency shall apply *mutatis mutandis* to shipping agency agreements.

Article 67

Claims - Liability of shipping agents

1. Shipping agents shall be entitled to a fee for their services and to reimbursement of the relevant costs they have incurred.

2. Shipping agents shall be liable for any fault in the performance of their work.

Article 68

Agency powers of shipping agents

1. Shipping agents act in the name of and on behalf of their principals.

2. Limitations on the agency powers of shipping agents may be invoked vis-à-vis third parties where the third parties were or, given the circumstances, ought to have been aware of such limitations.

3. With regard to the affairs assigned to them, shipping agents function as process agents for their principals.

CHAPTER V

SPECIAL LIABILITY REGIMES

Article 69

Liability for oil pollution damage

1. Liability for oil pollution damage shall be governed exclusively by the 1992 International Convention on Civil Liability for Oil Pollution Damage, ratified by Presidential Decree 197/1995 (Government Gazette, Series I, Issue 106) and as in force in Greece from time to time (International Convention on Liability for Oil Pollution Damage).

2. Without prejudice to more specific provisions, Articles 49 and 62 of this Code shall apply to pollution damage not falling within the scope of the International Convention referred to in paragraph 1.

3. The procedure for limiting liability and constituting a fund pursuant to Article VI of the International Convention on Liability for Oil Pollution Damage shall be governed by Chapter II of Part Nine of this Code.

Άρθρο 70

Ευθύνη για ζημίες ρύπανσης από πετρέλαιο κίνησης

1. Η ευθύνη για ζημίες ρύπανσης από πετρέλαιο κίνησης διέπεται αποκλειστικά από τη Διεθνή Σύμβαση του 2001 αναφορικά με την αστική ευθύνη για ζημίες ρύπανσης από πετρέλαιο κίνησης, όπως κυρώθηκε με τον ν. 3393/2005 (Α' 242) και εκάστοτε ισχύει στην Ελλάδα (Διεθνής Σύμβαση ευθύνης για πετρέλαιο κίνησης).

2. Με την επιφύλαξη ειδικότερων ρυθμίσεων, για ζημίες ρύπανσης που δεν εμπίπτουν στο πεδίο εφαρμογής της διεθνούς σύμβασης της παρ. 1, εφαρμόζονται τα άρθρα 49 και 62 του παρόντος.

3. Η ευθύνη για τις αναφερόμενες στις παρ. 1 και 2 ζημίες περιορίζεται με βάση τη Διεθνή Σύμβαση Περιορισμού, όπως εκάστοτε ισχύει στην Ελλάδα. Η διαδικασία περιορισμού και σύστασης κεφαλαίου διέπεται από το Κεφάλαιο Β' του Ένατου Μέρους του παρόντος.

Άρθρο 71

Ευθύνη για ζημίες από τη μεταφορά επικίνδυνων και επιβλαβών ουσιών

1. Η ευθύνη για ζημίες από τη μεταφορά επικίνδυνων και επιβλαβών ουσιών διέπεται αποκλειστικά από τη Διεθνή Σύμβαση του 2010 αναφορικά με την αστική ευθύνη και αποζημίωση για ζημίες σχετικές με τη μεταφορά επικίνδυνων και επιβλαβών ουσιών, όπως εκάστοτε ισχύει στην Ελλάδα (Διεθνής Σύμβαση ευθύνης για επικίνδυνες και επιβλαβείς ουσίες).

2. Με την επιφύλαξη ειδικότερων ρυθμίσεων, για ζημίες που δεν εμπίπτουν στο πεδίο εφαρμογής της διεθνούς σύμβασης της παρ. 1, εφαρμόζονται τα άρθρα 49 και 62 του παρόντος.

3. Η διαδικασία περιορισμού της ευθύνης και σύστασης κεφαλαίου δυνάμει του άρθρου 9 της διεθνούς σύμβασης της παρ. 1, διέπεται από το Κεφάλαιο Β' του Ένατου Μέρους του παρόντος.

Article 70

Liability for bunker oil pollution damage

1. Liability for bunker oil pollution damage shall be governed exclusively by the 2001 International Convention on Civil Liability for Bunker Oil Pollution Damage, ratified by Law 3393/2005 (Government Gazette, Series I, Issue 242) and as in force in Greece from time to time since its ratification (International Convention on Liability for Bunker Oil Pollution Damage).

2. Without prejudice to more specific provisions, Articles 49 and 62 of this Code shall apply to pollution damage not falling within the scope of the International Convention referred to in paragraph 1.

3. Liability for the damage referred to in paragraphs 1 and 2 shall be limited on the basis of the International Convention on Limitation of Liability, as in force in Greece from time to time. The procedure for limiting liability and constituting a fund shall be governed by Chapter II of Part Nine of this Code.

Article 71

Liability for damage in connection with the carriage of hazardous and noxious substances

1. Liability for damage in connection with the carriage of hazardous and noxious substances shall be governed exclusively by the 2010 International Convention on Liability and Compensation for Damage in Connection with the Carriage of Hazardous and Noxious Substances by Sea, as in force in Greece from time to time (International Convention on Liability for Hazardous and Noxious Substances).

2. Without prejudice to more specific provisions, Articles 49 and 62 of this Code shall apply to damage not falling within the scope of the International Convention referred to in paragraph 1.

3. The procedure for limiting liability and constituting a fund pursuant to Article 9 of the International Convention referred to in paragraph 1 shall be governed by Chapter II of Part Nine of this Code.

ΜΕΡΟΣ ΤΕΤΑΡΤΟ
ΝΑΥΛΩΣΗ

ΚΕΦΑΛΑΙΟ Α'
ΟΡΙΣΜΟΣ - ΓΕΝΙΚΑ

Άρθρο 72
Έννοια

Με τη σύμβαση ναύλωσης ο εκναυλωτής παραχωρεί έναντι ανταλλάγματος (ναύλος) τη χρήση πλοίου στον ναυλωτή για τη διενέργεια θαλάσσιας μεταφοράς πράγματων ή προσώπων ή άλλο συμφωνηθέντα σκοπό.

Άρθρο 73
Δικαιοπρακτική αυτονομία

Το περιεχόμενο της σύμβασης ναύλωσης καθορίζεται ελεύθερα από τα συμβαλλόμενα μέρη, εκτός αν ορίζεται διαφορετικά στον παρόντα.

Άρθρο 74
Κατάρτιση της σύμβασης ναύλωσης

1. *Για τη σύναψη της σύμβασης ναύλωσης δεν απαιτείται η τήρηση τύπου. Η απόδειξη των όρων της γίνεται εγγράφως ή με ηλεκτρονικό μέσο (ναυλοσύμφωνο).*

2. *Σε περίπτωση έκδοσης φορτωτικής σε εκτέλεση σύμβασης ναύλωσης (φορτωτική ναυλοσυμφώνου), οι όροι του ναυλοσυμφώνου διέπουν τη σχέση των συμβαλλομένων στη σύμβαση ναύλωσης μερών. Στις σχέσεις με τρίτους ισχύει το Πέμπτο Μέρος.*

3. *Τα συμβαλλόμενα στη ναύλωση μέρη μπορούν να συμφωνούν εκ των προτέρων, με αναφορά στο ναυλοσύμφωνο, ότι οι μεταξύ τους σχέσεις διέπονται από τη Διεθνή Σύμβαση των Βρυξελλών του 1924 για την ενοποίηση ορισμένων κανόνων σχετικά με τις φορτωτικές με τα μεταγενέστερα Πρωτόκολλα αυτής, όπως κυρώθηκε με το άρθρο πρώτο του ν. 2107/1992 (Α' 203) και εκάστοτε ισχύει στην Ελλάδα (Κανόνες Χάγης-Βίσμπυ).*

Άρθρο 75
Ερμηνεία της σύμβασης ναύλωσης

Κατά την ερμηνεία των όρων της σύμβασης ναύλωσης αναζητείται η αληθινή βούληση των συμβαλλομένων μερών, όπως αυτή δηλώθηκε στη σύμβαση, λαμβανομένων υπόψη της καλής πίστης και των συναλλακτικών ηθών στην οικεία αγορά. Σε περίπτωση αντίφασης όρων που περιλαμβάνονται στην ίδια σύμβαση, προκρίνεται η ερμηνεία που διασφαλίζει την ενότητα της σύμβασης.

PART FOUR
CHARTERING

CHAPTER I
DEFINITION - GENERAL

Article 72
Concept

By means of a charter contract, the shipowner cedes use of the ship, for a fee (freight), to the charterer for the carriage of goods or persons by sea or for a different purpose agreed upon.

Article 73
Freedom of contract

Unless otherwise provided for in this Code, the content of the charter contract shall be freely determined by the contracting parties.

Article 74
Drafting of charter contracts

1. A charter contract need not be entered into in any particular format. Its terms shall be proven either in writing or using electronic means (charter-party).

2. Where a bill of lading is issued in performance of a charter contract (charter-party bill of lading), the terms of the charter-party shall govern the relationship between the parties to the charter contract. Part Five [of this Code] shall apply to relationships with third parties.

3. The parties to the charter contract may agree in advance, making reference to the charter-party, that the relationship between them shall be governed by the 1924 Brussels International Convention for the Unification of Certain Rules of Law relating to Bills of Lading and the subsequent Protocols thereto, ratified by the first Article of Law 2107/1992 (Government Gazette, Series I, Issue 203) and as in force in Greece from time to time (Hague-Visby Rules).

Article 75
Interpretation of charter contracts

Interpretation of the terms of a charter contract consists of seeking out the actual intent of the contracting parties, as declared in the contract, taking into consideration good faith and business usages in the market in question. In the event of contradiction between terms contained in the same contract, an interpretation that safeguards the unity of the contract shall be preferred.

Άρθρο 76
Υποναύλωση

1. Η υποναύλωση του πλοίου από τον ναυλωτή επιτρέπεται, εκτός εάν τα μέρη στη ναύλωση συμφωνήσουν διαφορετικά.

2. Ο υποναυλωτής υπέχει έναντι του εκναυλωτή τις υποχρεώσεις του ναυλωτή που προβλέπονται στον παρόντα. Ο ναυλωτής ευθύνεται έναντι του εκναυλωτή για το πταίσμα του υποναυλωτή.

3. Σε περίπτωση μη καταβολής του ναύλου από τον ναυλωτή, ο εκναυλωτής ειδοποιεί τον υποναυλωτή για την ύπαρξη και το ύψος της απαίτησής του κατά του ναυλωτή και τον καλεί να καταβάλει σε αυτόν τον υποναύλο. Από τον χρόνο της ειδοποίησης, ο εκναυλωτής έχει ευθεία αξίωση κατά του υποναυλωτή έως το ποσό που ο τελευταίος οφείλει στον ναυλωτή.

Άρθρο 77
Είδη ναύλωσης

1. Τα κύρια είδη της σύμβασης ναύλωσης, που ρυθμίζονται στα άρθρα 93 έως 116 είναι:

(α) η ναύλωση κατά χρόνο (χρονοναύλωση),

(β) η ναύλωση κατά πλου (ταξίδι),

(γ) η ναύλωση γυμνού πλοίου, και

(δ) η ναύλωση-πλαίσιο.

2. Δεν αποκλείεται σύμβαση ναύλωσης με διαφορετικά χαρακτηριστικά ή με συνδυασμό των κύριων χαρακτηριστικών των αναφερομένων στην παρ. 1 συμβάσεων.

3. Σε περίπτωση αμφιβολίας, το είδος της ναύλωσης και οι απορρέουσες από αυτό συνέπειες κρίνονται από τα κύρια χαρακτηριστικά της, όπως αυτά προκύπτουν από τη συμφωνία των μερών.

4. Η ναύλωση μπορεί να είναι ολική ή μερική, εκτός αν ειδικές διατάξεις ορίζουν διαφορετικά.

5. Σε περίπτωση μερικής ναύλωσης, είναι δυνατή η ναύλωση είτε συγκεκριμένου ποσοστού χωρητικότητας είτε συγκεκριμένου αποθηκευτικού χώρου του πλοίου.

6. Με την επιφύλαξη ειδικότερης ρύθμισης, τα άρθρα 78 έως 92 εφαρμόζονται σε όλα τα είδη ναύλωσης.

ΚΕΦΑΛΑΙΟ Β'
ΥΠΟΧΡΕΩΣΕΙΣ ΕΚΝΑΥΛΩΤΗ

Άρθρο 78
Υποχρέωση παράδοσης του πλοίου

1. Ο εκναυλωτής υποχρεούται, κατόπιν σχετικής ειδοποίησης, να παραχωρήσει το συμφωνημένο πλοίο στον ναυλωτή κατά τόπο και χρόνο σύμφωνα με τη σύμβαση ναύλωσης (παράδοση).

2. Εάν στη σύμβαση ναύλωσης το πλοίο δεν εξατομικεύεται, το δικαίωμα επιλογής ανήκει στον εκναυλωτή.

3. Σε περίπτωση που οι όροι ως προς τον συμφωνημένο χρόνο ή τόπο παράδοσης του πλοίου δεν τηρήθηκαν ή κατέστη απολύτως βέβαιο ότι δεν θα τηρηθούν, εάν δεν υπάρχει αντίθετη συμφωνία, ο ναυλωτής δικαιούται να καταγγείλει τη σύμβαση ναύλωσης. Σε περίπτωση πταίσματος του εκναυλωτή, δεν αποκλείεται η αποκατάσταση ζημίας που υπέστη ο ναυλωτής κατά τις κοινές διατάξεις.

4. Εκτέλεση της σύμβασης ναύλωσης από τρίτο δεν είναι δυνατή χωρίς τη συναίνεση του ναυλωτή.

Article 76
Sub-chartering

1. Unless otherwise agreed upon by the parties to the charter contract, the charterer may sub-charter the ship.

2. The sub-charterer shall have the obligations of a charterer provided for in this Code towards the shipowner. The charterer shall be liable to the shipowner for any fault of the sub-charterer.

3. Where the charterer fails to pay the freight, the shipowner shall notify the sub-charterer of the existence and amount of its claim against the charterer and call upon the sub-charterer to pay the sub-freight to the shipowner. From the time of notification, the shipowner shall have a direct claim against the sub-charterer up to the amount the latter owes to the charterer.

Article 77
Types of charter

1. The main types of charter contracts regulated under Articles 93 to 116 are:

(a) time charter;

(b) voyage charter;

(c) bareboat charter; and

(d) contract of affreightment.

2. Charter contracts may have characteristics different to or combine the key characteristics of the contracts referred to in paragraph 1.

3. In case of doubt, the type of charter and the resulting consequences shall be determined on the basis of its key characteristics, as clear from the contract entered into between the parties.

4. Unless otherwise stipulated in specific provisions, chartering may be full or partial.

5. In cases of a partial charter, either a specific tonnage percentage or a specific storage space within the ship may be chartered.

6. Without prejudice to more specific provisions, Articles 78 to 92 shall apply to all types of charter.

CHAPTER II
OBLIGATIONS OF THE SHIPOWNER

Article 78
Obligation to deliver the ship

1. Following notice to this effect, the shipowner shall be obligated to hand over the agreed-upon ship to the charterer at the time and place indicated in the charter contract (delivery).

2. If the ship is not individually specified in the charter contract, the shipowner shall be entitled to choose [the ship].

3. Unless otherwise agreed upon, where the terms concerning the agreed-upon time or place of delivery of the ship are not complied with or where it became absolutely certain that they will not be complied with, the charterer shall have the right to terminate the charter contract. In the event of fault by the shipowner, restitution of the losses incurred by the charterer in accordance with the ordinary provisions may not be precluded.

4. A third party may not perform the charter contract without the charterer's consent.

Άρθρο 79

Υποχρέωση αξιοπλοΐας

1. Ο εκναυλωτής υποχρεούται, πριν και κατά την έναρξη του πλου, να επιδείξει την προσήκουσα επιμέλεια για να έχει το πλοίο αξιόπλοο ως προς τη συμφωνημένη χρήση. Αντίθετη συμφωνία των μερών που να καθιστά ευνοϊκότερη τη θέση του εκναυλωτή δεν είναι δυνατή.

2. Πρόσθετοι όροι καταλληλότητας, σύμφωνα με τη σύμβαση ναύλωσης, δεν θίγουν τον χαρακτηρισμό του πλοίου ως αξιόπλοου.

3. Εάν απαιτούνται ειδικά μέτρα διατήρησης του φορτίου, ο εκναυλωτής δεν φέρει ευθύνη για ζημία στο φορτίο, σε περίπτωση που αυτά δεν του γνωστοποιήθηκαν εγκαίρως και με σαφήνεια από τον φορτωτή ή τον ναυλωτή.

Άρθρο 80

Ετοιμότητα προς φόρτωση

1. Ο εκναυλωτής οφείλει να έχει το πλοίο έτοιμο προς φόρτωση κατά τον συμφωνημένο χρόνο και στον συμφωνημένο τόπο.

2. Κατά την άφιξη του πλοίου στον λιμένα φόρτωσης ο εκναυλωτής υποχρεούται να ειδοποιήσει τον ναυλωτή ή άλλα πρόσωπα που θα του υποδείξει ο τελευταίος, με οποιοδήποτε πρόσφορο τρόπο, για την ετοιμότητα του πλοίου προς φόρτωση (ειδοποίηση ετοιμότητας προς φόρτωση).

3. Η υποχρέωση της παρ. 2 ισχύει και κατά την άφιξη στον λιμένα εκφόρτωσης.

Άρθρο 81

Έκδοση φορτωτικής

1. Ο εκναυλωτής υποχρεούται να εκδώσει φορτωτική, εφόσον τούτο ζητηθεί από τον ναυλωτή, με λήπτη πρόσωπο που του υποδεικνύει ο τελευταίος.

2. Ως προς το περιεχόμενο και τις λειτουργίες της φορτωτικής ισχύουν τα άρθρα 122 έως 131.

Άρθρο 82

Απαγόρευση φόρτωσης επί του καταστρώματος

Η φόρτωση επί του καταστρώματος απαγορεύεται, εκτός αν συμφωνείται διαφορετικά ή συνιστά συνήθη ναυτιλιακή πρακτική.

Άρθρο 83

Απαγόρευση μεταφόρτωσης

Η μεταφόρτωση φορτίου απαγορεύεται, εκτός εάν συμφωνείται διαφορετικά ή επιβάλλεται από τις περιστάσεις.

Άρθρο 84

Υποχρέωση παράδοσης του φορτίου

1. Ο εκναυλωτής παραδίδει το φορτίο στον ναυλωτή ή στο υποδεικνυόμενο από αυτόν πρόσωπο.

2. Εάν έχει εκδοθεί φορτωτική ή άλλο ισοδύναμο έγγραφο μεταφοράς, η παράδοση γίνεται στο νομιμοποιούμενο πρόσωπο σύμφωνα με τα άρθρα 121, 126, την παρ. 3 του άρθρου 127 και τις παρ. 1 και 3 του άρθρου 144.

3. Εάν, κατ' εκτέλεση οδηγιών του ναυλωτή, το φορτίο παραδοθεί σε μη νομιμοποιούμενο πρόσωπο, ο ναυλωτής υποχρεούται να αποκαταστήσει τη ζημία που προκαλείται στον εκναυλωτή από το γεγονός αυτό.

Article 79
Obligation of seaworthiness

1. Before and at the beginning of the voyage, the shipowner shall be obligated to exercise due diligence to keep the ship seaworthy for the agreed-upon use. An agreement to the contrary between the parties which puts the shipowner in a more favourable position shall not be possible.

2. Any additional seaworthiness conditions laid down in the charter contract shall not affect the ship's classification as seaworthy.

3. Where special cargo preservation measures are required, the shipowner shall bear no liability for damage to the cargo if such measures were not notified to the shipowner clearly and in good time by the shipper or the charterer.

Article 80
Readiness for loading

1. The shipowner shall be obligated to have the ship ready for loading at the time and place agreed upon.

2. When the ship calls at the port of loading, the shipowner shall be obligated to notify the charterer or other persons indicated by the latter, using any expedient means, that the ship is ready for loading (notice of readiness for loading).

3. The obligation laid down in paragraph 2 shall also apply at the time the ship calls at the port of discharge.

Article 81
Issuance of bills of lading

1. The shipowner shall be obligated to issue a bill of lading, if so requested by the charterer, whose consignee is a person indicated by the charterer.

2. Articles 122 to 131 shall apply to the content of bills of lading and their function.

Article 82
Prohibition of loading on deck

Loading on deck is prohibited, unless otherwise agreed upon or where it constitutes common maritime practice.

Article 83
Prohibition of transhipment

Transhipment is prohibited, unless otherwise agreed upon or required under the circumstances.

Article 84
Obligation to deliver the cargo

1. The shipowner shall deliver the cargo to the charterer or the person indicated by the latter.

2. If a bill of lading or other equivalent transport document has been issued, delivery shall be made to the authorised person, in accordance with Articles 121, 126, 127(3) and 144(1) and (3).

3. Where, in performance of the charterer's instructions, the cargo is delivered to an unauthorised person, the charterer shall be obligated to make good the losses incurred by the shipowner due to this fact.

Άρθρο 85

Ευθύνη εκναυλωτή

1. Ο εκναυλωτής ευθύνεται απέναντι στον ναυλωτή ή στον δικαιούχο του φορτίου για κάθε ζημία από απώλεια ή βλάβη στο μεταφερόμενο φορτίο ή σε σχέση με αυτό, κατά τα άρθρα 3, 4, 4β και 6 των Κανόνων Χάγης-Βίσμπυ, όπως εκάστοτε ισχύουν.

2. Για τις ζημίες της παρ. 1, ο εκναυλωτής δικαιούται να περιορίσει την ευθύνη του σύμφωνα με την παρ. 5 του άρθρου 4 των Κανόνων Χάγης-Βίσμπυ, όπως εκάστοτε ισχύουν. Εάν η καθυστέρηση προκάλεσε οικονομική ζημία, η αποζημίωση δεν δύναται να υπερβεί ποσό ίσο με το τριπλάσιο του καταβλητέου ναύλου.

3. Με την επιφύλαξη ειδικότερων διατάξεων, ο εκναυλωτής ευθύνεται για κάθε άλλη ζημία που υφίσταται ο ναυλωτής από την υπαίτια αδυναμία εκτέλεσης ή την πλημμελή εκτέλεση της σύμβασης ναύλωσης. Ευθύνεται, επίσης, για κάθε ζημία του ναυλωτή λόγω ανακριβών δηλώσεών του σχετικά με τα χαρακτηριστικά του πλοίου, ιδίως τη χωρητικότητα και την ταχύτητα. Οι ανακριβείς δηλώσεις συνιστούν σπουδαίο λόγο καταγγελίας της σύμβασης ναύλωσης από τον ναυλωτή, ανεξάρτητα από την επέλευση της ζημίας, εφόσον υπερβαίνουν το εύλογο μέτρο κατά τα συναλλακτικά ήθη της οικείας αγοράς.

4. Με την επιφύλαξη του πρώτου εδαφίου του άρθρου 332 του Αστικού Κώδικα, τα μέρη μπορούν να συμφωνήσουν διαφορετικά από τα προβλεπόμενα στις παρ. 1, 2 και 3 του παρόντος.

ΚΕΦΑΛΑΙΟ Γ'

ΥΠΟΧΡΕΩΣΕΙΣ ΝΑΥΛΩΤΗ

Άρθρο 86

Υποχρέωση καταβολής ναύλου - Ικανοποίηση εκναυλωτή

1. Το ύψος του ναύλου, ο υπολογισμός και ο τρόπος καταβολής του συμφωνούνται από τα μέρη. Αν ελλείπει συμφωνία ως προς την καταβολή, εφαρμόζεται το παρόν Μέρος, με βάση τον οικείο τύπο ναύλωσης.

2. Σε περίπτωση μη καταβολής του οφειλόμενου ναύλου και των λοιπών οφειλών από τη σύμβαση ναύλωσης, όπως εν γένει λιμενικών εξόδων και τελών, εξόδων πλοήγησης και ρυμούλκησης, συνεισφοράς σε κοινή αβαρία, οφειλόμενης αποζημίωσης σε τρίτο λόγω απώλειας ή ζημίας στο φορτίο, ο εκναυλωτής δικαιούται σε μεσεγγύηση του φορτίου.

3. Ο εκναυλωτής διορίζεται μεσεγγυούχος του φορτίου με απόφαση του μονομελούς πρωτοδικείου κατά τη διαδικασία των ασφαλιστικών μέτρων.

4. Εάν υπάρχει φανερή ανάγκη, ή αν η διατήρηση του φορτίου είναι δυσχερής λόγω της φύσης και του είδους του ή για λόγους οικονομικούς, μετά από αίτημα του εκναυλωτή, το μονομελές πρωτοδικείο μπορεί να διατάξει, δικάζοντας κατά τη διαδικασία των ασφαλιστικών μέτρων, την εκποίηση του φορτίου με εκούσιο πλειστηριασμό, ορίζοντας συγχρόνως τους όρους διενέργειας αυτού. Η απόφαση που διατάσσει τον εκούσιο πλειστηριασμό προσδιορίζει την αμοιβή και τα έξοδα του μεσεγγυούχου. Αμφότερα τα ποσά προαφαιρούνται από το εκπλειστηρίασμα. Έπειτα από τη διενέργεια του πλειστηριασμού ακολουθεί διαδικασία αναγγελιών και κατάταξης.

Article 85

Liability of the shipowner

1. The shipowner shall be liable vis-à-vis the charterer or the person entitled to the cargo for any losses due to loss of or damage to or in connection with the cargo being transported, in accordance with Articles III, IV, IV bis and VI of the Hague-Visby Rules, as in force from time to time.

2. In the event of the losses referred to in paragraph 1, the shipowner shall be entitled to limitation of liability in accordance with Article IV(5) of the Hague-Visby Rules, as in force from time to time. If the delay caused financial losses, the compensation may not exceed three times the freight payable.

3. Without prejudice to more specific provisions, the shipowner shall be liable for any other losses incurred by the charterer due to culpable failure to perform or improper performance of the charter contract. Furthermore, the shipowner shall be liable for any losses incurred by the charterer due to misrepresentations made by the shipowner concerning the characteristics of the ship and, in particular, its tonnage and speed. Misrepresentations shall constitute good cause for the charterer terminating the charter contract, irrespective of whether or not losses were incurred, where such misrepresentations exceed what is reasonable according to business usages in the market in question.

4. Without prejudice to the first subparagraph of Article 332 of the Civil Code, the parties may reach an agreement diverging from the provisions of paragraphs 1, 2 and 3 of this Article.

CHAPTER III

OBLIGATIONS OF THE CHARTERER

Article 86

Obligation to pay freight - Satisfaction of shipowner [claims]

1. The parties shall agree on the amount, calculation and manner of payment of the freight. Where there is no agreement on payment, this Part shall apply, on the basis of the type of charter in question.

2. In the event of failure to pay the freight owed and other debts arising from the charter contract, such as port costs and charges in general, pilotage and towage costs, general average contributions, compensation owed to third parties due to loss of or damage to the cargo, the shipowner shall be entitled to detain the cargo [under the rules of sequestration].

3. The shipowner shall be appointed as sequestrator of the cargo pursuant to a judgment handed down by the single-member court of first instance, trying the matter under interim measures proceedings.

4. Where there is a clear need or where preservation of the cargo is difficult due to its nature and type or due to financial reasons, the single-member court of first instance may, following a request from the shipowner and trying the matter under interim measures proceedings, hand down a judgment ordering that the cargo be sold at voluntary auction and laying down the terms for holding the auction. The sequestrator's fee and costs shall be specified in the judgment ordering the voluntary auction. Both these amounts shall be deducted in advance from the auction price. After the auction has been completed, the procedure for the lodgement and ranking [of claims] shall take place.

5. Οι αξιώσεις του εκναυλωτή για τον ναύλο και τις λοιπές οφειλές από τη σύμβαση ναύλωσης ικανοποιούνται προνομιακά πριν από οποιαδήποτε άλλη απαίτηση.

6. Στις περιπτώσεις της παρ. 2, ο εκναυλωτής αποκτά, επίσης, νόμιμο ενέχυρο στο καύσιμο κίνησης που βρίσκεται στο πλοίο, όταν το εν λόγω καύσιμο κατά κυριότητα ανήκει στον ναυλωτή. Τεκμαίρεται ότι καύσιμο κίνησης, το οποίο παραγγέλλεται από τον ναυλωτή και παραδίδεται στο πλοίο στο πλαίσιο εκτέλεσης της σύμβασης ναύλωσης, ανήκει κατά κυριότητα σε αυτόν.

7. Στις περιπτώσεις της παρ. 2 ο εκναυλωτής δικαιούται επίσης να αρνηθεί την προσέγγιση του πλοίου στον προβλήτα και τη φόρτωση ή την εκφόρτωση του φορτίου. Δεν αποκλείεται περαιτέρω αξίωση του εκναυλωτή κατά του ναυλωτή κατά τις κοινές διατάξεις.

Άρθρο 87
Απαγόρευση φόρτωσης επικίνδυνου φορτίου

1. Ο ναυλωτής υποχρεούται να μην φορτώνει στο πλοίο εκρηκτικά, εύφλεκτα ή επικίνδυνα εμπορεύματα, για τη φόρτωση των οποίων ο εκναυλωτής ή ο πλοίαρχος δεν έχουν συμφωνήσει, γνωρίζοντας τη φύση και τα χαρακτηριστικά τους. Κατά τα λοιπά, εφαρμόζεται η παρ. 6 του άρθρου 4 των Κανόνων Χάγης-Βίσμπυ, όπως εκάστοτε ισχύουν.

2. Σε κάθε περίπτωση τηρούνται οι όροι των ισχυουσών διεθνών συμβάσεων σε σχέση με τη μεταφορά επικίνδυνων φορτίων και οι οικείες διατάξεις του Εθνικού Τελωνειακού Κώδικα (ν. 2961/2001, Α' 265).

Άρθρο 88
Υποχρέωση υπόδειξης ασφαλούς λιμένα

1. Ο ναυλωτής υποχρεούται να κατευθύνει το πλοίο σε ασφαλείς λιμένες και τόπους φόρτωσης και εκφόρτωσης.

2. Ο εκναυλωτής δικαιούται να αρνηθεί την είσοδο ή παραμονή του πλοίου σε μη ασφαλή λιμένα ή τόπο φόρτωσης ή εκφόρτωσης, εάν τούτο δεν έχει συμφωνηθεί ρητά ή εάν ο λιμένας ή ο τόπος φόρτωσης ή εκφόρτωσης καταστεί μη ασφαλής εκ των υστέρων.

Άρθρο 89
Φόρτωση - στοιβασία - εκφόρτωση

1. Ο ναυλωτής διενεργεί με δικές του δαπάνες τη φόρτωση, στοιβασία και εκφόρτωση του φορτίου και ευθύνεται για κάθε ζημία από αυτές, εκτός εάν η ζημία οφείλεται σε πταίσμα του πλοιάρχου ή του πληρώματος.

2. Ο ναυλωτής υποχρεούται να παραδίδει στον εκναυλωτή όλα τα έγγραφα που σχετίζονται με τη φόρτωση και την εκφόρτωση.

3. Ο πλοίαρχος μπορεί να αρνηθεί ή να διακόψει τη φόρτωση, εάν από αυτή επηρεάζεται η αξιοπλοΐα του πλοίου. Το ίδιο ισχύει και για την εκφόρτωση.

Άρθρο 90
Ζημία από τη συμμόρφωση στις οδηγίες του ναυλωτή

Ο ναυλωτής υποχρεούται να αποκαταστήσει κάθε ζημία που υφίσταται ο εκναυλωτής λόγω συμμόρφωσης στις οδηγίες του ναυλωτή.

5. The shipowner's claims concerning freight and other debts arising from the charter contract shall receive preferential satisfaction prior to any other claim.

6. In the cases referred to in paragraph 2, the shipowner shall also acquire a legal pledge on the motor fuel located on the ship, where the fuel in question is owned by the charterer. The motor fuel ordered by the charterer and delivered to the ship in the context of performance of the charter contract shall be presumed to belong to the charterer.

7. In the cases referred to in paragraph 2, the shipowner shall also be entitled to refuse to allow the ship to approach the pier and to load or discharge the cargo. Further claims by the shipowner against the charterer in accordance with the ordinary provisions may not be precluded.

Article 87
Prohibition on loading dangerous cargoes

1. The charterer shall be obligated not to load the ship with explosive, inflammable or dangerous goods to whose loading the shipowner or master has not consented, with knowledge of their nature and character. In all other respects, Article IV(6) of the Hague-Visby Rules, as in force from time to time, shall apply.

2. In all cases, the terms of international treaties and conventions in force on the carriage of dangerous goods and the relevant provisions of the National Customs Code (Law [2960]/2001, Government Gazette, Series I, Issue 265) shall be complied with.

Article 88
Obligation to indicate a safe harbour

1. The charterer shall be obligated to direct the ship towards safe harbours and places of loading and discharge.

2. The shipowner shall be entitled to refuse to allow the ship to call or remain at an unsafe harbour or place of loading or discharge if this has not been expressly agreed upon or if the port or place of loading or discharge subsequently becomes unsafe.

Article 89
Loading - Stowage - Discharge

1. The charterer shall load, stow and discharge the cargo at its own expense and shall be liable for any losses arising from such loading, stowage and unloading, unless the losses are due to the fault of the master or crew.

2. The charterer shall be obligated to hand over all documents relating to the loading and discharge to the shipowner.

3. The master may refuse to load or stop loading if this affects the seaworthiness of the ship. This shall also apply to discharge.

Article 90
Losses due to compliance with the charterer's instructions

The charterer shall be obligated to make good any losses incurred by the shipowner due to compliance with the charterer's instructions.

ΚΕΦΑΛΑΙΟ Δ'
ΛΥΣΗ ΤΗΣ ΣΥΜΒΑΣΗΣ ΝΑΥΛΩΣΗΣ

Άρθρο 91
Ανυπαίτια αδυναμία παροχής

1. Η σύμβαση ναύλωσης λύεται και τα μέρη ελευθερώνονται, αν η παροχή του εκναυλωτή καταστεί αδύνατη από γεγονός για το οποίο αυτός δεν έχει ευθύνη, ιδίως λόγω απώλειας του πλοίου ή οριστικής αδυναμίας παραχώρησης της χρήσης του από τυχηρό γεγονός, ανωτέρα βία ή επίταξη αυτού.

2. Ο εκναυλωτής υποχρεούται να ειδοποιήσει τον ναυλωτή για την αδυναμία παροχής χωρίς υπαίτια βραδύτητα. Σχετική ειδοποίηση απευθύνει και προς τον παραλήπτη του φορτίου, εφόσον είναι ευχερώς δυνατή η διακρίβωση της ταυτότητας αυτού.

3. Αν το γεγονός της αδυναμίας επέλθει σε χρόνο κατά τον οποίο το πλοίο είναι έμφορτο, ο εκναυλωτής μπορεί κατ' εύλογη κρίση, με βάση τις εκάστοτε συνθήκες, είτε να επιμεληθεί της αποστολής του φορτίου στον λιμένα προορισμού είτε να προκαλέσει την αποθήκευση αυτού στον εγγύτερο λιμένα. Σε περίπτωση που το φορτίο είναι ευπαθές ή υπάρχει κίνδυνος χειροτέρευσής του, ο εκναυλωτής δικαιούται να προσφύγει στο αρμόδιο δικαστήριο για την αναγκαστική ή εκούσια εκποίηση αυτού.

4. Ναύλος που καταβλήθηκε αναζητείται με τις διατάξεις για τον αδικαιολόγητο πλουτισμό. Ο ναυλωτής οφείλει να αποδώσει στον εκναυλωτή τις σχετικές με την προετοιμασία του πλοίου δαπάνες.

5. Αν η ναύλωση εκτελέσθηκε μερικώς, ο ναυλωτής οφείλει το αντίστοιχο τμήμα του ναύλου, περιλαμβανομένου του ναύλου που αφορά σε υπό έρμα πλου, καθώς και τις συναφείς με τη μερική εκτέλεση δαπάνες. Αν το φορτίο αφίχθηκε στον λιμένα προορισμού σύμφωνα με την παρ. 3, ο ναυλωτής οφείλει τον αρχικώς συμφωνηθέντα ναύλο.

Άρθρο 92
Καταγγελία της σύμβασης ναύλωσης

1. Η σύμβαση ναύλωσης λύεται με καταγγελία από οποιοδήποτε μέρος, αν συντρέχει σπουδαίος λόγος.

2. Η ανυπαίτια διακοπή ή παρεμπόδιση του πλου που έχει προσωρινό χαρακτήρα δεν συνιστά σπουδαίο λόγο.

3. Αν ο σπουδαίος λόγος συνίσταται σε γεγονός για το οποίο το ένα μέρος έχει ευθύνη, το αντισυμβαλλόμενο μέρος που καταγγέλλει τη σύμβαση ναύλωσης μπορεί να αξιώσει αποζημίωση. Σε περίπτωση καταγγελίας χωρίς σπουδαίο λόγο ή καταχρηστικής καταγγελίας, το αντισυμβαλλόμενο μέρος έχει δικαίωμα να ζητήσει αποκατάσταση της ζημίας που υπέστη από αυτήν, όχι όμως να αξιώσει εκπλήρωση της σύμβασης.

4. Σε περίπτωση καταγγελίας της σύμβασης ναύλωσης, όταν το πλοίο είναι έμφορτο, εφαρμόζεται αναλόγως η παρ. 3 του άρθρου 91. Ο ναυλωτής διατηρεί σε κάθε περίπτωση το δικαίωμα να αναλάβει το φορτίο με δικές του δαπάνες και απαλλάσσεται από το τμήμα του ναύλου που αντιστοιχεί στον πλου που δεν εκτελέσθηκε.

5. Αν η ναύλωση καταγγελθεί από τον εκναυλωτή για σπουδαίο λόγο που δεν ανάγεται στο πρόσωπό του, ο εκναυλωτής ευθύνεται έναντι του ναυλωτή, ως προς τη διατήρηση του φορτίου, μόνο για δόλο και βαριά αμέλεια.

CHAPTER IV
TERMINATION OF CHARTER CONTRACTS

Article 91
Non-culpable inability to provide performance

1. The charter contract shall be dissolved and the parties shall be released if the shipowner is unable to perform [the contract] due to circumstances for which the shipowner is not responsible and, in particular, due to loss of the ship or definitive inability to [deliver the ship] due to fortuity, force majeure or requisitioning of the ship.

2. The shipowner shall be obligated to notify without undue delay the charterer of the inability to provide performance. The shipowner shall also notify the consignee to this effect, where the identity of the latter can be readily established.

3. If the event giving rise to inability [to provide performance] occurs when the ship has already been loaded, the shipowner may, at its reasonable discretion and on the basis of the circumstances in question, take steps either to send the cargo to the port of destination or to store it at the nearest port. Where the cargo is perishable or is at risk of deterioration, the shipowner shall have the right to seek recourse to the competent court for the forced or voluntary sale of the cargo.

4. Any freight paid may be recovered in accordance with the provisions on unjust enrichment. The charterer shall be obligated to reimburse the shipowner for costs relating to preparation of the ship.

5. If the charter was performed in part, the charterer shall owe the corresponding portion of the freight, including the freight concerning a ballast voyage, as well as the costs relating to partial performance. If the cargo arrived at the port of destination in accordance with paragraph 3, the charterer shall owe the freight originally agreed upon.

Article 92
Termination of charter contracts

1. A charter contract may be terminated by either party for good cause.

2. Non-culpable, temporary interruption or hindering of a voyage shall not constitute good cause.

3. If the good cause concerns circumstances for which one party is responsible, the counterparty terminating the charter contract may seek compensation. In the event of termination without good cause or abusive termination, the counterparty shall have the right to seek restitution of the losses incurred due to said termination, but not to claim performance of the contract.

4. Where the charter contract is terminated after the ship has already been loaded, Article 91(3) shall apply *mutatis mutandis*. In all cases, the charterer shall reserve the right to undertake the cargo at its own expense and shall be released from the part of the freight corresponding to the voyage not carried out.

5. If the charter is terminated by the shipowner for good cause unrelated to the shipowner, the shipowner shall be liable to the charterer, with regard to preservation of the cargo, solely for *dolus* and gross negligence.

ΚΕΦΑΛΑΙΟ Ε'
ΕΙΔΙΚΟΤΕΡΕΣ ΔΙΑΤΑΞΕΙΣ ΓΙΑ ΤΗ ΝΑΥΛΩΣΗ ΚΑΤΑ ΧΡΟΝΟ

Άρθρο 93
Ναύλωση κατά χρόνο - Έννοια

1. Στη ναύλωση κατά χρόνο ο εκναυλωτής παραχωρεί στον ναυλωτή τη χρήση πλοίου έναντι ναύλου για ορισμένο χρονικό διάστημα. Ο εκναυλωτής διατηρεί την τεχνική διεύθυνση του πλοίου και ασκεί την εμπορική του εκμετάλλευση.

2. Ο ναύλος υπολογίζεται με βάση την πραγματική διάρκεια της σύμβασης.

3. Στη ναύλωση κατά χρόνο ο πλοίαρχος και το πλήρωμα ναυτολογούνται από τον εκναυλωτή ή για λογαριασμό του και θεωρούνται προστηθέντες του.

Άρθρο 94
Εκτέλεση πλόων

Ο εκναυλωτής υποχρεούται να εκτελεί τους συμφωνημένους πλόες χωρίς υπαίτια καθυστέρηση.

Άρθρο 95
Καταβολή ναύλου

1. Εάν δεν ορίζεται ρητά ο χρόνος καταβολής του ναύλου, αυτός προκαταβάλλεται ανά περίοδο δεκαπέντε (15) ημερών.

2. Η υποχρέωση καταβολής ναύλου αναστέλλεται για όσο χρονικό διάστημα η χρήση του πλοίου από τον ναυλωτή κωλύεται από πράξεις ή παραλείψεις του εκναυλωτή ή των προστηθέντων του. Η καταβολή ναύλου αναστέλλεται, επίσης, σε περιπτώσεις μη δικαιολογημένης παρέκκλισης από την ενδεδειγμένη πορεία, κατά την έννοια της παρ. 1 του άρθρου 102.

Άρθρο 96
Εφοδιασμός του πλοίου

1. Ο ναυλωτής υποχρεούται να αγοράσει από τον εκναυλωτή το καύσιμο κίνησης που βρίσκεται στο πλοίο κατά τον χρόνο παράδοσης και να το πωλήσει σε αυτόν κατά τον χρόνο επαναπαράδοσης. Εάν δεν συμφωνείται συγκεκριμένη αξία στη σύμβαση ναύλωσης, λαμβάνεται υπόψη η τρέχουσα αξία στον λιμένα παράδοσης ή επαναπαράδοσης ή στον εγγύτερο λιμένα κατά τον χρόνο παράδοσης και επαναπαράδοσης, αντίστοιχα.

2. Ο ναυλωτής υποχρεούται, για την περίοδο της ναύλωσης, να εφοδιάζει με δικές του δαπάνες το πλοίο με καύσιμο κίνησης που πληροί τις εκάστοτε ισχύουσες νόμιμες προδιαγραφές. Το καύσιμο κίνησης πρέπει να ανταποκρίνεται διαρκώς στα συμφωνημένα μεταξύ των μερών χαρακτηριστικά και σε κάθε περίπτωση να είναι γενικώς αποδεκτής ποιότητας.

Άρθρο 97
Λοιπές δαπάνες

Οι δαπάνες λιμένος, πλοήγησης και ρυμούλκησης βαρύνουν τον ναυλωτή.

CHAPTER V
SPECIFIC PROVISIONS ON TIME CHARTERS

Article 93
Time charter - Concept

1. In cases of time charter, the shipowner shall grant use of the ship, in exchange for freight, to the charterer for a specific period of time. The shipowner shall retain technical management of the ship and use it for commercial operations.

2. Freight shall be calculated on the basis of the actual duration of the contract.

3. In cases of time charter, the master and the crew shall be recruited by the shipowner or on the shipowner's behalf and shall be considered to be the shipowner's agents.

Article 94
Performance of voyages

The shipowner shall be obligated to perform the agreed-upon voyages without undue delay.

Article 95
Payment of freight

1. If the time when the freight is to be paid is not expressly specified, it shall be paid in advance for each 15-day period.

2. The obligation to pay freight shall be suspended while use of the ship by the charterer is impeded due to acts or omissions of the shipowner or its agents. Payment of the freight shall also be suspended in cases of unjustified deviation from the appropriate course, within the meaning of Article 102(1).

Article 96
Bunkering of ships

1. The charterer shall be obligated to purchase the motor fuel on board the ship at the time of delivery from the shipowner, and to sell it back to the shipowner at the time of re-delivery. If no specific price is agreed upon in the charter contract, account shall be taken of the current value at the port of delivery or re-delivery or at the nearest port at the time of delivery and re-delivery, as appropriate.

2. Throughout the charter period, the charterer shall be obligated to bunker the ship, at its own expense, with motor fuel which meets the lawful specifications in force from time to time. The motor fuel must always have the properties agreed upon between the parties and, in all cases, be of generally acceptable quality.

Article 97
Other costs

The port, pilotage and towage costs shall be borne by the charterer.

Άρθρο 98
Επαναπαράδοση του πλοίου

1. Ο ναυλωτής υποχρεούται να επαναπαραδώσει το πλοίο στον εκναυλωτή στην κατάσταση που ήταν κατά την παράδοσή του.

2. Πρόωρη επαναπαράδοση του πλοίου συνιστά υπαίτια καταγγελία της σύμβασης από τον ναυλωτή.

ΚΕΦΑΛΑΙΟ ΣΤ'
ΕΙΔΙΚΟΤΕΡΕΣ ΔΙΑΤΑΞΕΙΣ ΓΙΑ ΤΗ ΝΑΥΛΩΣΗ ΚΑΤΑ ΤΑΞΙΔΙ

Άρθρο 99
Ναύλωση κατά ταξίδι - Έννοια

1. Στη ναύλωση κατά ταξίδι, ο εκναυλωτής παραχωρεί στον ναυλωτή τη χρήση πλοίου, έναντι ναύλου, για ορισμένο πλου. Ο εκναυλωτής διατηρεί την τεχνική διεύθυνση του πλοίου και ασκεί την εμπορική του εκμετάλλευση.

2. Ο ναύλος υπολογίζεται κατ' αποκοπή ή με βάση τα χαρακτηριστικά του πλου και την ποσότητα του φορτίου.

3. Στη ναύλωση κατά ταξίδι ο πλοίαρχος και το πλήρωμα ναυτολογούνται από τον εκναυλωτή ή για λογαριασμό του και θεωρούνται προστηθέντες του.

Άρθρο 100
Ετοιμότητα προς φόρτωση

1. Ο εκναυλωτής οφείλει να έχει το πλοίο έτοιμο προς φόρτωση, κατά την παρ. 1 του άρθρου 80.

2. Σε περίπτωση παραβίασης της υποχρέωσης αυτής, ο ναυλωτής μπορεί να ασκήσει το δικαίωμα που προβλέπει η παρ. 1 του άρθρου 92.

Άρθρο 101
Εφοδιασμός του πλοίου

Ο εκναυλωτής προμηθεύει το πλοίο με καύσιμο κίνησης και εφόδια για την εκτέλεση των συμφωνημένων ταξιδιών.

Άρθρο 102
Εκτέλεση πλόων

1. Ο εκναυλωτής υποχρεούται να εκτελεί τους συμφωνημένους πλόες χωρίς παρέκκλιση και κατά την ενδεικνυόμενη πορεία. Αλλαγή πορείας επιτρέπεται για την προστασία ζωής ή περιουσίας ή για άλλη εύλογη αιτία.

2. Σε περίπτωση παρέκκλισης ή αλλαγής πορείας κατ' εντολή του ναυλωτή, οφείλονται επιπρόσθετος ναύλος για την επιπλέον απόσταση, ο οποίος υπολογίζεται με βάση τις προβλέψεις περί υπεραναμονής, και οι αντίστοιχες δαπάνες.

Article 98

Re-delivery of ships

1. The charterer shall be obligated to re-deliver the ship to the shipowner in the condition it was in at the time of delivery.

2. Early re-delivery of the ship shall constitute culpable termination of the contract by the charterer.

CHAPTER VI

SPECIFIC PROVISIONS ON VOYAGE CHARTERS

Article 99

Voyage charter - Concept

1. In cases of voyage charter, the shipowner shall grant use of the ship, in exchange for freight, to the charterer for a specific voyage. The shipowner shall retain technical management of the ship and use it for commercial operations.

2. Freight shall be calculated as a lump sum or on the basis of the characteristics of the voyage and the quantity of cargo.

3. In cases of voyage charter, the master and the crew shall be recruited by the shipowner or on the shipowner's behalf and shall be considered to be the shipowner's agents.

Article 100

Readiness for loading

1. The shipowner must have the ship ready for loading in accordance with Article 80(1).

2. Where this obligation is breached, the charterer may exercise the right provided for in Article 92(1).

Article 101

Bunkering [and stocking] of ships

The shipowner shall supply the ship with motor fuel and stores to carry out the voyages agreed upon.

Article 102

Performance of voyages

1. The shipowner shall be obligated to perform voyages agreed upon without deviations and in accordance with the appropriate course. Changes of course shall be permitted in order to protect life or property or for other reasonable cause.

2. In the event of deviation or change of course at the charterer's instructions, additional freight for the additional distance, calculated on the basis of the provisions on demurrage, and the corresponding costs shall be owed.

Άρθρο 103
Αναμονή - Υπεραναμονή

1. Ο εκναυλωτής οφείλει να αναμένει να ολοκληρωθεί η φόρτωση στον συμφωνηθέντα χρόνο, ή σε αυτόν που επιβάλλεται από τις περιστάσεις, χωρίς αντάλλαγμα (αναμονή). Ο χρόνος της αναμονής αρχίζει με την άφιξη του πλοίου στον λιμένα φόρτωσης και την αποστολή προσήκουσας ειδοποίησης ετοιμότητας προς φόρτωση.

2. Όταν παρέλθει ο χρόνος αναμονής και δεν έχει ολοκληρωθεί η φόρτωση, οφείλεται επιπλέον αντάλλαγμα στον εκναυλωτή για την περίοδο μέχρι την ολοκλήρωση της φόρτωσης (υπεραναμονή). Εάν το αντάλλαγμα δεν έχει συμφωνηθεί στη σύμβαση, οφείλεται το επιβαλλόμενο από τις περιστάσεις, αφού ληφθούν υπόψη και οι συνθήκεςτης ναυλαγοράς.

3. Οι παρ. 1 και 2 εφαρμόζονται και στην εκφόρτωση.

4. Εάν η υπεραναμονή είναι υπέρμετρη, ο εκναυλωτής δικαιούται επιπρόσθετο αντάλλαγμα, το οποίο υπολογίζεται με βάση το αντάλλαγμα της υπεραναμονής, προσαυξημένο κατά είκοσι πέντε τοις εκατό (25%).

5. Σε περίπτωση ολοκλήρωσης της φόρτωσης ή της εκφόρτωσης χωρίς εξάντληση της αναμονής, οφείλεται αντάλλαγμα στον ναυλωτή ίσο με το μισό του ανταλλάγματος για την υπεραναμονή, εάν τούτο συνηθίζεται στην οικεία αγορά.

Άρθρο 104
Λοιπές δαπάνες

Τα έξοδα λιμένος, πλοήγησης και ρυμούλκησης βαρύνουν τον εκναυλωτή.

Άρθρο 105
Καταβολή ναύλου

Εάν δεν ορίζεται ρητά ο χρόνος καταβολής του ναύλου, αυτός καταβάλλεται κατά το ήμισυ αμέσως μετά από το πέρας της φόρτωσης και κατά το ήμισυ αμέσως μετά από το πέρας της εκφόρτωσης.

Άρθρο 106
Υποχρεώσεις ναυλωτή που αφορούν το φορτίο

1. Ο ναυλωτής οφείλει να έχει διαθέσιμο προς φόρτωση το συμφωνημένο φορτίο στον συμφωνημένο τόπο και χρόνο και στην ενδεδειγμένη θέση. Εάν φορτώθηκε φορτίο λιγότερο από το συμφωνημένο, ο ναυλωτής οφείλει τον μισό ναύλο για το φορτίο που δεν φορτώθηκε.

2. Εάν το φορτίο απωλέσθηκε από τυχηρό γεγονός πριν από τη φόρτωσή του, η σύμβαση λύεται, τα μέρη ελευθερώνονται και ο ναυλωτής οφείλει να καταβάλει στον εκναυλωτή τις δαπάνες του.

3. Ο ναυλωτής οφείλει να παραδώσει στον πλοίαρχο όλα τα απαραίτητα προς φόρτωση φορτωτικά έγγραφα.

Article 103

Laytime - Demurrage

1. The shipowner must, without consideration, await completion of loading at the time agreed upon or the time required under the circumstances (laytime). Laytime shall commence when the ship arrives at the port of loading and the appropriate notice of readiness for loading is sent.

2. Where the laytime ends and loading has not been completed, additional consideration shall be owed to the shipowner for the time required until loading is complete (demurrage). If the consideration has not been agreed upon in the contract, the consideration required under the circumstances shall be owed, taking freight market conditions into consideration.

3. Paragraphs 1 and 2 shall also apply to discharge.

4. In cases of excessive demurrage, the shipowner shall be entitled to additional consideration, calculated on the basis of the demurrage consideration, augmented by 25%.

5. Where the loading or discharge is completed without exhausting the laytime, consideration equal to half the demurrage consideration shall be owed to the charterer, if this is common practice in the market in question.

Article 104

Other costs

The port, pilotage and towage costs shall be borne by the shipowner.

Article 105

Payment of freight

If the time of payment of the freight is not expressly specified, half shall be paid immediately after loading has been completed and half immediately after discharge has been completed.

Article 106

Cargo-related obligations of the charterer

1. The charterer shall be obligated to have the agreed-upon cargo ready for loading at the time and place agreed upon and at the appropriate location. If less cargo than that agreed upon is loaded, the charterer shall owe half the freight for the cargo not loaded.

2. If, prior to being loaded, the cargo was lost due to fortuity, the contract shall be dissolved, the parties shall be released, and the charterer shall be obligated to pay the shipowner its costs.

3. The charterer shall be obligated to hand over all the documents necessary for loading to the master.

ΚΕΦΑΛΑΙΟ Ζ'

ΕΙΔΙΚΟΤΕΡΕΣ ΔΙΑΤΑΞΕΙΣ ΓΙΑ ΤΗ ΝΑΥΛΩΣΗ ΓΥΜΝΟΥ ΠΛΟΙΟΥ

Άρθρο 107

Ναύλωση γυμνού πλοίου - Έννοια

1. Στη ναύλωση γυμνού πλοίου, τούτο ναυλώνεται χωρίς πλοίαρχο και πλήρωμα, η ναυτολόγηση των οποίων γίνεται από τον ναυλωτή και για λογαριασμό του. Ο ναυλωτής αποκτά την τεχνική διεύθυνση και την εμπορική εκμετάλλευση του πλοίου.

2. Αν δεν συμφωνήθηκε διαφορετικά, εφαρμόζονται αναλόγως οι διατάξεις περί χρονοναύλωσης στο μέτρο που είναι συμβατές με τη ναύλωση γυμνού πλοίου.

Άρθρο 108

Υποχρεώσεις

1. Το πλοίο κατά τη χρονική στιγμή της παράδοσης πρέπει να βρίσκεται σε κατάσταση κατάλληλη για τη συμφωνηθείσα χρήση.

2. Κατά τη διάρκεια της ναύλωσης, ο ναυλωτής οφείλει να το συντηρεί, να διατηρεί την κλάση του και όλα τα πιστοποιητικά του σε ισχύ και να το διατηρεί κατάλληλο για τη συμφωνηθείσα χρήση. Ο ναυλωτής δεν δικαιούται να εγγράψει το υπό ελληνική σημαία πλοίο σε αλλοδαπό νηολόγιο.

3. Με τη λήξη της ναύλωσης το πλοίο επαναπαραδίδεται στην παραληφθείσα κατάσταση, εξαιρουμένης της συνήθους φθοράς που προκαλείται από τη συμφωνηθείσα χρήση.

Άρθρο 109

Ευθύνη

1. Οι προϋποθέσεις ευθύνης για κάθε συμβαλλόμενο καθορίζονται στη σύμβαση ναύλωσης γυμνού πλοίου.

2. Ο εκναυλωτής υποχρεούται να αποκαταστήσει τη θετική και αποθετική ζημία του ναυλωτή λόγω μη εμφανούς πραγματικού ελαττώματος του πλοίου κατά τον χρόνο της παράδοσης, εφόσον αυτό εκδηλωθεί εντός δώδεκα (12) μηνών από την ως άνω παράδοση. Μη εμφανές θεωρείται το ελάττωμα που δεν μπορεί να διαπιστωθεί με την επιμέλεια του μέσου συνετού ναυλωτή.

Άρθρο 110

Ναύλος - Εξαγορά

1. Εφόσον δεν συμφωνηθεί διαφορετικά, η καταβολή του ναύλου είναι μηνιαία.

2. Τα συμβαλλόμενα μέρη μπορούν να συμφωνήσουν ότι η καταβολή του ναύλου αποτελεί τμηματική εξόφληση συμφωνηθέντος τιμήματος εξαγοράς του πλοίου.

3. Μέχρι την πλήρη εξόφληση η κυριότητα του πλοίου παραμένει στον εκναυλωτή.

4. Το άρθρο 532 του Αστικού Κώδικα εφαρμόζεται, εκτός αν συμφωνήθηκε διαφορετικά.

CHAPTER VII

SPECIFIC PROVISIONS ON BAREBOAT CHARTERS

Article 107

Bareboat charter - Concept

1. In cases of bareboat charter, the ship shall be chartered without a master and crew, who shall be recruited by and on behalf of the charterer. The charterer shall be responsible for technical management and commercial operation of the ship.

2. Unless otherwise agreed upon, the provisions on time charters shall apply *mutatis mutandis*, to the extent that they are compatible with bareboat charters.

Article 108

Obligations

1. At the time of delivery, the ship must be in a condition suitable for the use agreed upon.

2. Throughout the charter period, the charterer shall be obligated to maintain the ship, maintain its class, ensure that all its certificates remain in effect and keep the ship suitable for the use agreed upon. The charterer shall not be entitled to enter a ship flying a Greek flag in a foreign ship registry.

3. When the charter expires, the ship shall be re-delivered in the condition in which it was delivered, save ordinary wear and tear caused by the use agreed upon.

Article 109

Liability

1. The conditions for liability of each contracting party shall be set out in the bareboat charter contract.

2. The shipowner shall be obligated to make good any direct and consequential losses suffered by the charterer due to latent actual defects in the ship at the time of delivery, provided the defects manifest within 12 months from the aforesaid delivery. A latent defect is considered to be a defect which cannot be ascertained by the average prudent charterer exercising diligence.

Article 110

Freight - Acquisition

1. Unless otherwise agreed upon, freight shall be paid on a monthly basis.

2. The contracting parties may agree that the freight payment constitutes partial payment of the price agreed upon for acquiring the ship.

3. Until payment in full has taken place, the shipowner shall retain ownership of the ship.

4. Unless otherwise agreed upon, Article 532 of the Civil Code shall apply.

Άρθρο 111

Υποναύλωση

Με την επιφύλαξη αντίθετης συμφωνίας, περαιτέρω υποναύλωση του πλοίου ως γυμνού δεν επιτρέπεται.

Άρθρο 112

Απαγόρευση εκποίησης - υποθήκευσης

Κατά τη διάρκεια της γυμνής ναύλωσης, ο εκναυλωτής δεν δικαιούται να εκποιήσει το πλοίο σε τρίτο ή να συστήσει ναυτική υποθήκη σε αυτό, χωρίς τη σύμφωνη γνώμη του ναυλωτή, εφόσον η σύμβαση γυμνής ναύλωσης έχει καταχωρισθεί στο νηολόγιο.

Άρθρο 113

Ανέλκυση ναυαγίου

Αν το πλοίο κατά την περίοδο της γυμνής ναύλωσης καταστεί ναυάγιο, ο εκναυλωτής διατηρεί δικαίωμα αναγωγής κατά του υπαίτιου ναυλωτή για τη δαπάνη ανέλκυσης.

Άρθρο 114

Προστασία από τρίτους

Ο ναυλωτής γυμνού πλοίου επιδεικνύει κάθε επιμέλεια για την προστασία των δικαιωμάτων του εκναυλωτή από προσβολές τρίτων.

Άρθρο 115

Χρηματοδοτική μίσθωση με ναύλωση γυμνού πλοίου

1. Η χρηματοδοτική μίσθωση πλοίου επιτρέπεται.

2. Στη ναύλωση γυμνού σκάφους που συνάπτεται στο πλαίσιο χρηματοδοτικής μίσθωσης εφαρμόζεται το παρόν Κεφάλαιο.

ΚΕΦΑΛΑΙΟ Η'

ΕΙΔΙΚΟΤΕΡΕΣ ΔΙΑΤΑΞΕΙΣ ΓΙΑ ΤΗ ΝΑΥΛΩΣΗ - ΠΛΑΙΣΙΟ

Άρθρο 116

Χαρακτηριστικά - Εφαρμογή

1. Για την εκπλήρωση της ναύλωσης-πλαισίου συνομολογούνται ειδικότερες εκτελεστικές συμβάσεις ναύλωσης.

2. Στη ναύλωση-πλαίσιο εφαρμόζονται οι γενικές διατάξεις περί ναύλωσης.

Article 111

Sub-chartering

Without prejudice to any agreement to the contrary, further sub-chartering of a bare boat shall not be permitted.

Article 112

Prohibition on sale - mortgaging

Throughout the bareboat charter period, the shipowner shall not be entitled to sell the ship to a third party or establish a mortgage on the ship without the assent of the charterer, provided the bareboat charter has been entered in the ship registry.

Article 113

Removal of shipwrecks

Where a ship becomes shipwrecked during the bareboat charter period, the shipowner shall retain a right of recourse against the culpable charterer for the removal costs.

Article 114

Protection from third parties

The bareboat charterer shall exercise all due diligence to protect the rights of the shipowner from being infringed by third parties.

Article 115

Financial leases under a bareboat charter

1. Financial leases of ships shall be permitted.

2. This Chapter shall apply to bareboat charters entered into in the context of a financial lease.

CHAPTER VIII

SPECIFIC PROVISIONS ON CONTRACTS OF AFFREIGHTMENT

Article 116

Characteristics - Application

1. In order to perform contracts of affreightment, more specific executory charter contracts shall be entered into.

2. The general provisions on chartering shall apply to contracts of affreightment.

ΜΕΡΟΣ ΠΕΜΠΤΟ
ΘΑΛΑΣΣΙΑ ΜΕΤΑΦΟΡΑ ΠΡΑΓΜΑΤΩΝ

ΚΕΦΑΛΑΙΟ Α'
ΠΕΔΙΟ ΕΦΑΡΜΟΓΗΣ

Άρθρο 117
Έννοια θαλάσσιας μεταφοράς θαλάσσιου μεταφορέα

1. Με τη σύμβαση θαλάσσιας μεταφοράς πραγμάτων ο μεταφορέας αναλαμβάνει, έναντι ανταλλάγματος, την υποχρέωση μεταφοράς με πλοίο των πραγμάτων που αποτελούν αντικείμενο της σύμβασης από τον λιμένα φόρτωσης στον λιμένα εκφόρτωσης και παράδοσης αυτών στον νομιμοποιούμενο παραλήπτη.

2. Η μεταφορά μπορεί να εκτελείται μερικώς ή ολικώς από πρόσωπο διαφορετικό από το πρόσωπο που έχει συμβληθεί ως μεταφορέας στη σύμβαση θαλάσσιας μεταφοράς (πραγματικός μεταφορέας).

3. Αντικείμενο της σύμβασης μπορεί να είναι και η μεταφορά ορισμένης κατ' ανώτατο ή κατώτατο όριο ή οριστής από το ένα μέρος ποσότητας πραγμάτων, με διαδοχικές φορτώσεις στο ίδιο ή σε διαφορετικά πλοία, εντός ορισμένης χρονικής περιόδου (σύμβαση όγκου).

Άρθρο 118
Εφαρμοστέοι κανόνες

1. Η διεθνής θαλάσσια μεταφορά πραγμάτων που εκτελείται στο πλαίσιο υπηρεσίας τακτικών γραμμών διέπεται από τη Διεθνή Σύμβαση των Βρυξελλών του 1924 για την ενοποίηση ορισμένων κανόνων σχετικά με τις φορτωτικές με τα μεταγενέστερα Πρωτόκολλα αυτής, όπως κυρώθηκε με το άρθρο πρώτο του ν. 2107/1992 (Α' 203) και εκάστοτε ισχύει στην Ελλάδα (Κανόνες Χάγης-Βίσμπυ), ανεξαρτήτως της έκδοσης φορτωτικής ή ισοδυνάμου εγγράφου μεταφοράς.

2. Η υπηρεσία μεταφοράς με τακτικές γραμμές προσφέρεται στο κοινό με δημόσια ανακοίνωση και εκτελείται με πλοία που ταξιδεύουν με τακτικό δρομολόγιο μεταξύ καθορισμένων λιμένων, σύμφωνα με χρονοδιάγραμμα δρομολογίων που είναι διαθέσιμο στο κοινό.

3. Η διεθνής θαλάσσια μεταφορά που εκτελείται με μη τακτικές γραμμές, στο πλαίσιο ναύλωσης, διέπεται, επίσης, από τους Κανόνες Χάγης-Βίσμπυ, όπως εκάστοτε ισχύουν στην Ελλάδα, εφόσον έχει εκδοθεί γι' αυτήν θαλάσσια φορτωτική ή ισοδύναμο έγγραφο μεταφοράς, σύμφωνα με την παρ. 2 του άρθρου 74.

4. Η θαλάσσια μεταφορά πραγμάτων μεταξύ ελληνικών λιμένων και εν γένει εντός ελληνικών χωρικών υδάτων διέπεται, σε κάθε περίπτωση, από τους Κανόνες Χάγης-Βίσμπυ, όπως εκάστοτε ισχύουν στην Ελλάδα.

PART FIVE
CARRIAGE OF GOODS BY SEA

CHAPTER I
SCOPE

Article 117
Concept of carriage by sea undertaken by a carrier by sea

1. By virtue of a contract for the carriage of goods by sea, the carrier shall undertake, in exchange for consideration, the obligation to carry by ship the goods constituting the subject-matter of the contract from the port of loading to the port of discharge and deliver them to the authorised consignee.

2. Carriage may be performed, in whole or in part, by a person other than the carrier named in the contract entered into for carriage by sea (actual carrier).

3. The subject-matter of the contract may also be the carriage of a minimum, maximum or certain quantity of goods, specified by one party, in a series of shipments by the same or different ships within a specific time period (volume contract).

Article 118
Applicable rules

1. The international carriage of goods by sea performed in the context of liner services shall be governed by the 1924 Brussels International Convention for the Unification of Certain Rules of Law relating to Bills of Lading and the subsequent Protocols thereto, ratified by the first Article of Law 2107/1992 (Government Gazette, Series I, Issue 203) and as in force in Greece from time to time (the Hague-Visby Rules), irrespective of whether or not a bill of lading or equivalent transport document was issued.

2. Carriage via liner services shall be offered to the general public by means of public notice and performed by ships carrying out scheduled sailings between designated ports, in accordance with a schedule of sailings made available to the general public.

3. International carriage by sea performed by tramp services, in the context of chartering, shall also be governed by the Hague-Visby Rules, as in force in Greece from time to time, provided a maritime bill of lading or equivalent transport document has been issued for such, in accordance with Article 74(2).

4. Carriage of goods by sea between Greek ports and, generally, within Greek territorial waters shall be governed, in all cases, by the Hague-Visby Rules, as in force in Greece from time to time.

Άρθρο 119
Κανόνες αναγκαστικού δικαίου

1. Συμφωνίες που απαλλάσσουν τον μεταφορέα ή τον φορτωτή από την ευθύνη τους ή διαφοροποιούν τους όρους αυτής ή τις υποχρεώσεις αυτών κατά τρόπο ευνοϊκότερο για τον καθένα από αυτούς, είναι άκυρες, εκτός αν άλλως προβλέπεται ρητά.

2. Η ακυρότητα των συμφωνιών αυτών δεν θίγει το κύρος της σύμβασης μεταφοράς.

3. Οι Κανόνες Χάγης-Βίσμπυ, όπως εκάστοτε ισχύουν στην Ελλάδα, εφαρμόζονται σε διαφορές που εισάγονται σε ελληνικό δικαστήριο, ακόμη και αν δεν ισχύουν στο δίκαιο που επέλεξαν με συμφωνία τα μέρη.

Άρθρο 120
Χρονικό πεδίο εφαρμογής

1. Οι Κανόνες Χάγης-Βίσμπυ, όπως εκάστοτε ισχύουν στην Ελλάδα, καλύπτουν την περίοδο από τον χρόνο της φόρτωσης των πραγμάτων στο πλοίο μέχρι την εκφόρτωσή τους από αυτό.

2. Για τις περιόδους πριν από τη φόρτωση και μετά την εκφόρτωση εφαρμόζονται η παρ. 2 του άρθρου 132 και το άρθρο 13**5.**

ΚΕΦΑΛΑΙΟ Β'
ΘΑΛΑΣΣΙΑ ΦΟΡΤΩΤΙΚΗ ΚΑΙ ΛΟΙΠΑ ΕΓΓΡΑΦΑ ΜΕΤΑΦΟΡΑΣ

Άρθρο 121
Θαλάσσια φορτωτική - Έννοια - Χαρακτηριστικά

1. Η θαλάσσια φορτωτική αποδεικνύει έναντι παντός τη σύμβαση μεταφοράς και την παραλαβή των πραγμάτων από τον μεταφορέα προς φόρτωση (φορτωτική παραλαβής) ή τη φόρτωση αυτών στο πλοίο (φορτωτική φόρτωσης). Ως αξιόγραφο ενσωματώνει την αξίωση παράδοσης των πραγμάτων στον νομιμοποιούμενο κομιστή και τη νομή αυτών.

2. Με τη χρήση του όρου «φορτωτική» στον παρόντα νοείται η θαλάσσια φορτωτική.

Άρθρο 122
Έκδοση φορτωτικής

1. Ο μεταφορέας υποχρεούται να εκδώσει φορτωτική μετά από την παραλαβή των πραγμάτων, ύστερα από αίτημα του φορτωτή. Τη φορτωτική μπορούν να εκδώσουν, για λογαριασμό του μεταφορέα, και ο πλοίαρχος, ο πράκτορας ή ο ναυλωτής, εφόσον τους παρέχεται η δυνατότητα από τη σύμβαση ναύλωσης.

2. Μετά από τη φόρτωση των πραγμάτων, η φορτωτική παραλαβής ισχύει ως φορτωτική φόρτωσης, ύστερα από αίτημα του φορτωτή, όταν πληρούνται οι προϋποθέσεις της παρ. 7 του άρθρου 3 των Κανόνων Χάγης-Βίσμπυ, όπως εκάστοτε ισχύουν στην Ελλάδα.

3. Ο μεταφορέας μπορεί να εκδώσει επιμέρους φορτωτικές ή διαταγές παράδοσης για τμήματα του φορτίου, αν τούτο του ζητηθεί από τον φορτωτή και εφόσον επιστραφεί ή καταστεί ανίσχυρη η ενιαία φορτωτική, σε περίπτωση που η τελευταία έχει ήδη εκδοθεί.

4. Αντίγραφο της φορτωτικής παραμένει στην κατοχή του πλοιάρχου.

Article 119

Mandatory rules

1. Unless otherwise expressly provided for, covenants releasing the carrier or shipper from their liability or modifying the terms of such liability or their obligations in a manner which is more favourable for either of them shall be null and void.

2. Nullity of such covenants shall not affect the validity of the contract of carriage.

3. The Hague-Visby Rules, as in force in Greece from time to time, shall apply to disputes brought before Greek courts, even if not valid under the law chosen by agreement of the parties.

Article 120

Temporal scope

1. The Hague-Visby Rules, as in force in Greece from time to time, shall cover the period from the time of loading of the goods onto the ship until the time of their discharge from the ship.

2. Articles 132(2) and 135 shall apply to the time periods prior to loading and subsequent to discharge.

CHAPTER II

MARITIME BILL OF LADING AND OTHER TRANSPORT DOCUMENTS

Article 121

Maritime bill of lading - Concept - Characteristics

1. A maritime bill of lading constitutes proof *erga omnes* of the contract of carriage and the receipt of the goods by the carrier for loading (received for shipment bill of lading) or the loading of the goods onto the ship (shipped bill of lading). As a security, it embodies the claim for delivery to its authorised bearer of the goods and possession of said goods.

2. Where used in this Code, the term "bill of lading" shall be understood to mean a maritime bill of lading.

Article 122

Issue of bills of lading

1. At the request of the shipper, the carrier shall be obligated to issue a bill of lading upon taking receipt of the goods. The bill of lading may also be issued on the carrier's behalf by the master, the agent or the charterer, where empowered to do so in the charter contract.

2. After the goods have been loaded, a received for shipment bill of lading shall be a shipped bill of lading, if the shipper so demands, where the conditions laid down in Article III(7) of the Hague-Visby Rules, as in force in Greece from time to time, are met.

3. The carrier may issue separate bills of lading or delivery orders concerning sections of the cargo, if the shipper so demands and provided the single bill of lading, if issued, has been returned or rendered invalid.

4. A copy of the bill of lading shall remain in the possession of the master.

Άρθρο 123

Δικαιούχος φορτωτικής

1. Η φορτωτική εκδίδεται, κατ' επιλογή του φορτωτή, ως ονομαστική, σε διαταγή ή στον κομιστή.

2. Η φορτωτική με κατονομαζόμενο δικαιούχο τεκμαίρεται ότι έχει εκδοθεί σε διαταγή, εκτός αν περιέχει τη ρήτρα «όχι σε διαταγή».

3. Φορτωτική που εκδίδεται υπέρ προσώπου που κατονομάζεται με τη ρήτρα «στον κομιστή» ή άλλη ισοδύναμη φράση ή χωρίς σημείωση του δικαιούχου ισχύει ως φορτωτική στον κομιστή.

Άρθρο 124

Περιεχόμενο φορτωτικής

1. Η φορτωτική περιέχει:

α) την ονομασία «θαλάσσια φορτωτική» ή «φορτωτική» αναφερόμενη στο κείμενο του τίτλου,

β) την περιγραφή των παραληφθέντων ή φορτωθέντων πραγμάτων,

γ) τον προσδιορισμό του πλοίου,

δ) τον λιμένα φόρτωσης,

ε) τον λιμένα προορισμού,

στ) τον ναύλο και τον τρόπο καταβολής αυτού,

ζ) τη χρονολογία και τον τόπο έκδοσης και

η) την υπογραφή του εκδότη.

Αν δεν έχει σημειωθεί ο τόπος έκδοσης, ως τέτοιος εκλαμβάνεται ο τόπος που σημειώνεται δίπλα στο όνομα του εκδότη. Η υπογραφή μπορεί να τίθεται και με μηχανικά ή ηλεκτρονικά μέσα. Αν ελλείπουν και δεν αναπληρώνονται νομίμως τα υπό α, β, γ', δ, ζ' και η' στοιχεία, το έγγραφο δεν ισχύει ως φορτωτική.

2. Η περιγραφή των πραγμάτων στη φορτωτική περιλαμβάνει τα προβλεπόμενα στην παρ. 3 του άρθρου 3 των Κανόνων Χάγης-Βίσμπυ, όπως εκάστοτε ισχύουν στην Ελλάδα.

3. Επιφυλάξεις του μεταφορέα επί της φορτωτικής σχετικά με την περιγραφή των πραγμάτων κατά την παρ. 3 του άρθρου 3 των Κανόνων Χάγης-Βίσμπυ, όπως εκάστοτε ισχύουν στην Ελλάδα, είναι ισχυρές, εφόσον περιέχουν μνεία της αιτίας για την οποία τέθηκαν.

Άρθρο 125

Ηλεκτρονική φορτωτική

1. Η φορτωτική μπορεί να εκδίδεται και σε άυλη μορφή, ως ηλεκτρονικό αρχείο, εφόσον συμφωνούν σε αυτό ο μεταφορέας και ο φορτωτής.

2. Η έκδοση, κατοχή και μεταβίβαση της ηλεκτρονικής φορτωτικής έχουν την ίδια ισχύ και τις ίδιες συνέπειες με την έκδοση, κατοχή και μεταβίβαση της έγχαρτης φορτωτικής.

3. Με σύμφωνη γνώμη μεταφορέα και νόμιμου κομιστή, η έγχαρτη φορτωτική μπορεί να αντικαθίσταται από ηλεκτρονική φορτωτική και αντιστρόφως.

Article 123

Beneficiary of bill of lading

1. At the shipper's choice, the bill of lading shall be issued as a registered bill of lading, a to order bill of lading, or a to bearer bill of lading.

2. A bill of lading with a named beneficiary shall be presumed to have been issued to order, unless it contains the phrase "not to order".

3. A bill of lading issued in favour of a named person including the phrase "to bearer" or other equivalent phrase or without indicating a beneficiary shall be a bearer bill of lading.

Article 124

Content of bill of lading

1. The bill of lading shall contain:

a) the phase "maritime bill of lading" or "bill of lading" in the text of the title;

b) a description of the goods received or loaded;

c) the particulars of the ship;

d) the port of loading;

e) the port of destination;

f) the freight and manner of its payment;

g) the time and date of issue; and

h) the signature of the issuer.

If the place of issue is not indicated, the place indicated next to the issuer's name shall be considered to be the place of issue. Signatures may also be placed using mechanical or electronic means. If the information required under points (a), (b), (c), (d), (g) and (h) is absent and is not duly filled out, the document shall not function as a bill of lading.

2. The description of the goods in the bill of lading shall include the information required under Article III(3) of the Hague-Visby Rules, as in force in Greece from time to time.

3. Qualifications expressed by the carrier concerning the description of the goods in the bill of lading, in accordance with Article III(3) of the Hague-Visby Rules, as in force in Greece from time to time, shall be effective provided the reason for which they were expressed is given.

Article 125

Electronic bills of lading

1. The bill of lading may also be issued in dematerialised format, as an electronic file, provided the carrier and the shipper agree to this.

2. Issuing, possessing and transferring an electronic bill of lading shall have the same effects and the same consequences as issuing, possessing and transferring a physical bill of lading.

3. With the assent of the carrier and the lawful bearer, a physical bill of lading may be replaced by an electronic bill of lading, and vice versa.

Άρθρο 126
Μεταβίβαση φορτωτικής

1. Η ονομαστική φορτωτική μεταβιβάζεται με εκχώρηση.

2. Η φορτωτική σε διαταγή μεταβιβάζεται με οπισθογράφηση. Ως προς τα αποτελέσματα της οπισθογράφησης και τις ενστάσεις που μπορούν να αντιταχθούν κατά του κομιστή, εφαρμόζονται αναλόγως οι διατάξεις που ισχύουν για το αξιόγραφο της συναλλαγματικής.

3. Η φορτωτική στον κομιστή μεταβιβάζεται με συμφωνία και παράδοση.

4. Η μεταβίβαση της φορτωτικής σύμφωνα με τις παρ. 1 και 2 ισοδυναμεί, ως προς τα πράγματα που περιγράφονται σε αυτήν, με παράδοση της νομής αυτών.

5. Τα τεκμήρια της παρ. 4 του άρθρου 3 των Κανόνων Χάγης-Βίσμπυ, όπως εκάστοτε ισχύουν στην Ελλάδα, εφαρμόζονται αναλόγως.

Άρθρο 127
Δελτίο θαλάσσιας μεταφοράς

1. Το δελτίο θαλάσσιας μεταφοράς αποδεικνύει τη σύμβαση μεταφοράς και την παραλαβή από τον μεταφορέα των αναγραφόμενων σε αυτό πραγμάτων. Περιέχει επίσης υπόσχεση του μεταφορέα για παράδοση των πραγμάτων στον κατονομαζόμενο παραλήπτη.

2. Το δελτίο θαλάσσιας μεταφοράς αποτελεί έγγραφο μεταφοράς ισοδύναμο της φορτωτικής, για τους σκοπούς της παρ. 3 του άρθρου 118.

3. Ο φορτωτής δύναται να τροποποιήσει εγγράφως το όνομα του παραλήπτη μέχρι την παράδοση των πραγμάτων, εκτός αν άλλως προβλέπεται στο δελτίο, καταβάλλοντας στον μεταφορέα τις προκαλούμενες από την τροποποίηση εύλογες δαπάνες.

4. Η νομιμοποίηση του παραλήπτη γίνεται με την κατοχή του πρωτότυπου δελτίου, ή αντιγράφου αυτού και του τυχόν τροποποιητικού εγγράφου, καθώς και με τα στοιχεία της ταυτότητάς του.

5. Στο δελτίο θαλάσσιας μεταφοράς εφαρμόζονται αναλόγως η παρ. 2 του άρθρου 124, το άρθρο 125, η παρ. 5 του άρθρου 126 και το άρθρο 130.

Άρθρο 128
Διαφορτωτική - Διαδοχική θαλάσσια μεταφορά

1. Η διαφορτωτική, που εκδίδεται όταν τα πράγματα μεταφέρονται με περισσότερους του ενός θαλάσσιους μεταφορείς και καλύπτει το σύνολο της θαλάσσιας μεταφοράς, έχει τη λειτουργία και τις συνέπειες της φορτωτικής.

2. Η διαφορτωτική μπορεί να εκδίδεται και σε άυλη μορφή, ως ηλεκτρονικό αρχείο, σύμφωνα με το άρθρο 125.

Άρθρο 129
Φορτωτική συνδυασμένης μεταφοράς

1. Το έγγραφο μεταφοράς που εκδίδεται για ενιαία σύμβαση συνδυασμένης μεταφοράς με θαλάσσιο σκέλος, κατά την έννοια του άρθρου 147, ισχύει ως φορτωτική για το θαλάσσιο σκέλος, εφόσον περιέχει τα στοιχεία που προβλέπονται στην παρ. 1 του άρθρου 124.

2. Η φορτωτική συνδυασμένης μεταφοράς μπορεί να εκδίδεται και σε άυλη μορφή, ως ηλεκτρονικό αρχείο, σύμφωνα με το άρθρο 125.

Article 126

Transfer of bills of lading

1. A registered bill of lading may be transferred by assigning it.

2. A to order bill of lading may be transferred by endorsing it. The provisions applicable to bills of exchange shall apply *mutatis mutandis* to the effects of endorsement and the pleas that may be raised against the bearer.

3. A bearer bill of lading may be transferred by agreement and hand-over.

4. Transfer of a bill of lading in accordance with paragraphs 1 and 2 shall be equivalent, in respect of the goods described in the bill of lading, to handing over possession of the goods.

5. The *prima facie* evidence referred to in Article III(4) of the Hague-Visby Rules, as in force in Greece at any given time, shall apply *mutatis mutandis*.

Article 127

Sea waybill

1. A sea waybill constitutes proof of the contract of carriage and of receipt of the goods indicated in the waybill by the carrier. It also contains a promise by the carrier to deliver the goods to the named consignee.

2. For the purposes of Article 118(3), a sea waybill shall constitute a transport document equivalent to a bill of lading.

3. The shipper may change the name of the consignee in writing until the time of delivery of the goods, unless otherwise provided for in the waybill, paying the carrier the reasonable costs arising from this change.

4. The consignee shall [prove their entitlement to receive the consignment] by producing the original waybill or a copy thereof and any amending document, as well as their identity particulars.

5. Articles 124(2), 125, 126(5) and 130 shall apply *mutatis mutandis* to sea waybills.

Article 128

Through bill of lading - Successive carriage by sea

1. A through bill of lading, issued when goods are carried by several carriers by sea and covering the entirety of carriage by sea, shall function and generate the same effects as a bill of lading.

2. A through bill of lading may also be issued in dematerialised format, as an electronic file, in accordance with Article 125.

Article 129

Multimodal transport bill of lading

1. A transport document issued for a single contract of multimodal transport involving a sea leg, within the meaning of Article 147, shall function as a bill of lading for the sea leg, provided it contains the information required by Article 124(1).

2. A multimodal transport bill of lading may also be issued in dematerialised format, as an electronic file, in accordance with Article 125.

Άρθρο 130

Ρήτρες παρέκτασης δικαιοδοσίας

1. Ρήτρες δικαιοδοσίας που περιέχονται στη φορτωτική και ορίζουν ως παρεκτεινόμενο δικαστήριο κράτους μέλους της Ευρωπαϊκής Ένωσης είναι έγκυρες, εφόσον πληρούνται οι προϋποθέσεις του άρθρου 25 του Κανονισμού (ΕΕ) 1215/2012 του Ευρωπαϊκού Κοινοβουλίου και του Συμβουλίου της 12ης Δεκεμβρίου 2012 «για τη διεθνή δικαιοδοσία, την αναγνώριση και την εκτέλεση αποφάσεων σε αστικές και εμπορικές υποθέσεις» (L 351/1) και δεσμευτικές έναντι του τρίτου κομιστή.

2. Για τις ρήτρες δικαιοδοσίας που περιέχονται στη φορτωτική και ορίζουν ως παρεκτεινόμενο δικαστήριο τρίτου κράτους εφαρμόζεται αναλόγως η παρ. 1, με την επιφύλαξη της παρ. 3.

3. Οι ρήτρες της παρ. 2 δεν εφαρμόζονται όταν καθιστούν δυσχερή την παροχή έννομης προστασίας στον ζημιωθέντα ή παρεκτείνουν τη δικαιοδοσία σε έννομες τάξεις που περιορίζουν ουσιωδώς την προβλεπόμενη από τους Κανόνες Χάγης-Βίσμπυ ευθύνη του μεταφορέα.

Άρθρο 131

Ρήτρες ναυλοσυμφώνου

1. Σε περίπτωση έκδοσης φορτωτικής ναυλοσυμφώνου, οι όροι του ναυλοσυμφώνου είναι δεσμευτικοί για τον τρίτο κομιστή της φορτωτικής, εφόσον πληρούνται σωρευτικώς οι ακόλουθες προϋποθέσεις:

(α) Η φορτωτική περιλαμβάνει ρήτρα παραπομπής (ενσωμάτωσης) στους όρους του συγκεκριμένου ναυλοσυμφώνου,

(β) οι όροι του ναυλοσυμφώνου δεν αντίκεινται στους Κανόνες Χάγης-Βίσμπυ, όπως εκάστοτε ισχύουν στην Ελλάδα και αρμόζουν στις σχέσεις μεταφορέα και δικαιούχου του φορτίου και

(γ) ο κομιστής είχε τη δυνατότητα να λάβει γνώση των όρων αυτών κατά τον χρόνο έκδοσης ή οπισθογράφησης της φορτωτικής.

2. Οι ρήτρες δικαιοδοσίας και διαιτησίας ενσωματώνονται ρητώς στη φορτωτική ναυλοσυμφώνου. Ειδική αναφορά σε ρήτρα διαιτησίας που περιέχεται στο ναυλοσύμφωνο συνιστά συμφωνία διαιτησίας.

ΚΕΦΑΛΑΙΟ Γ'

ΚΑΘΕΣΤΩΣ ΕΥΘΥΝΗΣ ΘΑΛΑΣΣΙΟΥ ΜΕΤΑΦΟΡΕΑ

Άρθρο 132

Εφαρμοστέοι κανόνες

1. Οι υποχρεώσεις του θαλάσσιου μεταφορέα και οι προϋποθέσεις ευθύνης του διέπονται από τους Κανόνες Χάγης-Βίσμπυ, όπως εκάστοτε ισχύουν στην Ελλάδα, και το παρόν Κεφάλαιο.

2. Με την επιφύλαξη του άρθρου 136, η παρ. 1 εφαρμόζεται και στα στάδια από την παραλαβή των πραγμάτων προς μεταφορά μέχρι τη φόρτωσή τους και από την εκφόρτωση μέχρι την παράδοση αυτών.

3. Ο μεταφορέας υποχρεούται σε κάθε επιμέλεια.

Article 130

Prorogation of jurisdiction clauses

1. Jurisdiction clauses contained in a bill of lading and specifying the court of a European Union Member State as the prorogued court shall be valid, provided the conditions laid down in Article 25 of Regulation (EU) No 1215/2012 of the European Parliament and of the Council of 12 December 2012 on jurisdiction and the recognition and enforcement of judgments in civil and commercial matters (OJ L 351/1) are met, and shall be binding on third-party bearers.

2. Without prejudice to paragraph 3, paragraph 1 shall apply *mutatis mutandis* to jurisdiction clauses contained in a bill of lading and specifying the court of a third state as the prorogued court.

3. The clauses referred to in paragraph 2 shall not apply where they hinder the provision of legal protection to the prejudiced party or prorogue jurisdiction to legal systems which materially restrict the carrier's liability provided for in the Hague-Visby Rules.

Article 131

Charter-party clauses

1. Where a charter-party bill of lading is issued, the terms of the charter-party shall be binding on the third-party bearer of the bill of lading, provided all the following conditions are met:

(a) the bill of lading includes a clause citing (incorporating) the terms of the specific charter-party;

(b) the terms of the charter-party are not contrary to the Hague-Visby Rules, as in force in Greece from time to time, and are appropriate to the relationship between the carrier and the beneficiary of the cargo; and

(c) the bearer was able to take cognisance of these terms at the time the bill of lading was issued or endorsed.

2. Jurisdiction and arbitration clauses shall be expressly incorporated in the charter-party bill of lading. Specific reference to an arbitration clause contained in the charter-party shall constitute an arbitration agreement.

CHAPTER III

LIABILITY REGIME FOR CARRIERS BY SEA

Article 132

Applicable rules

1. The obligations of carriers by sea and the conditions for their liability shall be governed by the Hague-Visby Rules, as in force in Greece from time to time, and this Chapter.

2. Without prejudice to Article 136, paragraph 1 shall also apply to the stages from receipt of the goods for carriage until their loading and from discharge until their delivery.

3. Carriers shall be obligated to exercise all due diligence.

4. Η ευθύνη του μεταφορέα καταλαμβάνει κάθε ζημία σχετική με την απώλεια ή βλάβη των πραγμάτων που προκλήθηκε από την παραλαβή των πραγμάτων προς μεταφορά μέχρι την παράδοση αυτών, καθώς και τη ζημία από καθυστέρηση στην εκτέλεση της θαλάσσιας μεταφοράς σύμφωνα με το άρθρο 133.

5. Ο μεταφορέας ευθύνεται για το πταίσμα των προσώπων που χρησιμοποιεί για την εκτέλεση της θαλάσσιας μεταφοράς. Δεν ευθύνεται για απώλεια ή βλάβη του φορτίου ή άλλη ζημία που προκαλείται κατά τη διάρκεια της φόρτωσης και εκφόρτωσης του φορτίου από πταίσμα προσώπου, τις υπηρεσίες του οποίου υποχρεούται από τον νόμο να δεχθεί.

Άρθρο 133
Ευθύνη από καθυστέρηση

1. Ο μεταφορέας οφείλει να εκτελέσει τη θαλάσσια μεταφορά εντός του συμφωνηθέντος χρόνου, ελλείψει δε συμφωνίας περί αυτού, εντός του απαιτούμενου από τις περιστάσεις εύλογου χρόνου.

2. Ο μεταφορέας ευθύνεται σε αποζημίωση για τη θετική και την αποθετική ζημία του κομιστή της φορτωτικής ή του νομιμοποιούμενου στην παραλαβή του φορτίου προσώπου που προκαλούνται από υπαίτια καθυστέρηση κατά την εκτέλεση της θαλάσσιας μεταφοράς και την παράδοση του φορτίου, εκτός αν αποδείξει ότι δεν τον βαραίνει πταίσμα. Οι λόγοι απαλλαγής από την ευθύνη που προβλέπονται στην παρ. 2 του άρθρου 4 των Κανόνων Χάγης-Βίσμπυ όπως εκάστοτε ισχύουν στην Ελλάδα, εφαρμόζονται αναλόγως.

3. Για να οφείλεται η κατά την παρ. 2 αποζημίωση απαιτείται γραπτή ή ηλεκτρονική ειδοποίηση του μεταφορέα από τον κομιστή της φορτωτικής ή το νομιμοποιούμενο στην παραλαβή του φορτίου πρόσωπο εντός είκοσι μίας (21) ημερών από την παράδοση των πραγμάτων, με την οποία εξειδικεύεται το είδος της ζημίας και ορίζεται κατά προσέγγιση το ύψος αυτής.

Άρθρο 134
Ευθύνη πραγματικού μεταφορέα

1. Τα άρθρα 132, 133 και 138 ισχύουν ως προς την ευθύνη του πραγματικού μεταφορέα για το μέρος της μεταφοράς που εκτελείται από αυτόν.

2. Όταν η εκτέλεση της μεταφοράς ή μέρους αυτής έχει ανατεθεί σε πραγματικό μεταφορέα, ο συμβατικός μεταφορέας παραμένει υπεύθυνος για θαλάσσια μεταφορά σύμφωνα με τον παρόντα. Ο συμβατικός και ο πραγματικός μεταφορέας ευθύνονται από κοινού και εις ολόκληρον.

3. Δικαίωμα αναγωγής μεταξύ του συμβατικού και του πραγματικού μεταφορέα δεν αποκλείεται.

Άρθρο 135
Μεταφορά στο κατάστρωμα - Εμπορευματοκιβώτια

1. Μεταφορά πραγμάτων στο κατάστρωμα επιτρέπεται όταν έχει συμφωνηθεί στη σύμβαση μεταφοράς, όταν επιβάλλεται εκ του νόμου, ή όταν συνιστά συνήθη ναυτιλιακή πρακτική.

2. Η μεταφορά των εμπορευματοκιβωτίων στο κατάστρωμα συνιστά συνήθη ναυτιλιακή πρακτική, εφόσον διενεργείται με πλοίο ειδικώς διαρρυθμισμένο και εξοπλισμένο προς τούτο.

4. The carrier's liability shall extend to all losses concerning loss of or damage to the goods caused between the time the carrier took them over for carriage and the time of their delivery, as well as losses resulting from delay in performance of the carriage by sea, in accordance with Article 133.

5. The carrier shall be liable for faults of the persons engaged by the carrier to perform the carriage by sea. The carrier shall not be liable for loss of or damage to the cargo or other losses caused during the loading and discharge of the cargo due to fault of a person whose services the carrier is under statutory obligation to accept.

Article 133

Liability due to delay

1. The carrier shall be obligated to perform the carriage by sea within the time agreed upon and, absent an agreement on such time, within the reasonable time required under the circumstances.

2. The carrier shall be liable to pay compensation for any direct and consequential losses incurred by the bearer of the bill of lading or person entitled to take receipt of the cargo and resulting from undue delay in performance of the carriage by sea and delivery of the cargo, unless the carrier can prove that it is not at fault. The grounds for release from liability set out in Article IV(2) of the Hague-Visby Rules, as in force in Greece from to time time, shall apply *mutatis mutandis*.

3. In order for the compensation referred to in paragraph 2 to be owed, the carrier must be notified, in writing or electronically, by the bearer of the bill of lading or the person entitled to take receipt of the cargo within 21 days from the date the goods were delivered, specifying the type of losses and their approximate amount.

Article 134

Liability of the actual carrier

1. Articles 132, 133 and 138 shall apply to the liability of the actual carrier for that part of the carriage performed by the actual carrier.

2. Where performance of the carriage or part of the carriage has been assigned to an actual carrier, the contracting carrier shall remain liable for the carriage by sea in accordance with this Code. The contracting carrier and the actual carrier shall be jointly and severally liable.

3. A right of recourse between the contracting carrier and the actual carrier may not be precluded.

Article 135

Carriage on deck - Containers

1. Carriage of goods on deck shall be permitted where agreed upon in the contract of carriage, where required by law, or where this constitutes common maritime practice.

2. Carriage of containers on deck shall constitute common maritime practice, provided it is performed by a ship specially configured and equipped for this purpose.

3. Σε περίπτωση που δεν πληρούνται οι προϋποθέσεις των παρ. 1 και 2, η απώλεια ή η ζημία των πραγμάτων που μεταφέρονται στο κατάστρωμα τεκμαίρεται ότι οφείλεται σε πταίσμα του μεταφορέα κατά τη μεταχείριση των πραγμάτων.

4. Η υποχρέωση του μεταφορέα να μεριμνά για το φορτίο καταλαμβάνει και την κατάσταση των εμπορευματοκιβωτίων όταν αυτά παρέχονται από τον ίδιο, καθώς και την εγκιβωτίωση, εφόσον πραγματοποιείται από τον μεταφορέα.

Άρθρο 136
Ρήτρες για τα ακραία στάδια μεταφοράς

Με την επιφύλαξη της παρ. 4 του άρθρου 135 και του πρώτου εδαφίου του άρθρου 332 του Αστικού Κώδικα, για το χρονικό διάστημα πριν από τη φόρτωση και μετά την εκφόρτωση των πραγμάτων, τα μέρη μπορούν να συμφωνήσουν στον περιορισμό των υποχρεώσεων και της ευθύνης του μεταφορέα, καθώς και στην τροποποίηση των κανόνων για το βάρος απόδειξης.

Άρθρο 137
Ειδικές κατηγορίες εμπορευμάτων

Με την επιφύλαξη του πρώτου εδαφίου του άρθρου 332 του Αστικού Κώδικα, τα μέρη μπορούν να συμφωνήσουν στον περιορισμό των υποχρεώσεων και της ευθύνης του μεταφορέα, καθώς και στην τροποποίηση των κανόνων για το βάρος απόδειξης στις ακόλουθες περιπτώσεις:

(α) μεταφορά ζωντανών ζώων,

(β) μεταφορά συγκεκριμένων εμπορευμάτων που εμπίπτει στο πεδίο του άρθρου 6 των Κανόνων Χάγης-Βίσμπυ, όπως εκάστοτε ισχύουν στην Ελλάδα,

(γ) μεταφορά πραγμάτων με συμβάσεις όγκου κατά την έννοια της παρ. 3 του άρθρου 117 του παρόντος.

Άρθρο 138
Ατομικός περιορισμός ευθύνης

1. Ο μεταφορέας δικαιούται να περιορίσει την ευθύνη του σύμφωνα με τους Κανόνες Χάγης-Βίσμπυ, όπως εκάστοτε ισχύουν στην Ελλάδα. Απώλεια του ανωτέρω δικαιώματος επέρχεται σύμφωνα με την παρ. 5α του άρθρου 4 των εν λόγω Κανόνων.

2. Εάν η καθυστέρηση προκάλεσε οικονομική ζημία, η συνολική αποζημίωση δεν δύναται να υπερβεί ποσό ίσο με το τριπλάσιο του καταβλητέου ναύλου.

3. Εάν η καθυστέρηση προκάλεσε συγχρόνως και βλάβη ή απώλεια του φορτίου, η συνολική αποζημίωση δεν δύναται να υπερβεί εκείνη που υπολογίζεται σύμφωνα με την παρ. 5α του άρθρου 4 των Κανόνων Χάγης-Βίσμπυ, όπως εκάστοτε ισχύουν στην Ελλάδα, για την ολική απώλεια των πραγμάτων.

4. Η μετατροπή των Ειδικών Τραβηκτικών Δικαιωμάτων σε ευρώ γίνεται με την ισοτιμία που ισχύει κατά τον χρόνο εκφόρτωσης των πραγμάτων ή κατά τον χρόνο που έπρεπε να λάβει χώρα η εκφόρτωση.

3. Where the conditions laid down in paragraphs 1 and 2 are not met, loss of or damage to the goods carried on deck shall be presumed to be due to fault of the carrier in handling the goods.

4. The carrier's obligation to safeguard the cargo shall extend to the condition of the containers, where these are provided by the carrier, and to containerisation, where this is done by the carrier.

Article 136

Clauses on the stages prior and subsequent to carriage

Without prejudice to Article 135(4) and the first subparagraph of Article 332 of the Civil Code, with regard to the period prior to the loading and after the discharge of the goods, the parties may agree on limitation of the obligations and liability of the carrier, as well as on altering the burden of proof rules.

Article 137

Special categories of merchandise

Without prejudice to the first subparagraph of Article 332 of the Civil Code, the parties may agree on limitation of the obligations and liability of the carrier, as well as on altering the burden of proof rules in the following cases:

(a) carriage of live animals;

(b) carriage of particular merchandise falling within the scope of Article VI of the Hague-Visby Rules, as in force in Greece from time to time;

(c) carriage of goods pursuant to volume contracts, within the meaning of Article 117(3) of this Code.

Article 138

Personal limitation of liability

1. The carrier shall be entitled to limitation of liability in accordance with the Hague-Visby Rules, as in force in Greece from time to time. This right may be lost in accordance with Article IV(5)(a) of the Hague-Visby Rules.

2. If the delay caused financial losses, the total compensation may not exceed three times the freight payable.

3. If the delay also caused damage to or loss of the cargo, the total compensation may not exceed the compensation calculated in accordance with Article IV(5)(a) of the Hague-Visby Rules, as in force in Greece from time to time, for the total loss of the goods.

4. The Special Drawing Rights shall be converted into euros at the exchange rate applicable at the time the goods were or ought to have been discharged.

ΚΕΦΑΛΑΙΟ Δ'

ΥΠΟΧΡΕΩΣΕΙΣ ΚΑΙ ΕΥΘΥΝΗ ΦΟΡΤΩΤΗ

Άρθρο 139

Υποχρέωση καταβολής του ναύλου

1. Ο φορτωτής υποχρεούται να καταβάλει στον θαλάσσιο μεταφορέα τον συμφωνηθέντα ναύλο και τις λοιπές από τη σύμβαση και τον νόμο παροχές. Ο ναύλος υπολογίζεται με βάση την ποσότητα των μεταφερόμενων πραγμάτων. Αν δεν έχει συμφωνηθεί ναύλος, οφείλεται ο συνήθης ναύλος κατά τον χρόνο της φόρτωσης στον λιμένα φόρτωσης για παρόμοιες μεταφορές και φορτία. Αν φορτώθηκαν πράγματα καθ' υπέρβαση της ποσότητας που είχε συμφωνηθεί, οφείλεται ο αναλογών επί πλέον ναύλος.

2. Ο ναύλος είναι καταβλητέος μετά τη φόρτωση, εκτός αν συμφωνηθεί διαφορετικά.

3. Ο παραλήπτης καθίσταται μαζί με τον φορτωτή εις ολόκληρον οφειλέτης του ναύλου και κάθε άλλης οφειλής από τη σύμβαση θαλάσσιας μεταφοράς και τον νόμο, εκτός αν συμφωνηθεί ρητά διαφορετικά επί της φορτωτικής ή άλλου ισοδύναμου εγγράφου μεταφοράς.

Άρθρο 140

Δικαιώματα του μεταφορέα επί μη καταβολής του ναύλου

1. Σε περίπτωση μη καταβολής του ναύλου ή των λοιπών πρόσθετων παροχών, ο μεταφορέας δικαιούται σε μεσεγγύηση του φορτίου. Το δικαίωμα τούτο δεν υφίσταται, όταν ο ναύλος φέρεται να έχει προκαταβληθεί κατά τους όρους της φορτωτικής.

2. Ο μεταφορέας διορίζεται μεσεγγυούχος του φορτίου σύμφωνα με τις διατάξεις περί ασφαλιστικών μέτρων.

3. Εάν υπάρχει φανερή ανάγκη, ή αν η διατήρηση του φορτίου είναι δυσχερής λόγω της φύσης και του είδους του ή για λόγους οικονομικούς, μετά από αίτημα του μεταφορέα, το μονομελές πρωτοδικείο μπορεί να διατάξει, δικάζοντας κατά τη διαδικασία των ασφαλιστικών μέτρων, την εκποίηση του φορτίου με εκούσιο πλειστηριασμό, ορίζοντας συγχρόνως τους όρους διενέργειας αυτού. Η απόφαση που διατάσσει τον εκούσιο πλειστηριασμό προσδιορίζει την αμοιβή και τα έξοδα του μεσεγγυούχου. Αμφότερα τα ποσά προαφαιρούνται από το εκπλειστηρίασμα. Μετά από τη διενέργεια του πλειστηριασμού ακολουθεί διαδικασία αναγγελιών και κατάταξης.

4. Οι αξιώσεις του μεταφορέα για τον ναύλο και την υπεραναμονή ικανοποιούνται προνομιακά πριν από οποιαδήποτε άλλη απαίτηση.

Άρθρο 141

Υποχρέωση παράδοσης των πραγμάτων προς φόρτωση

1. Αν δεν συμφωνήθηκε διαφορετικά, ο φορτωτής υποχρεούται να φέρει τα πράγματα επί της προκυμαίας ή επί της φορτηγίδας παραπλεύρως του πλοίου και στην ενδεδειγμένη για τη φόρτωση θέση και στον συμφωνηθέντα προς τούτο χρόνο.

CHAPTER IV

OBLIGATIONS AND LIABILITY OF THE SHIPPER

Article 139

Obligation to pay freight

1. The shipper shall be obligated to pay the carrier by sea the freight agreed upon and any other amounts required under the contract and by law. The freight shall be calculated on the basis of the quantity of goods carried. If no freight has been agreed upon, the usual freight rate at the time of loading at the port of loading for similar types of carriage and cargo shall be payable. If the goods loaded exceed the quantity agreed upon, corresponding additional freight shall be payable.

2. Unless otherwise agreed upon, the freight shall be payable after loading.

3. The consignee and the shipper shall jointly owe the freight and all other debts arising from the contract of carriage by sea and law, unless expressly agreed otherwise in the bill of lading or other equivalent transport document.

Article 140

Rights of the carrier in cases of failure to pay freight

1. If the freight or other additional amounts are not paid, the carrier shall be entitled to detain the cargo [under the rules of sequestration]. This right shall not apply where the freight was purportedly paid in advance according to the terms of the bill of lading.

2. The carrier shall be appointed as sequestrator of the cargo in accordance with the provisions on interim measures.

3. Where there is a clear need or where preservation of the cargo is difficult due to its nature and type or due to financial reasons, the single-member court of first instance may, following a request from the carrier and trying the matter under interim measures proceedings, hand down a judgment ordering that the cargo be sold at voluntary auction and laying down the terms for holding the auction. The sequestrator's fee and costs shall be specified in the judgment ordering the voluntary auction. Both these amounts shall be deducted in advance from the auction price. After the auction has been completed, the procedure for the lodgement and ranking [of claims] shall take place.

4. The carrier's claims concerning freight and demurrage shall receive preferential satisfaction prior to any other claim.

Article 141

Obligation to deliver the goods to be loaded

1. Unless otherwise agreed, the shipper shall be obligated to bring the goods to the quay or aboard a lighter alongside the ship, at the position appropriate for loading and at the time agreed upon.

2. Αν δεν συμφωνήθηκε διαφορετικά, ο φορτωτής υποχρεούται να παραδώσει τα πράγματα στον μεταφορέα κατάλληλα προς μεταφορά και δεόντως συσκευασμένα κατά τη συνήθη εμπορική πρακτική, ώστε να παραμείνουν άθικτα και ασφαλή στη διάρκεια της θαλάσσιας μεταφοράς, συμπεριλαμβανομένων των σταδίων της φόρτωσης, του χειρισμού, της στοιβασίας και της εκφόρτωσης, να μην θέτουν σε κίνδυνο την ασφάλεια του πλοίου και να μην προκαλέσουν σωματική ή περιουσιακή βλάβη.

3. Όταν ένα εμπορευματοκιβώτιο παραδίδεται προς μεταφορά συσκευασμένο από τον φορτωτή ή ένα όχημα φορτώνεται με πράγματα συσκευασμένα από τον φορτωτή, ο τελευταίος υποχρεούται να συσκευάζει το περιεχόμενο εντός του εμπορευματοκιβωτίου ή του οχήματος προσηκόντως και να το ασφαλίζει, ώστε να μην προκαλείται κίνδυνος για την ασφάλεια του πλοίου ή κίνδυνος βλάβης της υγείας προσώπων και περιουσίας.

Άρθρο 142

Υποχρέωση παράδοσης εγγράφων και παροχής πληροφοριών

1. Ο φορτωτής υποχρεούται:

(α) Να παραδίδει στον μεταφορέα κατά τον χρόνο της φόρτωσης όλα τα έγγραφα που σχετίζονται με τη φόρτωση και την εκφόρτωση.

(β) Να παρέχει στον μεταφορέα τις πληροφορίες που προβλέπει η παρ. 5 του άρθρου 3 των Κανόνων ΧάγηςΒίσμπυ, όπως εκάστοτε ισχύουν στην Ελλάδα, καθώς και κάθε άλλη πληροφορία που είναι απαραίτητη για τον κατάλληλο χειρισμό και τη μεταφορά των πραγμάτων, συμπεριλαμβανομένων των προφυλάξεων που πρέπει να ληφθούν από τον μεταφορέα, καθώς και πληροφοριών και εγγράφων για τη συμμόρφωση του μεταφορέα προς τον νόμο σε σχέση με την υπό εκτέλεση θαλάσσια μεταφορά.

(γ) Να ενημερώνει τον μεταφορέα, όταν τα υπό μεταφορά πράγματα είναι επικίνδυνα και να προβαίνει στην απαιτούμενη σήμανση σύμφωνα με τις ισχύουσες διατάξεις. Κατά τα λοιπά εφαρμόζεται η παρ. 6 του άρθρου 4 των Κανόνων Χάγης-Βίσμπυ, όπως εκάστοτε ισχύουν στην Ελλάδα.

(δ) Να παρέχει στον μεταφορέα εγκαίρως ακριβείς πληροφορίες που απαιτούνται για τη συμπλήρωση των στοιχείων της σύμβασης θαλάσσιας μεταφοράς και την έκδοση των εγγράφων μεταφοράς ή των ηλεκτρονικών αρχείων μεταφοράς, όπως το όνομα του παραλήπτη, εάν υπάρχει, και το όνομα του προσώπου, εις διαταγήν του οποίου θα εκδοθεί η φορτωτική ή το ισοδύναμο έγγραφο μεταφοράς ή το ηλεκτρονικό αρχείο μεταφοράς, εάν υπάρχει.

2. Με την επιφύλαξη της παρ. 5 του άρθρου 3 των Κανόνων Χάγης-Βίσμπυ, όπως εκάστοτε ισχύουν στην Ελλάδα, ο φορτωτής οφείλει να αποζημιώσει τον μεταφορέα για κάθε απώλεια ή ζημία, η οποία προκύπτει από την παραβίαση των ανωτέρω υποχρεώσεων, εκτός αν αποδείξει ότι δεν τον βαρύνει πταίσμα.

Άρθρο 143

Ευθύνη του φορτωτή

Ο φορτωτής ευθύνεται για κάθε απώλεια ή ζημία που υπέστη ο μεταφορέας συμπεριλαμβανομένου του πραγματικού μεταφορέα ή για ζημία που υπέστη το πλοίο, που προκλήθηκαν από πράξη ή παράλειψη δική του ή των προσώπων για τα οποία ευθύνεται, εκτός αν αποδείξει ότι δεν τον βαρύνει πταίσμα.

2. Unless otherwise agreed upon, the shipper shall be obligated to deliver the goods to the carrier fit for carriage and duly packaged according to usual commercial practice, so that the goods remain intact and safe during carriage by sea, including the stages of loading, handling, stowing and unloading, do not endanger the safety of the ship and do not cause personal injury or material damage.

3. Where a container, having been packed by the shipper, is delivered for carriage or a vehicle is loaded with goods packed by the shipper, the latter shall be obligated to duly pack the contents within the container or vehicle and to secure it so as not to endanger the safety of the ship or cause risk to the health of persons and to property.

Article 142

Obligation to deliver documents and provide information

1. The shipper shall be obligated:

(a) to deliver all documents relating to the loading and discharge to the carrier;

(b) to provide the carrier with the information required under Article III(5) of the Hague-Visby Rules, as in force in Greece from time to time, as well as all other information necessary for the appropriate handling and carriage of the goods, including the precautions to be taken by the carrier, and information and documents concerning the carrier's compliance with the law as regards the carriage by sea taking place;

(c) to notify the carrier when the goods being carried are dangerous and to make the necessary marking in accordance with the provisions in force. In all other respects, Article IV(6) of the Hague-Visby Rules, as in force in Greece from time to time, shall apply;

(d) to provide the carrier in good time with accurate information necessary for supplementing the information contained in the contract of carriage by sea and for issuing the transport documents or electronic transport files, such as the name of the consignee, where available, and the name of the person to whose order the bill of lading or equivalent transport document or electronic transport file, where available, will be issued.

2. Without prejudice to Article III(5) of the Hague-Visby Rules, as in force in Greece from time to time, the shipper shall be obligated to compensate the carrier for any loss or damage resulting from infringement of the above obligations, unless the shipper can prove that it is not at fault.

Article 143

Liability of the shipper

The shipper shall be liable for any loss or damage sustained by the carrier, including the actual carrier, or for damage sustained by the ship as a result of acts or omissions of the shipper or persons for whom the shipper is responsible, unless the shipper can prove that it is not at fault.

ΚΕΦΑΛΑΙΟ Ε'
ΠΑΡΑΔΟΣΗ ΤΩΝ ΠΡΑΓΜΑΤΩΝ

Άρθρο 144
Υποχρέωση παράδοσης των πραγμάτων

1. Με την επιφύλαξη της παρ. 3 του άρθρου 139 και του άρθρου 140, ο μεταφορέας υποχρεούται να παραδώσει τα πράγματα προς τον προσηκόντως νομιμοποιούμενο παραλήπτη, στον συμφωνηθέντα λιμένα εκφόρτωσης. Ο παραλήπτης υποχρεούται να παραλάβει τα πράγματα εντός του απολύτως αναγκαίου και εύλογου χρόνου από την εκφόρτωση.

2. Ο παραλήπτης νομιμοποιείται με βάση το άρθρο 123 και την παρ. 3 του άρθρου 127.

3. Η παράδοση των πραγμάτων αποδεικνύεται είτε με την επιστροφή στον μεταφορέα ή στον αντιπρόσωπό του της θαλάσσιας φορτωτικής ή άλλου ισοδύναμου εγγράφου μεταφοράς είτε με απόδοση του ιδιωτικού κωδικού, όταν πρόκειται για ηλεκτρονικό αρχείο μεταφοράς είτε με οποιονδήποτε άλλον πρόσφορο τρόπο.

Άρθρο 145
Εμφάνιση περισσότερων παραληπτών

1. Εάν εμφανίζονται περισσότεροι και έκαστος αξιώνει την παραλαβή των πραγμάτων, ο μεταφορέας, εάν δεν είναι εφικτό να διαπιστώσει ποιος νομιμοποιείται για την παραλαβή, δικαιούται να ζητήσει τον διορισμό μεσεγγυούχου κατά τη διαδικασία των ασφαλιστικών μέτρων και να προβεί σε ασφαλή αποθήκευση αυτών, με δαπάνη και κίνδυνο των φερομένων ως παραληπτών.

2. Η παρ. 1 δεν εφαρμόζεται, αν έχει τεθεί σε εφαρμογή η διαδικασία του άρθρου 140.

3. Εάν υπάρχει φανερή ανάγκη ή αν η διατήρηση των πραγμάτων είναι δυσχερής λόγω της φύσης και του είδους τους ή για λόγους οικονομικούς, ιδίως εάν το κόστος διατήρησης των πραγμάτων είναι δυσαναλόγως μεγάλο σε σχέση με την αξία τους, μετά από αίτηση του μεταφορέα ή του μεσεγγυούχου, που εκδικάζεται με τη διαδικασία των ασφαλιστικών μέτρων, το μονομελές πρωτοδικείο μπορεί να διατάξει εκποίηση των πραγμάτων με εκούσιο πλειστηριασμό, ορίζοντας συγχρόνως τους όρους διενέργειας αυτού. Στην απόφαση προσδιορίζονται η αμοιβή και τα έξοδα του μεσεγγυούχου. Αμφότερα τα ποσά προαφαιρούνται από το εκπλειστηρίασμα. Μετά τη διενέργεια του πλειστηριασμού ακολουθεί διαδικασία αναγγελιών και κατάταξης.

4. Ως προς την ικανοποίηση των αξιώσεων των παραληπτών και την υπεραναμονή εφαρμόζεται η παρ. 4 του άρθρου 140.

Άρθρο 146
Μη εμφάνιση παραλήπτη - άρνηση παραλαβής

1. Σε περίπτωση μη εμφάνισης του παραλήπτη προς παραλαβή των πραγμάτων στον λιμένα εκφόρτωσης ή σε περίπτωση καθυστερημένης εμφάνισής του ή όταν ο παραλήπτης αρνηθεί την παραλαβή για οποιονδήποτε λόγο, ο θαλάσσιος μεταφορέας δικαιούται να προβεί σε ασφαλή αποθήκευση αυτών με δαπάνη και κίνδυνο του παραλήπτη.

CHAPTER V

DELIVERY OF GOODS

Article 144

Obligation to deliver goods

1. Without prejudice to Articles 139(3) and 140, the carrier shall be obligated to deliver the goods to the duly authorised consignee at the port of discharge agreed upon. The consignee shall be obligated to take receipt of the goods within the period of time absolutely necessary and reasonable from the time of discharge.

2. The consignee shall [prove their entitlement to receive the consignment] on the basis of Articles 123 and 127(3).

3. Delivery of the goods shall be proven either by returning the maritime bill of lading or other equivalent transport document to the carrier or its agent, or by issuing a personalised password, in cases of an electronic transport file, or in any other expedient manner.

Article 145

Appearance of several consignees

1. If several persons appear and each seeks to take receipt of the goods, the carrier, where it cannot ascertain who is entitled to take receipt, shall be entitled to request that a sequestrator be appointed under interim measures proceedings and to place the goods in secure storage, at the expense and risk of the purported consignees.

2. Paragraph 1 shall not apply if the procedure laid down in Article 140 has been initiated.

3. Where there is a clear need or where preservation of the goods is difficult due to their nature and type or due to financial reasons and, in particular, if the cost of their preservation is disproportionately high in relation to their value, the single-member court of first instance may, following a request by the carrier or the sequestrator and trying the matter under interim measures proceedings, order that the goods be sold at voluntary auction and set the terms for holding the auction. The sequestrator's fee and costs shall be specified in the judgment. Both these amounts shall be deducted in advance from the auction price. After the auction has been completed, the procedure for the lodgement and ranking [of claims] shall take place.

4. Article 140(4) shall apply to satisfaction of claims of the consignees and demurrage.

Article 146

Failure of consignee to appear - refusal to take receipt [of goods]

1. If the consignee fails to appear in order to take receipt of the goods at the port of discharge or delays appearing or refuses to take receipt on any grounds, the carrier by sea shall be entitled to place the goods in secure storage, at the expense and risk of the consignee.

2. Ο μεταφορέας οφείλει να γνωστοποιήσει την αποθήκευση στον αναγραφόμενο στη φορτωτική παραλήπτη ή στον εμφανισθέντα και αρνηθέντα την παραλαβή του φορτίου, καθώς και στον φορτωτή, με κάθε πρόσφορο μέσο, και να θέσει εύλογη προθεσμία, μετά την παρέλευση της οποίας δικαιούται να προβεί σε εκποίηση των πραγμάτων με εκούσιο πλειστηριασμό, μετά από σχετική άδεια του μονομελούς πρωτοδικείου που δικάζει κατά τη διαδικασία των ασφαλιστικών μέτρων, ορίζοντας συγχρόνως τους όρους διενέργειας του πλειστηριασμού. Οι δαπάνες αποθήκευσης και εκποίησης προσδιορίζονται με την απόφαση και προαφαιρούνται από το εκπλειστηρίασμα. Μετά τη διενέργεια του πλειστηριασμού ακολουθεί διαδικασία αναγγελιών και κατάταξης.

3. Ως προς την ικανοποίηση των αξιώσεων του παραλήπτη και την υπεραναμονή εφαρμόζεται η παρ. 4 του άρθρου 140.

ΚΕΦΑΛΑΙΟ ΣΤ'
ΣΥΝΔΥΑΣΜΕΝΗ ΜΕΤΑΦΟΡΑ ΜΕ ΘΑΛΑΣΣΙΟ ΣΚΕΛΟΣ

Άρθρο 147
Σύμβαση συνδυασμένης μεταφοράς με θαλάσσιο σκέλος

Στη σύμβαση συνδυασμένης μεταφοράς με θαλάσσιο σκέλος ο μεταφορέας υποχρεούται να εκτελέσει τη μεταφορά του πράγματος με περισσότερα είδη μεταφορικών μέσων, ένα από τα οποία είναι πλοίο, με μεταφόρτωση του πράγματος από ένα μεταφορικό μέσο σε άλλο.

Άρθρο 148
Ευθύνη του μεταφορέα

1. Στην περίπτωση του άρθρου 147, η ευθύνη του μεταφορέα για ζημίες σχετικές με την ολική ή μερική απώλεια ή βλάβη των πραγμάτων ή καθυστέρηση στην παράδοση αυτών προσδιορίζεται από τους κανόνες που ρυθμίζουν το θαλάσσιο σκέλος της μεταφοράς, εφόσον το γεγονός που προκάλεσε την απώλεια, βλάβη ή καθυστέρηση στην παράδοση του πράγματος επήλθε στο σκέλος αυτό. Η απόδειξη ότι το εν λόγω γεγονός επήλθε στο θαλάσσιο σκέλος της μεταφοράς βαρύνει αυτόν που προβάλλει τον σχετικό ισχυρισμό.

2. Αν το στάδιο της μεταφοράς στο οποίο επήλθε το γεγονός που προκάλεσε την απώλεια, βλάβη ή καθυστέρηση στην παράδοση του πράγματος δεν αποδεικνύεται, η ευθύνη του μεταφορέα προσδιορίζεται από τους κανόνες που ρυθμίζουν το στάδιο της μεταφοράς στο οποίο προβλέπεται υψηλότερο όριο αποζημίωσης σε βάρος του μεταφορέα, εφόσον στο στάδιο αυτό θα μπορούσε να έχει προκύψει η σχετική ζημία.

Άρθρο 149
Επιφύλαξη εφαρμογής άλλων διατάξεων

Δεν θίγεται η εφαρμογή του άρθρου 2 της Διεθνούς Σύμβασης της Γενεύης του 1956 για τη διεθνή μεταφορά εμπορευμάτων οδικώς που κυρώθηκε με τον ν. 559/1977 (Α' 78), όπως εκάστοτε ισχύει στην Ελλάδα ή άλλων διεθνών συμβάσεων.

2. The carrier shall be obligated to use any expedient means to notify such storage to the consignee who is indicated in the bill of lading or who appeared and refused to take receipt of the cargo, as well as to the shipper, and to set a reasonable deadline, after the lapse of which the carrier shall be entitled to sell the goods at voluntary auction, with relevant permission from the single-member court of first instance, which shall try the matter under interim measures proceedings and lay down the terms for holding the auction. The storage and sale costs shall be specified in the judgment and deducted from the auction price [before it is paid to the carrier]. After the auction has been completed, the procedure for the lodgement and ranking [of claims] shall take place.

3. Article 140(4) shall apply to satisfaction of claims of the consignee and demurrage.

CHAPTER VI

MULTIMODAL TRANSPORT INVOLVING A SEA LEG

Article 147

Contract for multimodal transport involving a sea leg

In a contract for multimodal transport involving a sea leg, the carrier shall be obligated to perform carriage of the goods using several modes of transport, one of which is a ship, by transhipping the goods from one mode of transport to another.

Article 148

Liability of the carrier

1. In the case referred to in Article 147, the carrier's liability for losses concerning total or partial loss of or damage to the goods or delay in their delivery shall be determined by the rules regulating the sea leg of the carriage, provided the event which caused the loss, damage or delay in delivery of the goods occurred during the sea leg. The person making said assertion shall bear the burden of proving that the event in question occurred during the sea leg.

2. If it cannot be proven during which leg of the carriage the event which caused the loss of, damage to or delay in delivery of the goods occurred, the carrier's liability shall be determined by the rules regulating the leg of the carriage where a higher compensation limit is set for the carrier, provided the losses in question could have occurred during that leg.

Article 149

Operation of other provisions

Application of Article 2 of the 1956 Geneva Convention on the Contract for the International Carriage of Goods by Road, ratified by Law 559/1977 (Government Gazette, Series I, Issue 78), as in force in Greece from time to time, or of other international treaties or conventions shall not be prejudiced.

ΚΕΦΑΛΑΙΟ Ζ'

ΠΑΡΑΓΓΕΛΙΟΔΟΧΟΣ ΘΑΛΑΣΣΙΑΣ ΜΕΤΑΦΟΡΑΣ

Άρθρο 150

Σύμβαση παραγγελίας - Παραγγελιοδόχος θαλάσσιας μεταφοράς

1. Σύμβαση παραγγελίας θαλάσσιας μεταφοράς είναι η σύμβαση, δυνάμει της οποίας ένα φυσικό ή νομικό πρόσωπο (παραγγελιοδόχος) αναλαμβάνει την οργάνωση θαλάσσιας μεταφοράς και ιδίως την κατάρτιση σύμβασης θαλάσσιας μεταφοράς στο όνομά του για λογαριασμό του παραγγελέα.

2. Εκτός αν συμφωνήθηκε διαφορετικά, ο παραγγελιοδόχος θαλάσσιας μεταφοράς ευθύνεται για την προσήκουσα εκτέλεση της θαλάσσιας μεταφοράς εις ολόκληρον με τον μεταφορέα για τους ίδιους λόγους και στην ίδια έκταση που ευθύνεται ο τελευταίος. Ο παραγγελιοδόχος θαλάσσιας μεταφοράς ευθύνεται επίσης για τις πράξεις του μεσολαβούντος παραγγελιοδόχου.

Άρθρο 151

Παραγγελιοδόχος συνδυασμένης μεταφοράς με θαλάσσιο σκέλος

Εκτός αν συμφωνήθηκε διαφορετικά, ο παραγγελιοδόχος συνδυασμένης μεταφοράς με θαλάσσιο σκέλος ευθύνεται για την προσήκουσα εκτέλεση της μεταφοράς σύμφωνα με το πρώτο εδάφιο της παρ. 2 του άρθρου 150, το οποίο εφαρμόζεται αναλόγως.

CHAPTER VII
MARITIME FREIGHT FORWARDERS

Article 150
Commission contract - Maritime freight forwarders

1. A commission contract concerning carriage by sea is a contract pursuant to which a natural or legal person (freight forwarder) undertakes to organise carriage by sea and, in particular, the signing of a contract concerning carriage by sea in its name on behalf of the principal.

2. Unless otherwise agreed upon, the maritime freight forwarder shall be liable for proper performance of the carriage by sea jointly with the carrier on the same grounds for which and to the same extent to which the carrier is liable. The maritime freight forwarder shall also be held liable for the acts of the intermediary freight forwarder.

Article 151
Maritime freight forwarders for multimodal transport involving a sea leg

Unless otherwise agreed upon, the maritime freight forwarder for multimodal transport involving a sea leg shall be liable for proper performance of the carriage in accordance with the first subparagraph of Article 150(2), which shall apply *mutatis mutandis*.

ΜΕΡΟΣ ΕΚΤΟ
ΘΑΛΑΣΣΙΑ ΜΕΤΑΦΟΡΑ ΕΠΙΒΑΤΩΝ

ΚΕΦΑΛΑΙΟ Α'
ΕΝΝΟΙΑ - ΠΕΔΙΟ ΕΦΑΡΜΟΓΗΣ

Άρθρο 152
Θαλάσσια μεταφορά επιβάτη - Έννοια

1. Με τη σύμβαση θαλάσσιας μεταφοράς επιβάτη ο μεταφορέας αναλαμβάνει την υποχρέωση μεταφοράς δια θαλάσσης του επιβάτη και των αποσκευών του, συμπεριλαμβανομένου του οχήματός του, στον τόπο προορισμού έναντι ανταλλάγματος, όπου τούτο προβλέπεται.

2. Η σύμβαση θαλάσσιας μεταφοράς επιβάτη αποδεικνύεται με την έκδοση στον επιβάτη εισιτηρίου ή απόδειξης μεταφοράς οχήματος. Η έκδοση μπορεί να γίνει και ηλεκτρονικά.

3. Η θαλάσσια μεταφορά επιβάτη μπορεί να εκτελείται μερικώς ή ολικώς από πρόσωπο διαφορετικό από το πρόσωπο που έχει συμβληθεί ως μεταφορέας στη σύμβαση θαλάσσιας μεταφοράς (πραγματικός μεταφορέας).

Άρθρο 153
Εφαρμοστέοι κανόνες

1. Στη διεθνή και την εθνική θαλάσσια μεταφορά επιβάτη εφαρμόζονται η Διεθνής Σύμβαση των Αθηνών του 2002 σχετικά με τη θαλάσσια μεταφορά επιβατών και αποσκευών, η οποία κυρώθηκε με το άρθρο πρώτο του ν. 4195/2013 (Α' 211), όπως εκάστοτε ισχύει στην Ελλάδα (Διεθνής Σύμβαση Αθηνών) και ο Κανονισμός (ΕΚ) 392/2009 του Ευρωπαϊκού Κοινοβουλίου και του Συμβουλίου της 23ης Απριλίου 2009 «σχετικά με την ευθύνη των μεταφορέων που εκτελούν θαλάσσιες μεταφορές επιβατών, σε περίπτωση ατυχήματος» (L 131/24).

2. Οι διατάξεις του παρόντος Μέρους δεν θίγουν την εφαρμογή:

(α) του Κανονισμού (ΕΕ) 1177/2010 του Ευρωπαϊκού Κοινοβουλίου και του Συμβουλίου της 24ης Νοεμβρίου 2010 «σχετικά με τα δικαιώματα των επιβατών στις θαλάσσιες και εσωτερικές πλωτές μεταφορές» (L 334/1), όπως εκάστοτε ισχύει, και του Μέρους Γ' του Κώδικα θαλάσσιων ενδομεταφορών και δικαιωμάτων επιβατών (ν. 4948/2022, Α' 125) ως προς τη μεταφορά επιβάτη με δρομολογημένα πλοία στις θαλάσσιες ενδομεταφορές,

(β) του π.δ. 7/2018 (Α' 12), περί εναρμόνισης της νομοθεσίας με την Οδηγία (ΕΕ) 2015/2302 σχετικά με τα οργανωμένα ταξίδια και τους συνδεδεμένους ταξιδιωτικούς διακανονισμούς (L 326/1).

PART SIX
CARRIAGE OF PASSENGERS BY SEA

CHAPTER I
CONCEPT - SCOPE

Article 152
Carriage of passengers by sea - Concept

1. By virtue of a contract for the carriage of passengers by sea, the carrier undertakes the obligation to carry passengers and their luggage, as well as their vehicles, by sea to the place of destination in exchange for consideration, where such obligation is provided for.

2. The contract of carriage of passengers by sea shall be proven by issuing a ticket or vehicle carriage receipt to the passenger. Said ticket or carriage receipt may also be issued electronically.

3. The carriage of passengers by sea may be performed, in whole or in part, by a person other than the person entering into the contract of carriage by sea as the carrier (actual carrier).

Article 153
Applicable rules

1. The 2002 Athens Convention Relating to the Carriage of Passengers and their Luggage by Sea, ratified by the first Article of Law 4195/2013 (Government Gazette, Series I, Issue 211), as in force in Greece from time to time (the Athens Convention), and Regulation (EC) No 392/2009 of the European Parliament and of the Council of 23 April 2009 on the liability of carriers of passengers by sea in the event of accidents (OJ L 131/24) shall apply to national and international carriage of passengers by sea.

2. The provisions of this Part shall not prejudice the application of:

(a) Regulation (EU) No 1177/2010 of the European Parliament and of the Council of 24 November 2010 concerning the rights of passengers when travelling by sea and inland waterway (OJ L 334/1), as in force from time to time, and Part C of the Code of Maritime Cabotage and Rights of Passengers (Law 4948/2022, Government Gazette, Series I, Issue 125) concerning the carriage of passengers by ship carrying out scheduled maritime cabotage operations;

(b) Presidential Decree 7/2018 (Government Gazette, Series I, 12) on transposition of Directive (EU) 2015/2302 on package travel and linked travel arrangements (OJ L 326/1) into Greek law.

ΚΕΦΑΛΑΙΟ Β'
ΥΠΟΧΡΕΩΣΕΙΣ ΚΑΙ ΕΥΘΥΝΗ ΤΟΥ ΜΕΤΑΦΟΡΕΑ

Άρθρο 154
Υποχρεώσεις του μεταφορέα

Ο μεταφορέας υποχρεούται:

(α) Να εκτελεί τη θαλάσσια μεταφορά με αξιόπλοο για τον συγκεκριμένο πλου πλοίο, κατά τον προγραμματισμένο ή συμφωνημένο χρόνο, από και προς τους προγραμματισμένους ή συμφωνημένους τόπους και σύμφωνα με τους υπόλοιπους όρους της σύμβασης θαλάσσιας μεταφοράς.

(β) Να παρέχει υπηρεσίες θαλάσσιων μεταφορών χωρίς διακρίσεις μεταξύ των επιβατών, λαμβανομένων υπόψη της κατηγορίας, της θέσης, του τύπου του θαλάμου επιβατών, καθώς και των λοιπών συμφωνημένων παροχών.

(γ) Να τηρεί τους όρους ασφάλειας και υγιεινής των επιβατών του πλοίου και να λαμβάνει κάθε αναγκαίο μέτρο προς τον σκοπό αυτόν.

(δ) Να παρέχει στους επιβάτες επαρκείς πληροφορίες στα σημεία πώλησης, και πάντως το αργότερο κατά την αναχώρηση, σχετικά με τις υποχρεώσεις του και τα δικαιώματα των επιβατών σε περίπτωση ατυχήματος, καθυστέρησης ή ματαίωσης της μεταφοράς.

(ε) Να διασφαλίζει συνθήκες πρόσβασης χωρίς διακρίσεις και να παρέχει κάθε δυνατή συνδρομή και πληροφόρηση στα άτομα με αναπηρία ή στα άτομα μειωμένης κινητικότητας και στους συνοδούς αυτών, σύμφωνα με τους όρους του Κανονισμού (ΕΕ) 1177/2010 του Ευρωπαϊκού Κοινοβουλίου και του Συμβουλίου της 24ης Νοεμβρίου 2010 για τα δικαιώματα των επιβατών στις θαλάσσιες και εσωτερικές πλωτές μεταφορές και για την τροποποίηση του Κανονισμού (ΕΚ) 2006/2004 (L 334/1) και του Κώδικα θαλάσσιων ενδομεταφορών και δικαιωμάτων επιβατών.

(στ) Να παρέχει την απαιτούμενη συνδρομή σε περίπτωση καθυστέρησης ή ματαίωσης της μεταφοράς και να διευκολύνει την άσκηση των σχετικών δικαιωμάτων που προβλέπονται στο Κεφάλαιο III του Κανονισμού (ΕΕ) 1177/2010 και στο Μέρος Γ' του Κώδικα θαλάσσιων ενδομεταφορών και δικαιωμάτων επιβατών.

(ζ) Να διαθέτει προσβάσιμο μηχανισμό διεκπεραίωσης των παραπόνων ή διαμαρτυριών των επιβατών και να παρέχει σαφή πληροφόρηση για τις διαδικασίες αυτές.

Άρθρο 155
Ευθύνη του μεταφορέα

***1.** Η ευθύνη του μεταφορέα, συμπεριλαμβανομένου του πραγματικού μεταφορέα και των προστηθέντων αυτών, για ζημίες που έχουν σχέση με σωματικές βλάβες ή απώλεια ζωής επιβάτη και απώλεια ή βλάβη των αποσκευών του, διέπεται αποκλειστικά από τη Διεθνή Σύμβαση Αθηνών και τον Κανονισμό (ΕΚ) 392/2009 του Ευρωπαϊκού Κοινοβουλίου και του Συμβουλίου, της 23ης Απριλίου 2009, σχετικά με την ευθύνη των μεταφορέων που εκτελούν θαλάσσιες μεταφορές επιβατών, σε περίπτωση ατυχήματος (L 131/24), όπου οι διατάξεις του τελευταίου καλούνται σε εφαρμογή.*

***2.** Η παρ. 1 εφαρμόζεται:*

(α) στις θαλάσσιες περιηγήσεις και

(β) στη μεταφορά επιβατών με αερόστρωμνα οχήματα.

***3.** Η ευθύνη του μεταφορέα για καθυστέρηση αναχώρησης, άφιξης ή ματαίωσης της μεταφοράς διέπεται από τον Κανονισμό (ΕΕ) 1177/2010 και τον Κώδικα θαλάσσιων ενδομεταφορών και δικαιωμάτων επιβατών. Περαιτέρω αποζημίωση με βάση τις κοινές διατάξεις δεν αποκλείεται.*

CHAPTER II
OBLIGATIONS AND LIABILITY OF THE CARRIER

Article 154
Obligations of the carrier

The carrier shall be obligated:

(a) to perform the carriage by sea using a ship which is seaworthy for the voyage in question, at the time scheduled or agreed upon, to and from the places scheduled or agreed upon and in accordance with the other terms of the contract of carriage by sea;

(b) to provide carriage by sea services without discrimination between passengers with regard to the category, class, type of passenger cabin and other amenities agreed upon;

(c) to comply with the requirements concerning the health and safety of passengers aboard the ship, and to take all measures necessary to this end;

(d) to provide passengers with adequate information at points of sale and, in all cases, no later than during departure, concerning the carrier's obligations and the passengers' rights in the event of accident, delay or cancellation of the carriage;

(e) to ensure non-discriminatory access conditions and to provide all possible assistance and information to disabled persons and persons with reduced mobility and their accompanying persons, in accordance with the terms of Regulation (EU) No 1177/2010 of the European Parliament and of the Council of 24 November 2010 concerning the rights of passengers when travelling by sea and inland waterway and amending Regulation (EC) No 2006/2004 (OJ L 334/1) and the Code of Maritime Cabotage and Rights of Passengers;

(f) to provide the necessary assistance in the event of delay or cancellation of carriage, and to facilitate exercise of the relevant rights provided for in Chapter III of Regulation (EU) No 1177/2010 and Part III of the Code of Maritime Cabotage and Rights of Passengers;

(g) to have an accessible mechanism for handling complaints or grievances of passengers, and to provide clear information on such procedures.

Article 155
Liability of the carrier

1. The liability of the carrier, including the actual carrier and its agents, for losses relating to personal injury or loss of life of passengers and loss of or damage to their luggage shall be exclusively governed by the Athens Convention and Regulation (EC) No 392/2009 of the European Parliament and of the Council of 23 April 2009 on the liability of carriers of passengers by sea in the event of accidents (OJ L 131/24), where the provisions of the latter apply.

2. Paragraph 1 shall apply:

(a) to cruises; and

(b) to carriage of passengers by air-cushion vehicle.

3. The liability of the carrier for delayed departure, delayed arrival or cancellation of carriage shall be governed by Regulation (EU) No 1177/2010 and the Code of Maritime Cabotage and Rights of Passengers. Further compensation on the basis of the ordinary provisions may not be precluded.

Άρθρο 156
Περίοδος ευθύνης του μεταφορέα

Η ευθύνη του μεταφορέα, τόσο στην εσωτερική όσο και στη διεθνή θαλάσσια μεταφορά επιβατών και των αποσκευών τους, εκτείνεται στη χρονική περίοδο της παρ. 8 του άρθρου 1 της Διεθνούς Σύμβασης Αθηνών.

Άρθρο 157
Ρήτρες περιορισμού ευθύνης του μεταφορέα

Οποιοσδήποτε συμβατικός όρος που συνομολογείται προτού λάβει χώρα το συμβάν που προκάλεσε τον θάνατο ή τη σωματική βλάβη επιβάτη ή την απώλεια ή ζημία των αποσκευών του, συμπεριλαμβανομένου του οχήματός του, και απαλλάσσει τον μεταφορέα, συμβατικό ή πραγματικό, καθώς και τους προστηθέντες του, από την ευθύνη τους ή διαφοροποιεί τους όρους αυτής ή τις υποχρεώσεις τους ή μεταβάλλει το βάρος απόδειξης κατά τρόπο ευνοϊκότερο για αυτούς, ή περιορίζει τις επιλογές διεθνούς δικαιοδοσίας, είναι άκυρος, χωρίς να επηρεάζεται το κύρος της σύμβασης μεταφοράς, η οποία εξακολουθεί και υπόκειται στις ρυθμίσεις του παρόντος Μέρους.

Άρθρο 158
Ατομικός και συνολικός περιορισμός της ευθύνης

1. Ο μεταφορέας, συμπεριλαμβανομένου του πραγματικού μεταφορέα, και οι προστηθέντες αυτών δικαιούνται να προβούν σε ατομικό περιορισμό της ευθύνης τους, σύμφωνα με τα όρια και τις προϋποθέσεις των άρθρων 7, 8, 10, 11 και 13 της Διεθνούς Σύμβασης Αθηνών.

2. Ειδικώς για τους κινδύνους που αναφέρονται στο άρθρο 2.2. των Κατευθυντήριων Γραμμών του Διεθνούς Ναυτιλιακού Οργανισμού, ισχύουν τα προβλεπόμενα στις ως άνω Κατευθυντήριες Γραμμές όρια ευθύνης, σύμφωνα με το άρθρο τρίτο του ν. 4195/2013 (Α' 211) και την περ. β' της παρ. 1 του άρθρου 1 και το άρθρο 3 του Κανονισμού (ΕΚ) 392/2009.

3. Οι παρ. 1 και 2 δεν θίγουν το δικαίωμα συνολικού περιορισμού της ευθύνης για απαιτήσεις σχετικές με απώλεια ζωής ή σωματικές βλάβες επιβατών, σύμφωνα με τη Διεθνή Σύμβαση Περιορισμού όπως εκάστοτε ισχύει στην Ελλάδα.

4. Για τα πλοία που δεν εμπίπτουν στο πεδίο εφαρμογής του Κανονισμού (ΕΚ) 392/2009, τα ατομικά και συνολικά όρια της ευθύνης του μεταφορέα καθορίζονται και αναθεωρούνται με απόφαση του Υπουργού Ναυτιλίας και Νησιωτικής Πολιτικής.

Άρθρο 159
Υποχρεωτική ασφάλιση του πραγματικού μεταφορέα

1. Ο πλοιοκτήτης - πραγματικός μεταφορέας υποχρεούται να καλύψει ασφαλιστικά την αστική ευθύνη του ως προς τους επιβάτες ή να παράσχει άλλου είδους χρηματοοικονομική ασφάλεια, σύμφωνα με το άρθρο 4α της Διεθνούς Σύμβασης Αθηνών, λαμβανομένων υπόψη των επιφυλάξεων και των Κατευθυντηρίων Γραμμών του Διεθνούς Ναυτιλιακού Οργανισμού, που περιέχονται στο άρθρο 3 του ν. 4195/2013, και στο άρθρο 3 του Κανονισμού (ΕΚ) 392/2009.

2. Για τα πλοία που δεν εμπίπτουν στην εφαρμογή του Κανονισμού (ΕΚ) 392/2009, η υποχρεωτική ασφάλιση καλύπτει τα όρια της ευθύνης του πλοιοκτήτη - πραγματικού μεταφορέα, όπως καθορίζονται σύμφωνα με την παρ. 4 του άρθρου 158.

Article 156

Period of liability of the carrier

The liability of the carrier for both domestic and international carriage of passengers and their luggage by sea shall cover the period set forth in Article 1(8) of the Athens Convention.

Article 157

Carrier limitation of liability clauses

Any contractual term agreed upon prior to the incident resulting in death of or personal injury to a passenger or damage of or loss to their luggage, as well as their vehicle, and releasing the carrier, whether contractual or actual, and its agents from their liability, or altering the terms of such liability, or their obligations, or altering the burden of proof in a manner which benefits them, or limiting choice of forum shall be null and void, but shall not affect the validity of the contract of carriage, which shall persist and shall be subject to the provisions of this Part.

Article 158

Personal and global limitation of liability

1. The carrier, including the actual carrier, and their agents shall be entitled to personally limit their own liability, in accordance with the limits and conditions laid down in Articles 7, 8, 10, 11 and 13 of the Athens Convention.

2. With specific regard to the risks referred to in Article 2.2 of the IMO Guidelines [for the Implementation of the Athens Convention], the limits of liability laid down in the aforesaid Guidelines shall apply, in accordance with the third Article of Law 4195/2013 (Government Gazette, Series I, Issue 211) and Article 1(1)(b) and Article 3 of Regulation (EC) No 392/2009.

3. Paragraphs 1 and 2 shall not prejudice the right to global limitation of liability for claims in respect of loss of life or personal injury sustained by passengers, in accordance with the International Convention on Limitation of Liability, as in force in Greece from time to time.

4. In cases of ships not falling within the scope of Regulation (EC) No 392/2009, the personal and global limits of the carrier's liability shall be laid down and revised in a decision issued by the Minister of Maritime Affairs and Insular Policy.

Article 159

Obligatory insurance of the actual carrier

1. The owner-operator - actual carrier shall be obligated to cover its civil liability in respect of passengers with insurance or provide any other kind of financial security, in accordance with Article 4bis of the Athens Convention, having regard to the Reservation and Guidelines of the International Maritime Organisation contained in the [third Article] of Law 4195/2013 and Article 3 of Regulation (EC) No 392/2009.

2. In cases of ships not falling within the scope of Regulation (EC) No 392/2009, the obligatory insurance shall cover the limits of liability of the owner-operator - actual carrier, as laid down in accordance with Article 158(4).

ΚΕΦΑΛΑΙΟ Γ'
ΥΠΟΧΡΕΩΣΕΙΣ ΕΠΙΒΑΤΗ

Άρθρο 160
Εισιτήριο

1. Το αντίτιμο του εισιτηρίου προκαταβάλλεται.

2. Στην αξία του εισιτηρίου περιλαμβάνεται ο ναύλος της μεταφοράς. Δεν περιλαμβάνεται το αντίτιμο τροφοδοσίας κατά τον πλου, εκτός αν συμφωνήθηκε διαφορετικά.

3. Για τις αποσκευές του ο επιβάτης υποχρεώνεται σε καταβολή πρόσθετου ναύλου, εφόσον αυτές υπερβαίνουν το βάρος που προβλέπεται στον νόμο ή στη σύμβαση. Οι σχετικές ρυθμίσεις της θαλάσσιας ενδομεταφοράς εφαρμόζονται και στη διεθνή θαλάσσια μεταφορά.

4. Δεν επιτρέπεται η μεταβίβαση του εισιτηρίου χωρίς την έγκριση του μεταφορέα ή του εκδότη του εισιτηρίου.

Άρθρο 161
Έγκαιρη επιβίβαση

1. Ο επιβάτης οφείλει να επιβιβάζεται εγκαίρως στο πλοίο σύμφωνα με τους όρους της σύμβασης μεταφοράς και τους οικείους κανονισμούς.

2. Σε περίπτωση μη έγκαιρης προσέλευσης του επιβάτη προς επιβίβαση, ο μεταφορέας ελευθερώνεται, ο δε επιβάτης υποχρεούται στον πλήρη ναύλο.

3. Κατά τη διάρκεια του πλου, ο επιβάτης οφείλει να συμμορφώνεται προς τις οδηγίες του πλοιάρχου και του πληρώματος του πλοίου. Το άρθρο 43 του Κώδικα θαλάσσιων ενδομεταφορών και δικαιωμάτων επιβατών εφαρμόζεται και στη διεθνή θαλάσσια μεταφορά.

Άρθρο 162
Όροι υπαναχώρησης επιβάτη

1. Ο επιβάτης δικαιούται να υπαναχωρήσει από τη σύμβαση θαλάσσιας μεταφοράς πριν από την έναρξη του πλου.

2. Οι όροι και οι συνέπειες της υπαναχώρησης ως προς τον καταβληθέντα ναύλο που ισχύουν στη θαλάσσια ενδομεταφορά εφαρμόζονται και στη διεθνή θαλάσσια μεταφορά επιβατών.

3. Ο επιβάτης υποχρεώνεται στην καταβολή ολόκληρου του ναύλου εάν αποβιβασθεί σε ενδιάμεσο λιμένα. Εάν η διακοπή του πλου επέλθει λόγω ασθένειας ή άλλου τυχαίου συμβάντος που αφορά στον επιβάτη, αυτός υποχρεώνεται σε καταβολή μέρους του ναύλου ανάλογου με τον διανυθέντα πλου.

Άρθρο 163
Δήλωση περί απώλειας ή φθοράς αποσκευών

1. Ο επιβάτης οφείλει να δηλώσει, εγγράφως ή ηλεκτρονικώς, στον μεταφορέα τυχόν εμφανή φθορά των αποσκευών του, το αργότερο κατά τον χρόνο της αποβίβασης, εφόσον πρόκειται για αποσκευές καμπίνας, ή το αργότερο κατά τον χρόνο της παραλαβής για τις λοιπές αποσκευές.

2. Σε περίπτωση απώλειας ή μη εμφανούς φθοράς των αποσκευών, η δήλωση της παρ. 1 πρέπει να αποσταλεί εντός δεκαπέντε (15) ημερών από την αποβίβαση, ή την παραλαβή αντιστοίχως ή από τον χρόνο που η παραλαβή έπρεπε να λάβει χώρα.

CHAPTER III
OBLIGATIONS OF PASSENGERS

Article 160
Tickets

1. The price of the ticket shall be paid in advance.

2. The value of the ticket includes the fare for carriage. Unless otherwise agreed upon, the price of catering during the voyage shall not be included.

3. Where a passenger's luggage exceeds the statutory or contractual weight, the passenger shall be obligated to pay an additional fare. The relevant regulations on maritime cabotage shall also apply to international carriage by sea.

4. Tickets may not be transferred without the approval of the carrier or ticket issuer.

Article 161
Timely embarkation

1. Passengers must embark in good time, in accordance with the terms of the contract of carriage and the applicable regulations.

2. In the event of late arrival of a passenger for embarkation, the carrier shall be released and the passenger shall be obligated to pay the full fare.

3. During the voyage, passengers shall be obligated to comply with the instructions of the master and the crew of the ship. Article 43 of the Code of Maritime Cabotage and Rights of Passengers shall also apply to international carriage by sea.

Article 162
Conditions for passenger withdrawal

1. Passengers shall be entitled to withdraw from the contract of carriage by sea before the voyage commences.

2. The conditions for and consequences of withdrawal in respect of the fare paid applicable to maritime cabotage shall also apply to international carriage of passengers by sea.

3. If they disembark at an intermediate port, passengers shall be obligated to pay the entire fare. If the voyage is interrupted due to illness or other fortuity concerning a passenger, that passenger shall be obligated to pay a part of the fare in proportion to the voyage completed.

Article 163
Declaration concerning loss of or damage to luggage

1. Passengers shall be obligated to declare to the carrier, whether in writing or electronically, any apparent damage to their luggage, no later than the time of disembarkation in cases of cabin luggage, or no later than the time of redelivery in cases of other luggage.

2. In cases of loss of or damage to luggage which is not apparent, the declaration referred to in paragraph 1 must be sent within 15 days from the date of disembarkation or redelivery, respectively, or from the time when such redelivery ought to have taken place.

3. Δεν απαιτείται δήλωση, αν η φθορά ή η απώλεια διαπιστώθηκε με κοινή εξέταση κατά τον χρόνο της παραλαβής.

4. Ο επιβάτης που δεν συμμορφώνεται με τη διαδικασία του παρόντος, τεκμαίρεται ότι έχει παραλάβει τις αποσκευές χωρίς βλάβη, εκτός αν αποδείξει το αντίθετο.

Άρθρο 164
Σχέση με ναύλωση

1. Σε περίπτωση ναύλωσης του πλοίου με σκοπό την περιήγηση προσώπων, έστω και μη ορισμένου αριθμού, εφαρμόζονται η περ. (α) του άρθρου 154, η παρ. 1 του άρθρου 155, και τα άρθρα 156, 157 και 159, εφόσον τη ναυτική διεύθυνση του πλοίου διατηρεί ο εκμεταλλευόμενος αυτό.

2. Τα όρια ευθύνης και ασφαλιστικής κάλυψης στην περίπτωση της παρ. 1 καθορίζονται στο άρθρο 17 του ν. 4926/2022 (Α' 82).

3. No declaration shall be required if the damage or loss was ascertained by means of a simple check at the time of redelivery.

4. Passengers who fail to comply with the procedure laid down in this Article shall be presumed, unless they prove otherwise, to have received the luggage undamaged.

Article 164

Relationship to chartering

1. Where a ship has been chartered for the purpose of providing cruises to persons, even if indefinite in number, Articles 154(a), 155(1), 156, 157 and 159 shall apply, provided the person operating the ship retains its maritime management.

2. The limits of liability and insurance coverage in the case provided for in paragraph 1 are laid down in paragraph 1 in Article 17 of Law 4926/2022 (Government Gazette, Series I, Issue 82).

ΜΕΡΟΣ ΕΒΔΟΜΟ
ΝΑΥΤΙΚΗ ΕΡΓΑΣΙΑ

Άρθρο 165
Εφαρμοστέοι κανόνες

1. Η σύμβαση ναυτολόγησης, οι όροι εργασίας και τα δικαιώματα του ναυτικού ρυθμίζονται από τις συλλογικές συμβάσεις ναυτικής εργασίας που έχουν εφαρμογή, τη Διεθνή Σύμβαση Ναυτικής Εργασίας του 2006, όπως έχει κυρωθεί με τον ν. 4078/2012 (Α' 179) και εκάστοτε ισχύει στην Ελλάδα (Διεθνή Σύμβαση Ναυτικής Εργασίας), τις σχετικές ρυθμίσεις του ενωσιακού δικαίου και συμπληρωματικώς από το παρόν Μέρος.

2. Τα Κεφάλαια Α' και Β' του παρόντος Μέρους εφαρμόζονται και στον πλοίαρχο, εκτός αν άλλως ορίζεται ρητώς.

ΚΕΦΑΛΑΙΟ Α'
ΣΥΜΒΑΣΗ ΝΑΥΤΟΛΟΓΗΣΗΣ

Άρθρο 166
Κατάρτιση σύμβασης ναυτολόγησης

1. Η σύμβαση ναυτολόγησης συνομολογείται μεταξύ του ναυτικού και του πλοιοκτήτη ή του αντιπρόσωπου του ή του πλοιάρχου, εφόσον δεν είναι ο ίδιος ναυτολογούμενος. Καταρτίζεται εγγράφως και περιέχει τους όρους της ναυτολόγησης επί του πλοίου. Καθένας από τους συμβαλλομένους λαμβάνει υπογεγραμμένο πρωτότυπο της σύμβασης ναυτολόγησης.

2. Κατά την κατάρτιση της σύμβασης ναυτολόγησης ο ναυτικός πρέπει να έχει ενημερωθεί πλήρως σχετικά με το περιεχόμενο της σύμβασης, τα δικαιώματα και τις υποχρεώσεις του, καθώς και τους όρους εργασίας επί του πλοίου.

3. Η σύμβαση ναυτολόγησης καταχωρίζεται στο ναυτολόγιο του πλοίου. Η καταχώριση θεωρείται από τη λιμενική ή προξενική αρχή ή από τη Διεύθυνση Ναυτικής Εργασίας του Υπουργείου Ναυτιλίας και Νησιωτικής Πολιτικής.

4. Η τήρηση του ναυτολογίου, καθώς και κάθε πράξη και εγγραφή σε αυτό μπορεί να γίνεται και με ηλεκτρονικά μέσα.

PART SEVEN
MARITIME LABOUR

Article 165
Applicable rules

1. The employment agreement, the terms of employment and rights of seafarers shall be regulated by the maritime labour collective bargaining agreements in effect, by the International Maritime Labour Convention of 2006, as ratified by Law 4078/2012 (Government Gazette, Series I, Issue 179) and in force in Greece from time to time (International Maritime Labour Convention), by the relevant EU law provisions and, on a supplementary basis, by this Part.

2. Unless expressly provided for otherwise, Chapters I and II of this Part shall also apply to the master.

CHAPTER I
EMPLOYMENT AGREEMENT

Article 166
Drafting of employment agreements

1. The employment agreement shall be entered into by the seafarer and the owner-operator or its agent or the master, where the latter is not signed on. The agreement shall be drawn up in writing and shall contain the terms of employment aboard the ship. Each of the contracting parties shall receive a signed original of the employment agreement.

2. During the drafting of the employment agreement, the seafarer must have been fully informed about the content of the agreement, their rights and obligations, as well as the terms of labour on the ship.

3. The employment agreement shall be recorded in the ship's articles. The entry shall be certified by the port or consular authority or the Seafarer's Labour Directorate of the Ministry of Maritime Affairs and Insular Policy.

4. Electronic means may be used to keep the ship's articles and record any transaction and entry in them.

Άρθρο 167
Μορφές σύμβασης ναυτολόγησης

Η σύμβαση ναυτολόγησης μπορεί να είναι σύμβαση ορισμένου χρόνου, κατά ταξίδι ή αορίστου χρόνου.

Άρθρο 168
Περιεχόμενο της σύμβασης ναυτολόγησης

Η σύμβαση ναυτολόγησης περιέχει, εκτός από την ημερομηνία και τον τόπο κατάρτισής της, τα ακόλουθα στοιχεία:

(α) Το πλήρες όνομα του ναυτικού, τον τόπο και τον χρόνο της γέννησής του.

(β) Το πλήρες όνομα και τη διεύθυνση του πλοιοκτήτη ή του νόμιμου αντιπροσώπου του ή του πλοιάρχου.

(γ) Το όνομα του πλοίου, τον τύπο και τον αριθμό νηολογίου, τη χωρητικότητα, το διεθνές διακριτικό σήμα, τον διακριτικό αριθμό του Διεθνούς Ναυτιλιακού Οργανισμού.

(δ) Την ειδικότητα, με την οποία ναυτολογείται ο ναυτικός, και το κατεχόμενο αποδεικτικό ναυτικής ικανότητας.

(ε) Το ποσό του μισθού του ναυτικού και τον τύπο που χρησιμοποιείται για τον υπολογισμό του.

(στ) Τον χρόνο της ετήσιας άδειας μετ' αποδοχών ή αναλόγως, όταν έχει εφαρμογή, τον τύπο που χρησιμοποιείται για τον υπολογισμό της.

(ζ) Τον χρόνο διάρκειας της σύμβασης και τις προϋποθέσεις καταγγελίας αυτής.

(η) Τις παροχές υγείας και κοινωνικής προστασίας του πλοιοκτήτη προς τον ναυτικό.

(θ) Ρητή πρόβλεψη περί του δικαιώματος παλιννόστησης του ναυτικού, συμπεριλαμβανομένου του τόπου παλιννόστησης.

(ι) Την εφαρμοζόμενη συλλογική σύμβαση εργασίας, αντίτυπο της οποίας προσαρτάται στο ναυτολόγιο, καθώς και τυχόν επιπρόσθετους, συμφωνηθέντες από τα συμβαλλόμενα μέρη, όρους.

(ια) Ρητή πρόβλεψη περί της επίλυσης των διαφορών που τυχόν προκύπτουν από τη σύμβαση ναυτολόγησης.

Άρθρο 169
Προσύμφωνο ναυτολόγησης

1. Το προσύμφωνο ναυτολόγησης αποτελεί συμφωνία του πλοιοκτήτη ή του αντιπροσώπου του με τον ναυτικό, σύμφωνα με την οποία ο πρώτος αναλαμβάνει την υποχρέωση να συνάψει σύμβαση ναυτικής εργασίας με τον ναυτικό, όταν αυτός επιβιβασθεί στο πλοίο.

2. Ο πλοιοκτήτης υποχρεούται να καταβάλει στον ναυτικό τις δαπάνες μετακίνησής του στον λιμένα ναυλοχίας του πλοίου και παραμονής σε αυτόν, καθώς και τον αναλογούντα πλήρη μισθό για το χρονικό διάστημα από τη σύναψη του προσυμφώνου μέχρι την υπογραφή της σύμβασης ναυτολόγησης. Εάν υφίσταται ευνοϊκότερη ρύθμιση στην οικεία συλλογική σύμβαση ναυτικής εργασίας, ισχύει αυτή.

3. Σε περίπτωση που ο πλοιοκτήτης δεν συνάψει τη σύμβαση ναυτολόγησης, ο ναυτικός που μετέβη στον λιμένα ναυλοχίας δικαιούται τα προβλεπόμενα στην παρ. 2 καθώς και τις δαπάνες επιστροφής του στον τόπο αναχώρησης.

Article 167

Types of employment agreements

The employment agreement may be made for a definite period, for a voyage or for an indefinite period.

Article 168

Content of the employment agreement

In addition to specifying the time and place where it was drawn up, the employment agreement shall also contain the following information:

(a) the full name of the seafarer, the place and date of their birth;

(b) the full name and address of the owner-operator or its lawful agent or the master;

(c) the name of the ship, her type and ship registry number, tonnage, international call sign, and IMO number;

(d) the capacity in which the seafarer is being employed, and the certificate of competence held;

(e) the amount of the seafarer's wages and the formula used for calculating them;

(f) the amount of paid annual leave or, where applicable, the formula used for calculating it;

(g) the term of duration of the agreement and the conditions for its termination;

(h) the health and social protection benefits [to be provided] by the owner-operator to the seafarer;

(i) an express provision concerning the seafarer's entitlement to repatriation, including the place of repatriation;

(j) the applicable collective bargaining agreement, a copy of which shall be appended to the ship's articles, as well as any additional terms agreed upon between the contracting parties; [and]

(k) an express provision concerning the resolution of any disputes arising from the employment agreement.

Article 169

Preliminary employment agreement

1. A preliminary employment agreement is an agreement between the owner-operator or its agent and the seafarer whereby the former undertakes the obligation to enter into a seafarer employment agreement with the seafarer when the latter embarks.

2. The owner-operator shall be obligated to pay the seafarer the costs for travelling to the port of anchorage of the ship and their stay there, as well as the corresponding full wages for the period between the signing of the preliminary agreement and the signing of the employment agreement. If the applicable maritime labour collective bargaining agreement contains a more favourable provision, that provision shall apply.

3. Where the owner-operator does not enter into the employment agreement, the seafarer who travelled to the port of anchorage shall be entitled to the amounts provided for in paragraph 2 and the costs of returning to their place of departure.

Άρθρο 170
Σύμβαση ναυτολόγησης ορισμένου χρόνου

Η σύμβαση ναυτολόγησης ορισμένου χρόνου περιέχει την ημερομηνία λήξης της. Εάν η σύμβαση ναυτολόγησης λήξει κατά τη διάρκεια του πλου, παρατείνεται μέχρι τον κατάπλου του πλοίου στον επόμενο λιμένα, εφόσον είναι δυνατή η αποναυτολόγηση του ναυτικού σε αυτόν.

Άρθρο 171
Σύμβαση ναυτολόγησης κατά ταξίδι

1. Η σύμβαση ναυτολόγησης κατά ταξίδι αναφέρει τους λιμένες αναχώρησης και προορισμού του πλοίου και καθορίζει τον χρόνο αποναυτολόγησης του ναυτικού. Για τα φορτηγά πλοία ο χρόνος αυτός δεν μπορεί να προσδιορίζεται προγενέστερα από την εκφόρτωση του πλοίου.

2. Η σύμβαση ναυτολόγησης κατά ταξίδι περιλαμβάνει και τον πλου υπό έρμα.

3. Πλοία που ακολουθούν τακτική γραμμή θεωρείται ότι συμπληρώνουν το ταξίδι με την εκφόρτωση στον λιμένα της ναυτολόγησης.

Άρθρο 172
Σύμβαση ναυτολόγησης αορίστου χρόνου

Η σύμβαση ναυτολόγησης αορίστου χρόνου ορίζει τις προϋποθέσεις καταγγελίας της και την απαιτούμενη περίοδο κοινοποίησης αυτής.

Άρθρο 173
Λύση της σύμβασης ναυτολόγησης με συμφωνία

Η σύμβαση ναυτολόγησης λύνεται με συμφωνία των συμβαλλομένων.

Άρθρο 174
Αυτοδίκαιη λύση της σύμβασης ναυτολόγησης

Η σύμβαση ναυτολόγησης λύνεται αυτοδίκαια λόγω:

α) απώλειας του πλοίου,

β) εκποίησης του πλοίου σε δημόσιο πλειστηριασμό,

γ) διαγραφής του πλοίου από το ελληνικό νηολόγιο.

Άρθρο 175
Λύση της σύμβασης ναυτολόγησης με άτακτη καταγγελία από τον πλοιοκτήτη

Εάν ο ναυτικός παράνομα απουσιάζει από την υπηρεσία του ή παραβιάζει τις εργασιακές του υποχρεώσεις, έτσι ώστε να θέτει σε κίνδυνο την ασφάλεια του πλοίου, των επιβαινόντων, του φορτίου, καθώς και της ναυσιπλοΐας, η σύμβαση ναυτολόγησης λύνεται με καταγγελία του πλοιοκτήτη ή του αντιπροσώπου του ή του πλοιάρχου χωρίς τήρηση προθεσμίας.

Article 170

Employment agreement for a definite period

An employment agreement made for a definite period shall contain its expiry date. If the employment agreement expires during the voyage, it shall be extended until the ship calls at the next port, provided the seafarer can leave service at that port.

Article 171

Employment agreement for a voyage

1. An employment agreement made for a voyage shall indicate the ports of departure and destination of the ship and specify the time at which the seafarer will leave service. In cases of cargo ships, that time may not be set prior to the [time of] discharge of [cargo from] the ship.

2. An employment agreement made for a voyage shall also include ballast voyages.

3. Ships operating a liner service shall be considered to have completed their passage upon discharging [their cargo] at the port of recruitment.

Article 172

Employment agreement for an indefinite period

An employment agreement made for an indefinite period shall set out the conditions for its termination and the required notice period.

Article 173

Dissolution of employment agreement by consensus

The employment agreement shall be dissolved by consensus of the contracting parties.

Article 174

Automatic dissolution of the employment agreement

The employment agreement shall be automatically dissolved due to:

a) loss of the ship;

b) sale of the ship at public auction;

d) deregistration of the ship from the Greek ship registry.

Article 175

Dissolution of the employment agreement through termination without notice by the owner-operator

If a seafarer is unlawfully absent from service or in breach of their employment obligations and thus imperils the safety of the ship, the persons on board, the cargo and navigation, the employment agreement shall be terminated without notice by the owner-operator or its agent or the master.

Άρθρο 176
Λύση της σύμβασης ναυτολόγησης με τακτική καταγγελία από τον πλοιοκτήτη

1. Ο πλοιοκτήτης ή ο αντιπρόσωπός του, συμπεριλαμβανομένου του πλοιάρχου, μπορεί να καταγγείλει τη σύμβαση ναυτολόγησης ορισμένου ή αορίστου χρόνου των μελών του πληρώματος με τήρηση προθεσμίας τουλάχιστον επτά (7) ημερών και δήλωση του λόγου αυτής.

2. Ως λόγοι καταγγελίας σύμφωνα με την παρ. 1 θεωρούνται:

α) η πρόσκαιρη ανικανότητα του πλοίου για πλου και

β) ο παροπλισμός του πλοίου για διάστημα άνω των δεκαπέντε (15) ημερών.

Άρθρο 177
Άτακτη καταγγελία της σύμβασης ναυτολόγησης από τον ναυτικό

1. Ο ναυτικός μπορεί, χωρίς να τηρήσει προθεσμία, να καταγγείλει τη σύμβαση ναυτολόγησης λόγω βαρείας παράβασης των υποχρεώσεων, κατά περίπτωση, του πλοιοκτήτη ή του πλοιάρχου έναντι αυτού.

2. Ο ναυτικός μπορεί να καταγγείλει τη σύμβαση ναυτολόγησης σε περίοδο γνωστοποίησης μικρότερη των επτά (7) ημερών ή χωρίς προθεσμία για σοβαρούς προσωπικούς ή άλλους επείγοντες λόγους.

Άρθρο 178
Τακτική καταγγελία της σύμβασης ναυτολόγησης από τον ναυτικό

Ο ναυτικός μπορεί να καταγγείλει τη σύμβαση ναυτολόγησης αορίστου χρόνου μετά από την παρέλευση έξι (6) μηνών από τη συνομολόγησή της. Η λύση της σύμβασης ναυτολόγησης επέρχεται μετά την πάροδο επτά (7) ημερών από την καταγγελία. Η προθεσμία αυτή παρατείνεται μέχρι τον κατάπλου του πλοίου στον αμέσως επόμενο λιμένα.

Άρθρο 179
Σύμβαση ναυτολόγησης και ομηρία του ναυτικού

1. Η ομηρία του ναυτικού εντός ή εκτός του πλοίου λόγω πειρατείας ή ένοπλης βίας δεν επιφέρει λύση της σύμβασης ναυτολόγησης.

2. Σύμβαση ναυτολόγησης ορισμένου χρόνου δεν λύνεται, εάν επέλθει ο χρόνος λήξης της κατά τη διάρκεια ομηρίας του ναυτικού.

3. Καθ' όλη τη διάρκεια της ομηρίας, ο ναυτικός δικαιούται να λαμβάνει πλήρη μισθό σύμφωνα με το άρθρο 183.

Άρθρο 180
Αποζημίωση του ναυτικού λόγω λύσης της σύμβασης ναυτολόγησης

Σε περίπτωση λύσης της σύμβασης ναυτολόγησης για τους λόγους των περ. α), β) και γ) του άρθρου 174, των περ. α) και β) του άρθρου 176 και της παρ. 1 του άρθρου 177, ο ναυτικός δικαιούται αποζημίωσης, η οποία συνίσταται σε ποσό ίσο προς τον μισθό δεκαπέντε (15) ημερών. Εάν η λύση επήλθε στην αλλοδαπή, η αποζημίωση διπλασιάζεται όταν πρόκειται για λιμένα της Μεσογείου Θάλασσας, του Ευξείνου Πόντου, της Ερυθράς Θάλασσας ή της Ευρώπης, και τριπλασιάζεται όταν πρόκειται για οποιονδήποτε άλλο λιμένα.

Article 176

Dissolution of the employment agreement through termination with notice by the owner-operator

1. The owner-operator or its agent, including the master, may terminate an employment agreement for a definite or indefinite term with crew members by serving notice at least seven days beforehand and declaring the grounds for termination.

2. Grounds for termination under paragraph 1 are:

a) temporary unseaworthiness of the ship; and

b) laying-up for more than 15 days.

Article 177

Termination without notice of the employment agreement by the seafarer

1. The seafarer may terminate the employment agreement without notice due to serious infringement by the owner-operator or the master, as the case may be, of their obligations towards the seafarer.

2. The seafarer may terminate the employment agreement within a notice period shorter than seven days or without notice on serious personal or other urgent grounds.

Article 178

Termination with notice of the employment agreement by the seafarer

After six months have elapsed from the date an employment agreement for an indefinite period was entered into, the seafarer may terminate said agreement. The employment agreement shall end after seven days have elapsed from the date of termination. This deadline shall be extended until the ship calls at the next port.

Article 179

Employment agreements and seafarers taken hostage

1. Where a seafarer is taken hostage on or off board the ship due to piracy or armed violence, the employment agreement shall not end.

2. An employment agreement for a definite period shall not end if it expires while the seafarer is being held hostage.

3. Throughout the time they are being held hostage, the seafarer shall be entitled to full wages in accordance with Article 183.

Article 180

Compensation of seafarers due to dissolution of the employment agreement

Where the employment agreement is dissolved on the grounds set forth in Article 174(a), (b) and (c), Article 176(a) and (b), and Article 177(1), the seafarer shall be entitled to compensation equal to 15 days' wages. If the agreement was dissolved abroad, the compensation amount shall be doubled in cases of ports in the Mediterranean, the Black Sea, the Red Sea or Europe, and tripled in cases of any other port.

Άρθρο 181

Αστική ευθύνη του αντιπροσώπου του πλοιοκτήτη

1. Αν ο πλοιοκτήτης είναι αλλοδαπή ναυτιλιακή εταιρεία, ο αντιπρόσωπός του, ο οποίος συνάπτει για λογαριασμό του σύμβαση ή προσύμφωνο ναυτολόγησης στην Ελλάδα με ναυτικό, ευθύνεται εις ολόκληρον με τον πλοιοκτήτη για όλες τις υποχρεώσεις που προκύπτουν από ή με αφορμή τη σύμβαση ναυτολόγησης και θεωρείται αντίκλητος του πλοιοκτήτη ως προς τις υποχρεώσεις αυτές. Εάν ο αντιπρόσωπος είναι νομικό πρόσωπο ημεδαπό ή αλλοδαπό, ενέχονται με τον πλοιοκτήτη ατομικά και εις ολόκληρον, εκτός από το νομικό πρόσωπο και όλα τα φυσικά πρόσωπα που το εκπροσώπησαν ή το εκπροσωπούν από τη σύναψη της σύμβασης ή του προσυμφώνου ναυτολόγησης μέχρι την άσκηση των αξιώσεων από τον ναυτικό.

2. Εάν ο πλοιοκτήτης κηρυχθεί σε πτώχευση, ο αντιπρόσωπος του πλοιοκτήτη ευθύνεται μόνο για τις απαιτήσεις του ναυτικού που δημιουργήθηκαν τους τελευταίους έξι (6) μήνες πριν από την ημέρα της κήρυξης της πτώχευσης.

3. Οι αξιώσεις του ναυτικού κατά του αντιπροσώπου του πλοιοκτήτη υπόκεινται σε ετήσια παραγραφή, εκτός των αξιώσεων από εργατικό ατύχημα, οι οποίες υπόκεινται σε παραγραφή τριάντα (30) μηνών. Σε κάθε περίπτωση, η παραγραφή αρχίζει από τη λύση της σύμβασης ναυτολόγησης.

ΚΕΦΑΛΑΙΟ Β'

ΔΙΚΑΙΩΜΑΤΑ ΚΑΙ ΥΠΟΧΡΕΩΣΕΙΣ ΝΑΥΤΙΚΟΥ

Άρθρο 182

Προκαταβολή μισθού

1. Με την κατάρτιση της σύμβασης ναυτολόγησης ο ναυτικός δικαιούται προκαταβολή μισθού έως το ύψος του μηνιαίου πλήρους μισθού του, εκτός αν άλλως ορίζεται σε ισχύουσα συλλογική σύμβαση εργασίας.

2. Τα μέρη μπορούν να συμφωνούν προκαταβολή ποσού μεγαλύτερου από το προβλεπόμενο στην παρ. 1.

Άρθρο 183

Υπολογισμός του μισθού του ναυτικού

1. Ο ναυτικός δικαιούται πλήρη μισθό για την εργασία που παρέχει σύμφωνα με τη σύμβαση ναυτολόγησής του. Ο μισθός του ναυτικού καταβάλλεται σε τακτά χρονικά διαστήματα όχι μεγαλύτερα από έναν μήνα και σύμφωνα με τη συλλογική σύμβαση εργασίας που έχει εφαρμογή.

2. Ο ναυτικός δικαιούται πλήρη μισθό για τους μήνες και τις ημέρες που διήρκεσε η σύμβαση ναυτολόγησης. Εάν η σύμβαση ναυτολόγησης διήρκεσε λιγότερο από μήνα, ο ναυτικός δικαιούται τον πλήρη μισθό ενός μήνα.

3. Ως πλήρης μισθός νοούνται ο βασικός μισθός που αντιστοιχεί στις κανονικές ώρες εργασίας του ναυτικού, τα τακτικά επιδόματα που σχετίζονται με τον βασικό μισθό και το επίδομα τροφής.

4. Ως πλήρεις ημέρες θεωρούνται τόσο η πρώτη ημέρα ναυτολόγησης όσο και αυτή της απoναυτολόγησης.

Article 181

Civil liability of the owner-operator's agent

1. If the owner-operator is a foreign shipping company, its agent who entered into an employment agreement or preliminary employment agreement with a seafarer on the owner-operator's behalf, shall be jointly liable with the owner-operator for all obligations arising from or due to the employment agreement, and shall be considered to be the owner-operator's process agent in respect of said obligations. If the agent is a Greek or foreign legal person, in addition to that legal person, all natural persons who represented or have been representing it between the signing of the employment agreement or preliminary employment agreement and the date the seafarer brought their claim shall also be jointly and severally liable with the owner-operator.

2. If the owner-operator is declared bankrupt, the owner-operator's agent shall be liable only for the claims of the seafarer which arose during the six months prior to the date on which bankruptcy was declared.

3. The seafarer's claims against the owner-operator's agent shall become time-barred after one year, save claims arising from an occupational accident, which shall become time-barred after 30 months. In all events, the time-barring [period] shall commence on the date the employment agreement is dissolved.

CHAPTER II

SEAFARERS' ENTITLEMENTS AND OBLIGATIONS

Article 182

Advance payment of wages

1. Upon signing the employment agreement, the seafarer shall be entitled to advance payment of up to one month's full wages, unless otherwise provided for in a collective bargaining agreement in effect.

2. The parties may agree on an advance payment exceeding the amount provided for in paragraph 1.

Article 183

Calculation of seafarers' wages

1. Seafarers shall be entitled to full wages for the work they provide in accordance with the employment agreement. Seafarers' wages shall be paid at regular intervals no greater than one month and in accordance with the applicable collective bargaining agreement.

2. Seafarers shall be entitled to full wages for the months and days of duration of the employment agreement. If the employment agreement lasts less than one month, the seafarer shall be entitled to one month's full wages.

3. Full wages means the minimum wage corresponding to the ordinary working hours of the seafarer, the ordinary allowances related to the minimum wage and the food allowance.

4. Full days include both the first day of employment and the day on which the seafarer leaves service.

Άρθρο 184
Μισθός σε περίπτωση απώλειας του πλοίου - Αποζημίωση του ναυτικού για απώλεια των αντικειμένων του

1. Σε περίπτωση απώλειας του πλοίου, ο ναυτικός δικαιούται πλήρεις αποδοχές για τις ημέρες που εργάστηκε για τη διάσωση του πλοίου, των επιβαινόντων ή του φορτίου και επιπλέον πλήρη μισθό, μέχρι δύο (2) μηνών εφόσον δεν ναυτολογήθηκε σε άλλο πλοίο. Ο ναυτικός δικαιούται κατ' επιλογή του τον μισθό του παρόντος ή την αποζημίωση του άρθρου 180.

2. Ο ναυτικός δικαιούται επίσης αποζημίωση για την απώλεια των αντικειμένων της προσωπικής ή επαγγελματικής του χρήσης κατά τη διάρκεια πυρκαγιάς ή άλλων ατυχημάτων προερχόμενων από τυχηρό γεγονός.

Άρθρο 185
Δικαίωμα αδείας

1. Ο ναυτικός δικαιούται ετήσια άδεια σύμφωνα με τη Διεθνή Σύμβαση Ναυτικής Εργασίας, και με τις προβλεπόμενες στην παρ. 3 του άρθρου 183 του παρόντος αποδοχές. Συμφωνία παραίτησης του ναυτικού από το δικαίωμα της ετήσιας άδειας μετ' αποδοχών απαγορεύεται και είναι άκυρη.

2. Ειδικότεροι όροι της οικείας συλλογικής σύμβασης ναυτικής εργασίας που έχει εφαρμογή υπερισχύουν.

Άρθρο 186
Δικαιώματα του ναυτικού σε περίπτωση ασθένειας και ατυχήματος

1. Ο ναυτικός που ασθενεί δικαιούται πλήρη μισθό και νοσηλεύεται με δαπάνη του πλοιοκτήτη. Εάν η σύμβαση ναυτολόγησης λυθεί λόγω της ασθένειας και ο ναυτικός νοσηλεύεται εκτός του πλοίου, δικαιούται νοσήλια και πλήρη μισθό όσο διαρκεί η ασθένεια, όχι όμως πέραν των τεσσάρων (4) μηνών από τη λύση της σύμβασης ναυτολόγησης.

2. Η παρ. 1 εφαρμόζεται και σε περίπτωση ατυχήματος. Εάν ο ναυτικός καταστεί ανίκανος για εργασία, καθώς και σε περίπτωση θανάτου, εφαρμόζονται και οι ειδικές διατάξεις περί αποζημιώσεως όσων έπαθαν ατύχημα κατά την εργασία τους.

3. Ο πλοιοκτήτης υποχρεούται να συνάπτει σύμβαση ασφάλισης ή χρηματοοικονομικής ασφάλειας που να καλύπτει την ευθύνη του, σύμφωνα με τη Διεθνή Σύμβαση Ναυτικής Εργασίας. Ο ναυτικός έχει ευθεία αξίωση κατά του ασφαλιστή για τις απαιτήσεις των παρ. 1 και 2. Ο ασφαλιστής δεν μπορεί να αντιτάξει κατά του ναυτικού ενστάσεις που απορρέουν από την ασφαλιστική σύμβαση.

Άρθρο 187
Δικαίωμα παλιννόστησης

1. Σε περίπτωση λύσης της σύμβασης ναυτολόγησης, ο ναυτικός δικαιούται να επιστρέψει με δαπάνες του πλοιοκτήτη, κατ' επιλογή του, είτε στον τόπο κατοικίας του ή στον λιμένα έναρξης του πλου ή στον τόπο υπογραφής της σύμβασης ή σε οποιονδήποτε άλλο τόπο συμφωνηθεί κατά τη συνομολόγηση της σύμβασης ναυτολόγησης.

Article 184

Wages in cases of loss of ship - Seafarers' compensation for loss of their personal effects

1. In the event of loss of the ship, the seafarer shall be entitled to full pay for the days they worked to salvage the ship, rescue persons on board or salvage the cargo, and up to two months' additional full wages if the seafarer was not recruited to serve aboard another ship. The seafarer shall be entitled to choose between the wages provided for in this Article or the compensation provided for in Article 180.

2. The seafarer shall further be entitled to compensation for loss of their personal or occupational effects during a fire or other accidents caused by fortuity.

Article 185

Entitlement to leave

1. Seafarers shall be entitled to annual leave in accordance with the International Maritime Labour Convention with the pay provided for in Article 183(3) of this Code. Any agreement for the seafarer to forgo their entitlement to paid annual leave is prohibited and null and void.

2. Any more specific terms of the applicable maritime labour collective bargaining agreement shall prevail.

Article 186

Seafarers' entitlements in the event of sickness and injury

1. Seafarers who fall ill shall be entitled to full wages, and the cost of treatment shall be borne by the owner-operator. If the employment agreement ends due to sickness and the seafarer is treated off-ship, the seafarer shall be entitled to medical expenses and full wages while the sickness persists, but for no longer than four months from the date the employment agreement is dissolved.

2. Paragraph 1 shall also apply in cases of accidents. If the seafarer become incapable of working or in the event of their death, the specific provisions on compensation for those who suffered an accident during work shall also apply.

3. The owner-operator shall be obligated to enter into a contract for insurance or financial security to cover its liability, in accordance with the International Maritime Labour Convention. The seafarer shall have a direct claim against the insurer for the amounts referred to in paragraphs 1 and 2. The insurer may not raise pleas arising from the insurance policy against the seafarer.

Article 187

Entitlement to repatriation

1. Where the employment agreement is dissolved, the seafarer shall be entitled to return, at their own choice and at the owner-operator's expense, to their place of domicile, or to the port where the voyage commenced, or to the place where the agreement was signed, or to any other place agreed upon at the signing of the employment agreement.

2. Η παλιννόστηση λαμβάνει χώρα με τα πλέον πρόσφορα μέσα σύμφωνα με την εύλογη κρίση του πλοιοκτήτη, αφού ληφθεί υπόψη η βούληση του ναυτικού.
3. Το δικαίωμα παλιννόστησης αποσβέννυται, εάν ο ναυτικός δεν το ασκήσει εντός εύλογου χρόνου από την καθ' οιονδήποτε τρόπο λύση της σύμβασης ναυτολόγησης.

Άρθρο 188
Κόστος παλιννόστησης

1. Η παλιννόστηση καλύπτει το κόστος μετάβασης του ναυτικού στον τόπο που επελέγη, τη διαμονή και τη διατροφή του.
2. Το κόστος παλιννόστησης δεν παρακρατείται από τον μισθό του ναυτικού, εκτός εάν ο τελευταίος αποδεδειγμένα, με βάση τελεσίδικη δικαστική απόφαση, παραβίασε τα καθήκοντα και τις υποχρεώσεις του που απορρέουν από τη σύμβαση ναυτολόγησης.
3. Ο πλοιοκτήτης υποχρεούται να συνάπτει σύμβαση ασφάλισης ή χρηματοοικονομικής ασφάλειας που να καλύπτει την ευθύνη του, σύμφωνα με τη Διεθνή Σύμβαση Ναυτικής Εργασίας. Ο ναυτικός έχει ευθεία αξίωση κατά του ασφαλιστή για τις καλυπτόμενες απαιτήσεις. Ο ασφαλιστής δεν μπορεί να αντιτάξει κατά του ναυτικού ενστάσεις που απορρέουν από την ασφαλιστική σύμβαση.

Άρθρο 189
Σύννομη εκτέλεση των καθηκόντων του ναυτικού

1. Ο ναυτικός υποχρεούται να εκτελεί την υπηρεσία του σύμφωνα με τους νόμους, τους όρους της σύμβασης ναυτολόγησης, τους κανονισμούς και τις κρατούσες συνήθειες, με γνώμονα την ασφάλεια του πλοίου, των επιβαινόντων και του φορτίου, συμμορφούμενος προς τις εντολές των ιεραρχικώς προϊσταμένων του.
2. Κατά την εκτέλεση της υπηρεσίας του ο ναυτικός υποχρεούται να διατηρεί σε καλή κατάσταση το πλοίο, καθώς και τα αντικείμενα που του έχουν χορηγηθεί.

ΚΕΦΑΛΑΙΟ Γ'
Ο ΠΛΟΙΑΡΧΟΣ

Άρθρο 190
Ευθύνη πλοιάρχου

1. Ο πλοίαρχος διοικεί το πλοίο και μεριμνά για τη νόμιμη σύνθεση του πληρώματος σύμφωνα με τις οδηγίες του πλοιοκτήτη, καθώς και για την τήρηση των ισχυόντων νόμων και κανονισμών που άπτονται της ασφάλειας του πλοίου, του πληρώματος, των επιβαινόντων και του φορτίου.
2. Ο πλοίαρχος ευθύνεται για δόλο και βαριά αμέλεια, εκτός εάν ειδικός νόμος ορίζει διαφορετικά.

Άρθρο 191
Υποχρέωση για τη φύλαξη ναυτιλιακών εγγράφων

Ο πλοίαρχος φυλάσσει με προσωπική του ευθύνη επί του πλοίου τα ναυτιλιακά έγγραφα και βιβλία, πιστοποιητικά και φορτωτικά έγγραφα.

2. Repatriation shall take place using the most expedient means, at the reasonable discretion of the owner-operator, having taken the seafarer's wishes into consideration.
3. The entitlement to repatriation shall lapse if the seafarer does not claim it within a reasonable period of time from the date the employment agreement is dissolved in any manner.

Article 188
Cost of repatriation

1. Repatriation covers the cost of passage of the seafarer to the place chosen, accommodation and food.
2. The cost of repatriation shall not be withheld from the seafarer's wages, unless the seafarer demonstrably — on the basis of a *de jure* non-appealable court judgment — breached their duties and obligations under the employment agreement.
3. The owner-operator shall be obligated to enter into a contract for insurance or financial security to cover its liability, in accordance with the International Maritime Labour Convention. The seafarer shall have a direct claim against the insurer for the amounts covered. The insurer may not raise pleas arising from the insurance policy against the seafarer.

Article 189
Lawful performance of seafarers' duties

1. Seafarers shall be obligated to perform their duties in accordance with the law, the terms of the employment agreement, the regulations and prevailing custom, with a view to the safety of the ship, the persons on board and the cargo, in compliance with the orders issued by their superiors.
2. In the performance of their duties, seafarers shall be obligated to keep the ship and any articles provided to them in good working order.

CHAPTER III
THE MASTER

Article 190
Liability of the master

1. The master shall govern the ship and ensure the lawful composition of the crew, in accordance with the owner-operator's instructions, and compliance with the applicable laws and regulations relating to the safety of the ship, the crew, the persons on board and the cargo.
2. Unless otherwise provided for in a specific law, the master shall be liable for *dolus* and gross negligence.

Article 191
Obligation to safekeep shipping documents

The master shall be personally responsible for safekeeping the shipping documents, certificates and cargo documents aboard the ship.

Άρθρο 192
Αποτροπή επικείμενου κινδύνου από τον πλοίαρχο

Ο πλοίαρχος δικαιούται να χρησιμοποιήσει κάθε αντικείμενο που βρίσκεται επί του πλοίου και είναι αναγκαίο για την αποτροπή επικείμενου κινδύνου. Στην περίπτωση αυτή εφαρμόζεται το άρθρο 286 του Αστικού Κώδικα.

Άρθρο 193
Ανάθεση από τον πλοίαρχο πρόσθετων καθηκόντων σε ναυτικό

1. Σε εξαιρετικές περιπτώσεις, ο πλοίαρχος μπορεί να αναθέσει προσωρινά σε ναυτικό καθήκοντα πέραν εκείνων που έχει αναλάβει με τη σύμβαση ναυτολόγησης, εφόσον δεν είναι ασυμβίβαστα με την ειδικότητα και τον βαθμό του.

2. Στην περίπτωση της παρ. 1 καταβάλλεται πρόσθετη αμοιβή που καθορίζεται ανάλογα με τον συμφωνημένο μισθό και τις ειδικές περιστάσεις.

Άρθρο 194
Απαγόρευση φόρτωσης εμπορευμάτων για ίδιο λογαριασμό

Απαγορεύεται στον πλοίαρχο με ποινή αποζημίωσης να φορτώνει εμπορεύματα για ίδιο λογαριασμό, εάν δεν υπάρχει ρητή έγγραφη άδεια του πλοιοκτήτη ή του αντιπροσώπου του. Ομοίως, απαιτείται η ρητή άδεια του πλοιάρχου, προκειμένου να φορτώσει ο ναυτικός επί του πλοίου εμπορεύματα για ίδιο λογαριασμό.

Άρθρο 195
Ενεργητική και παθητική αντιπροσώπευση

1. Ο πλοίαρχος μπορεί, σε περίπτωση επείγουσας ανάγκης κατά τη διάρκεια του πλου, να κοινοποιεί έγγραφα στο όνομα του πλοιοκτήτη, να λαμβάνει ασφαλιστικά μέτρα και να εγείρει αγωγή για οτιδήποτε αφορά στο πλοίο ή το φορτίο.

2. Εάν το πλοίο ευρίσκεται σε τόπο διαφορετικό από την έδρα του πλοιοκτήτη, η κοινοποίηση διαδικαστικών ή εξωδίκων εγγράφων που αφορούν στο υπό την πλοιαρχία του πλοίο δύναται να γίνει στον πλοίαρχο.

Article 192

Averting of imminent peril by the master

The master shall be entitled to use any article aboard the ship which is necessary to avert an imminent peril. In this case, the provisions of Article 286 of the Civil Code shall apply.

Article 193

Assignment of additional duties to seafarers by the master

1. In exceptional circumstances, the master may temporarily assign to a seafarer duties beyond those undertaken by virtue of the employment agreement, provided such duties are not incompatible with the seafarer's capacity and rank.

2. In the case referred to in paragraph 1, an additional fee shall be paid, set in proportion to the wages agreed upon and taking into account the specific circumstances.

Article 194

Prohibition on loading merchandise for the master's own account

On penalty of compensation, the master shall be prohibited from loading merchandise for their own account without the express permission of the owner-operator or its agent in writing. Similarly, the master's express permission shall be required in order for seafarers to load merchandise onto the ship for their own account.

Article 195

Agency in an active and passive capacity

1. Where an emergency occurs during a voyage, the master may send documents in the owner-operator's name, take interim measures and file an action in regard to any matter concerning the ship or the cargo.

2. If the ship is situated away from the owner-operator's seat, any procedural or extra-judicial documents concerning the ship under the master's command may be notified to the master.

ΜΕΡΟΣ ΟΓΔΟΟ
ΘΑΛΑΣΣΙΑ ΑΡΩΓΗ - ΣΥΓΚΡΟΥΣΗ - ΚΟΙΝΗ ΑΒΑΡΙΑ

ΚΕΦΑΛΑΙΟ Α'
ΘΑΛΑΣΣΙΑ ΑΡΩΓΗ

Άρθρο 196
Εφαρμοστέοι κανόνες

1. Σε επιχείρηση επιθαλάσσιας αρωγής εφαρμόζεται η Διεθνής Σύμβαση για την επιθαλάσσια αρωγή του 1989 (Διεθνής Σύμβαση για την επιθαλάσσια αρωγή), η οποία κυρώθηκε με τον ν. 2391/1996 (Α' 55) και εκάστοτε ισχύει στην Ελλάδα. Σε θέματα που εξαιρούνται ή δεν ρυθμίζονται από τη Σύμβαση εφαρμόζονται τα άρθρα 197 και 198 του παρόντος.

2. Η Διεθνής Σύμβαση για την επιθαλάσσια αρωγή εφαρμόζεται και σε επιχείρηση επιθαλάσσιας αρωγής σε σταθερές ή πλωτές εξέδρες ή σε κινητές θαλάσσιες μονάδες γεώτρησης, όταν αυτές οι εξέδρες ή μονάδες ασχολούνται επί τόπου με την εξερεύνηση, εκμετάλλευση ή παραγωγή ορυκτού πλούτου από τον βυθό της θάλασσας.

Άρθρο 197
Κατανομή της αμοιβής

1. Αν την επιθαλάσσια αρωγή παρέχει πλοίο με ελληνική σημαία που δεν είναι κατ' επάγγελμα ναυαγοσωστικό, το ήμισυ της αμοιβής ανήκει στον πλοιοκτήτη ή εφοπλιστή του πλοίου, το ένα τέταρτο (1/4) στον πλοίαρχο και το υπόλοιπο ένα τέταρτο (1/4) στο πλήρωμα. Συμφωνία που περιορίζει το ποσό αμοιβής που αναλογεί στον πλοίαρχο και το πλήρωμα είναι άκυρη.

2. Το ποσό αμοιβής που αναλογεί στο πλήρωμα κατανέμεται με βάση πίνακα που συντάσσεται από τον πλοίαρχο κατά τον λόγο της προσωπικής συμβολής κάθε μέλους του πληρώματος στην επίτευξη του ωφέλιμου αποτελέσματος.

Άρθρο 198
Δικονομικές διατάξεις

1. Την αγωγή για πληρωμή αμοιβής της παρ. 1 του άρθρου 197 νομιμοποιείται να ασκήσει και ο πλοιοκτήτης ή εφοπλιστής του πλοίου που παρέχει την επιθαλάσσια αρωγή για ολόκληρο το ποσό αμοιβής που αναλογεί στον ίδιο, τον πλοίαρχο και το πλήρωμα, καθώς και ο πλοίαρχος για ολόκληρο το ποσό αμοιβής που αναλογεί στον ίδιο και τα μέλη του πληρώματος.

2. Στη δίκη της παρ. 1 ο πλοίαρχος εκπροσωπεί και τα μέλη του πληρώματος, εφόσον αυτά δεν παρίστανται αυτοπροσώπως ή με άλλον αντιπρόσωπο.

3. Αμφισβήτηση της κατάταξης με βάση τον πίνακα της παρ. 2 του άρθρου 197 επιλύεται από τη λιμενική ή προξενική αρχή, η απόφαση της οποίας μπορεί να προσβληθεί ενώπιον του μονομελούς πρωτοδικείου, το οποίο δικάζει με τη διαδικασία των ασφαλιστικών μέτρων.

PART EIGHT
SALVAGE - COLLISION - GENERAL AVERAGE

CHAPTER I
SALVAGE

Article 196
Applicable rules

1. The 1989 International Convention on Salvage, ratified by Law 2391/1996 (Government Gazette, Series I, Issue 55) and in force in Greece from time to time, shall apply to salvage operations. Articles 197 and 198 of this Code shall apply to matters exempt from or not regulated under the Convention.

2. The International Convention on Salvage shall also apply to salvage operations involving fixed or floating platforms or to mobile offshore drilling units when such platforms or units are on location engaged in the exploration, exploitation or production of sea-bed mineral resources.

Article 197
Apportionment of the reward

1. If salvage is rendered by a ship flying a Greek flag which is not operated as a salvage ship, half the reward shall belong to the owner-operator or operator of the ship, 1/4 to the master and the remaining 1/4 to the crew. Any agreement limiting the reward amount corresponding to the master and the crew is null and void.

2. The reward amount corresponding to the crew shall be apportioned on the basis of a table compiled by the master in proportion to the personal contribution of each crew member to achieving the useful result.

Article 198
Procedural provisions

1. The action for payment of the reward referred to in Article 197(1) may also be filed by the owner-operator or operator of the ship rendering salvage for the entire reward amount corresponding to the owner-operator or operator, the master and the crew, and by the master for the entire reward amount corresponding to the master and the crew members.

2. In the proceedings referred to in paragraph 1, the master shall also represent the crew members, provided they do not enter an appearance in person or via a different agent.

3. Any dispute concerning the ranking set out in the table referred to in Article 197(2) shall be resolved by the port or consular authority, whose decision may be contested before the single-member court of first instance, trying the matter under interim measures proceedings.

ΚΕΦΑΛΑΙΟ Β'
ΣΥΓΚΡΟΥΣΗ ΠΛΟΙΩΝ

Άρθρο 199
Πεδίο εφαρμογής

1. Οι διατάξεις του παρόντος κεφαλαίου διέπουν τις αξιώσεις αποζημίωσης που απορρέουν από τα περιστατικά του άρθρου 201, όταν δεν εφαρμόζεται η Διεθνής Σύμβαση των Βρυξελλών του 1910 περί ενοποίησης κανόνων τινών επί συγκρούσεως πλοίων, η οποία κυρώθηκε με τον ν. ΓΩΠΣΤ 3886/1911 (Α' 224).

2. Το παρόν κεφάλαιο εφαρμόζεται πάντοτε όταν όλα τα εμπλεκόμενα πλοία φέρουν την ελληνική σημαία, ανεξαρτήτως αν τα περιστατικά του άρθρου 201 έλαβαν χώρα στα ελληνικά χωρικά ή στα διεθνή ύδατα.

Άρθρο 200
Διεθνής δικαιοδοσία

1. Με την επιφύλαξη συμφωνίας παρέκτασης, η διεθνής δικαιοδοσία των ελληνικών δικαστηρίων για τις διαφορές του άρθρου 199 καθορίζεται από τη Διεθνή Σύμβαση των Βρυξελλών του 1952 για την αρμοδιότητα επίλυσης ιδιωτικών διαφορών από σύγκρουση πλοίων, η οποία κυρώθηκε με το ν.δ. 4407 της 4ης/11.11.1964 (Α' 213) και τη Διεθνή Σύμβαση των Βρυξελλών του 1952 για την ενοποίηση των κανόνων επί συντηρητικής κατάσχεσής τους, η οποία κυρώθηκε με το ν.δ. 4570/1966 (Α' 224), άλλως από τον Κανονισμό (ΕΕ) 1215/2012 του Ευρωπαϊκού Κοινοβουλίου και του Συμβουλίου της 12ης Δεκεμβρίου 2012 για τη διεθνή δικαιοδοσία, την αναγνώριση και την εκτέλεση αποφάσεων σε αστικές και εμπορικές υποθέσεις (L 351/1).

2. Σε κάθε άλλη περίπτωση τα ελληνικά δικαστήρια έχουν δικαιοδοσία:

α) όταν ο εναγόμενος κατοικεί ή διαμένει στην Ελλάδα,

β) αν ένα από τα εμπλεκόμενα πλοία είναι εγγεγραμμένο σε ελληνικό νηολόγιο,

γ) αν τα γεγονότα του άρθρου 201 συνέβησαν στα ελληνικά χωρικά ύδατα,

δ) αν το υπεύθυνο πλοίο κατασχέθηκε συντηρητικά στην Ελλάδα ή απαγορεύθηκε ο απόπλους του από ελληνικό λιμένα, έστω και αν η κατάσχεση ή η απαγόρευση έχουν αρθεί πριν από την έγερση της αγωγής με παροχή εγγυοδοσίας.

Άρθρο 201
Νόμιμος λόγος ευθύνης

1. Σε περίπτωση υλικής επαφής του κύτους ή των συστατικών ή των παραρτημάτων δύο (2) τουλάχιστον πλοίων που προκαλεί ζημία (άμεση σύγκρουση) ή σε περίπτωση που η ζημία προκαλείται χωρίς επαφή (έμμεση σύγκρουση), λόγω αναξιοπλοΐας ή παραβίασης των Κανόνων Αποφυγής Συγκρούσεων στη θάλασσα αποζημίωση οφείλεται μόνον αν η σύγκρουση προκλήθηκε με υπαιτιότητα.

2. Για την εφαρμογή της παρ. 1 είναι αδιάφορο:

α) αν τα πλοία πλέουν ή είναι ακινητοποιημένα εντός ή εκτός του λιμένα και

β) αν η σύγκρουση πραγματοποιείται στα ελληνικά χωρικά ή σε διεθνή ύδατα.

CHAPTER II
COLLISION OF VESSELS

Article 199
Scope

1. The provisions of this Chapter shall govern claims for compensation arising from the incidents referred to in Article 201, where the 1910 Brussels International Convention for the Unification of Certain Rules of Law with respect to Collisions between Vessels, ratified by Law 3886/1911 (Government Gazette, Series I, Issue 224) does not apply.

2. This Chapter shall always apply when all the ships involved fly the Greek flag, irrespective of whether the incidents referred to in Article 201 occurred in Greek territorial waters or international waters.

Article 200
Jurisdiction

1. Without prejudice to any prorogation agreement, the jurisdiction of the Greek courts regarding the disputes referred to in Article 199 shall be determined by the 1952 Brussels International Convention on certain rules concerning civil jurisdiction in matters of collision, ratified by Legislative Decree 4407 of 4/11 November 1964 (Government Gazette, Series I, 224), and by the 1952 Brussels International Convention for the unification of certain rules relating to arrest of sea-going ships, ratified by Legislative Decree 4570/1966 (Government Gazette, Series I, 224), otherwise by Regulation (EU) No 1215/2012 of the European Parliament and of the Council of 12 December 2012 on jurisdiction and the recognition and enforcement of judgments in civil and commercial matters (OJ L 351/1).

2. In all other events, the Greek courts shall have jurisdiction:

a) if the defendant is domiciled or resident in Greece;

b) if one of the ships involved is registered in a Greek ship registry;

c) if the incidents referred to in Article 201 occurred in Greek territorial waters; [or]

d) if the ship responsible was placed under preventive arrest in Greece or was detained from leaving a Greek port, even if the arrest or detention were lifted before the action was filed through payment of a surety amount.

Article 201
Legitimate grounds for liability

1. In the event of physical contact between the hulls or the constituent parts or accessories of at least two ships resulting in damage (direct collision) or damage caused without contact (indirect collision) due to unseaworthiness or breach of the Regulations for Preventing Collisions at Sea, compensation shall be owed solely if the party that caused the collision was at fault.

2. For the purposes of paragraph 1, it is irrelevant whether:

a) the ships are sailing or still within or beyond a port; and

b) the collision occurs in Greek territorial waters or international waters.

Άρθρο 202
Υποκείμενο της ευθύνης

1. Η ευθύνη προς αποκατάσταση των ζημιών βαρύνει αυτόν που εκμεταλλεύεται το υπεύθυνο για τη σύγκρουση πλοίο.

2. Αν το ζημιογόνο πλοίο τελεί υπό εφοπλισμό, ο κύριος αυτού ευθύνεται κατά τους όρους του άρθρου 63.

3. Η ευθύνη σύμφωνα με την παρ. 1 δεν αναιρείται όταν η σύγκρουση προκλήθηκε με υπαιτιότητα πλοηγού, έστω και αν η πρόσληψη αυτού ήταν υποχρεωτική.

4. Τα λοιπά υπαίτια για τη σύγκρουση πρόσωπα ενέχονται κατά τις κοινές διατάξεις περί αδικοπραξιών.

Άρθρο 203
Μέτρο της ευθύνης

1. Αν για τη σύγκρουση είναι υπεύθυνο ένα μόνον πλοίο, η ευθύνη βαρύνει αποκλειστικά το πρόσωπο που εκμεταλλεύεται το πλοίο αυτό.

2. Σε περίπτωση που η σύγκρουση προκλήθηκε με ευθύνη περισσοτέρων πλοίων, το πρόσωπο που εκμεταλλεύεται το καθένα τους βαρύνεται αναλόγως του βαθμού της συνυπαιτιότητάς του. Αν ο καθορισμός της αναλογίας δεν είναι εφικτός, η ευθύνη κατανέμεται ισομερώς.

3. Οι υλικές ζημίες που προκλήθηκαν στα πλοία, στα φορτία ή στους επιβάτες τους βαρύνουν τα συνυπαίτια πλοία κατά την αναλογία της παρ. 2.

4. Κατ' εξαίρεση, σε περίπτωση θανάτου ή σωματικής βλάβης, τα συνυπαίτια πλοία ευθύνονται εις ολόκληρον.

Άρθρο 204
Δικαιούχος της αποζημίωσης

1. Αποζημίωση δικαιούνται ο εκμεταλλευόμενος το ζημιωθέν από τη σύγκρουση πλοίο, ο πλοίαρχος, το πλήρωμα, οι επιβάτες και οι δικαιούχοι των μεταφερόμενων με αυτό πραγμάτων.

2. Εάν το ζημιωθέν πλοίο τελεί υπό εφοπλισμό, αξίωση αποζημιώσεως για τις υλικές ζημίες του έχει και ο κύριος αυτού.

3. Η αποζημίωση του προσώπου που πριν από τη σύγκρουση συνήψε σύμβαση με τον εκμεταλλευόμενο το ζημιογόνο πλοίο διέπεται από τους ειδικούς κανόνες της συγκεκριμένης έννομης σχέσης, ανεξαρτήτως της νομικής βάσης της απαίτησής του.

4. Σχετικά με την ευθύνη προς αποζημίωση για ζημίες σε πρόσωπα και πράγματα που κατά τον χρόνο της σύγκρουσης βρίσκονταν εκτός των πλοίων που συγκρούστηκαν δεν εφαρμόζεται το παρόν Κεφάλαιο.

Άρθρο 205
Έκταση της αποζημίωσης

1. Με την επιφύλαξη των δικαιωμάτων του οφειλέτη προς περιορισμό της ευθύνης του, η αποζημίωση είναι πλήρης και καλύπτει όλες τις υλικές και λοιπές περιουσιακές ζημίες.

2. Ο ζημιωθείς οφείλει να λάβει κάθε πρόσφορο μέτρο προς περιορισμό της έκτασης της ζημίας του.

Article 202
Liable party

1. Liability to provide compensation for the damage shall be borne by the party operating the ship responsible for the collision.

2. Where the ship which caused the collision is being operated [by an operator], its owner shall be held liable in accordance with the provisions of Article 63.

3. Liability under paragraph 1 shall not be affected when the collision was caused with a pilot being at fault, even when engaging a pilot was mandatory.

4. The other persons responsible for the collision shall be liable in accordance with the ordinary provisions on tort.

Article 203
Allocation of liability

1. Where only one ship is responsible for the collision, liability shall be borne exclusively by the person operating that ship.

2. Where several ships are responsible for the collision, the person operating each ship shall be held liable in proportion to their contributory fault. Where this proportional apportionment is not feasible, liability shall be apportioned equally.

3. Material damage caused to the ships, their cargoes or their passengers shall be covered by the ships with contributory fault according to the proportion referred to in paragraph 2.

4. By way of exception, in the event of death or personal injury, any ships with contributory fault shall be jointly liable.

Article 204
Person entitled to compensation

1. The person operating the ship damaged by the collision, the master, the crew, the passengers and the beneficiaries of the goods being carried on the ship shall be entitled to compensation.

2. If the damaged ship is being operated, its owner shall also have a claim to compensation for material damage to the ship.

3. The compensation for the person who, prior to the collision, entered into an agreement with the person operating the ship which caused the damage shall be governed by the special rules concerning the specific legal relationship, irrespective of the legal basis of their claim.

4. This Chapter shall not apply to liability to pay compensation for losses incurred by persons who and damage to goods which, at the time of collision, were not on the ships which collided.

Article 205
Extent of compensation

1. Without prejudice to the rights of the debtor to limitation of liability, compensation shall be full and shall cover all material and other damage to property.

2. The injured party shall be obligated to take all expedient measures to limit the extent of their losses.

3. Χρηματική ικανοποίηση για τις μη περιουσιακές ζημίες σύμφωνα με τους όρους του άρθρου 932 του Αστικού Κώδικα δεν αποκλείεται.

4. Τόκος οφείλεται από την ημέρα επέλευσης της ζημίας ή, σε περίπτωση αναγωγής, της πληρωμής.

Άρθρο 206
Λόγοι απαλλαγής

1. Ο ζημιώσας απαλλάσσεται ολικώς, αν η σύγκρουση προκλήθηκε από τυχαίο γεγονός ή ανωτέρα βία ή όταν υπάρχουν αμφιβολίες για τα αίτιά της. Στην περίπτωση αυτή οι ζημίες βαρύνουν αυτούς που τις υπέστησαν.

2. Αυτός που εκμεταλλεύεται το ζημιώσαν πλοίο απαλλάσσεται μερικώς αν αποδείξει συνυπαιτιότητα του εκμεταλλευομένου το ζημιωθέν. Η απαλλαγή επέρχεται κατά το ποσοστό της ζημίας που αναλογεί στον βαθμό της συνυπαιτιότητας. Αν δεν μπορεί να καθοριστεί η αναλογία, η ευθύνη κατανέμεται ισομερώς.

Άρθρο 207
Δικαίωμα αναγωγής

Στις περιπτώσεις της παρ. 4 του άρθρου 203, ο εκμεταλλευόμενος πλοίο που κατέβαλε αποζημίωση μεγαλύτερη από αυτή που του αναλογούσε σύμφωνα με το άρθρο 206 έχει δικαίωμα αναγωγής.

Άρθρο 208
Βάρος απόδειξης

1. Οι προϋποθέσεις της ευθύνης αποδεικνύονται από αυτόν που αξιώνει αποζημίωση.

2. Για την απόδειξη δεν ισχύει κανένα νόμιμο τεκμήριο.

Άρθρο 209
Εκπροσώπηση των δικαιούχων

1. Ο φορέας εκμετάλλευσης του πλοίου που συγκρούστηκε ή ο πλοίαρχός του νομιμοποιούνται να ασκήσουν αγωγή για λογαριασμό του πληρώματος, των δικαιούχων του φορτίου και των επιβατών του πλοίου για την αποκατάσταση των ζημιών που υπέστησαν από τη σύγκρουση.

2. Αυτός που ενεργεί σύμφωνα με την παρ. 1 υποχρεούται να προσεπικαλέσει στη δίκη τους εκπροσωπούμενους από αυτόν σε εύλογη προθεσμία πριν από τη συζήτηση της αγωγής.

Άρθρο 210
Υποχρεώσεις του πλοιάρχου

1. Μετά τη σύγκρουση ο πλοίαρχος καθενός από τα εμπλεκόμενα πλοία υποχρεούται να παράσχει αρωγή στα άλλα πλοία, στους επιβάτες και στο πλήρωμά τους, εφόσον μπορεί να το πράξει χωρίς να θέσει σε σοβαρό κίνδυνο το δικό του πλοίο, το πλήρωμα και τους επιβάτες του. Ομοίως υποχρεούται να γνωστοποιήσει στα άλλα πλοία, κατά τον πιο πρόσφορο υπό τις περιστάσεις τρόπο, κάθε πληροφορία που είναι αναγκαία για την ταυτοποίηση του δικού του πλοίου.

2. Για την παραβίαση των υποχρεώσεων της παρ. 1 δεν υπέχει ευθύνη το πρόσωπο που εκμεταλλεύεται το πλοίο.

3. Payment of compensation for non-material damage in accordance with the terms of Article 932 of the Civil Code may not be precluded.
4. Interest shall be owed from the day the damage occurred or, where recourse is sought, the day of payment.

Article 206
Grounds for release

1. The person causing the damage shall be wholly released [from liability] if the collision was caused by fortuity or force majeure or where there are doubts concerning the cause of collision. In this case, the losses shall be borne by the persons who incurred them.
2. The person operating the ship which caused the damage shall be partially released [from liability] if they can prove contributory fault of the person operating the damaged ship. Release shall apply pro rata to the loss corresponding to the extent of contributory fault. If the ratio cannot be determined, liability shall be apportioned equally.

Article 207
Right of recourse

In the cases referred to in Article 203(4), the person operating a ship who paid compensation higher than the one corresponding to them under Article 206 shall have a right of recourse.

Article 208
Burden of proof

1. The requirements for [establishing] liability shall be proven by the person claiming compensation.
2. No legal presumptions shall apply to the evidence.

Article 209
Representation of persons entitled to compensation

1. The person operating the ship involved in a collision or its master may file an action on behalf of the crew, the beneficiaries of the cargo and the passengers of the ship for compensation for the damage they suffered due to the collision.
2. The person taking the steps referred to in paragraph 1 shall be obligated to implead the persons they represent in the proceedings within a reasonable deadline before the action is heard.

Article 210
Obligations of the master

1. After the collision, the master of each of the ships involved shall be obligated to render salvage to the other ships, their passengers and their crews, provided they can do so without seriously imperilling their own ship, crew and passengers. The master of each of the ships involved shall be further obligated to provide the other ships, using the means most expedient in the circumstances, with all information necessary for the identification of the master's ship.
2. The person operating the ship shall not be liable for any breach of the obligations laid down in paragraph 1.

ΚΕΦΑΛΑΙΟ Γ'

ΚΟΙΝΗ ΑΒΑΡΙΑ

Άρθρο 211

Κοινή αβαρία - Ορισμός

Κοινή αβαρία υπάρχει μόνον όταν έκτακτη θυσία ή δαπάνη, εκούσια και εύλογη, πραγματοποιήθηκε με σκοπό την προστασία πλοίου και φορτίου από θαλάσσιο κίνδυνο που έχει συμβεί σε κοινή ναυτική αποστολή.

Άρθρο 212

Εφαρμογή διατάξεων

Τις θυσίες και δαπάνες της κοινής αβαρίας φέρουν τα θυσιασθέντα και διασωθέντα συμφέροντα του πλοίου, του φορτίου και του ναύλου, τα οποία συνεισφέρουν σε αυτήν, σύμφωνα με το παρόν Κεφάλαιο.

Άρθρο 213

Κοινή ναυτική αποστολή

1. Κοινή ναυτική αποστολή υπάρχει όταν οι θαλάσσιοι κίνδυνοι απειλούν ταυτόχρονα το πλοίο, το φορτίο ή/ και τον ναύλο.

2. Κοινή ναυτική αποστολή υπάρχει και όταν ένα ή περισσότερα πλοία ρυμουλκούν ή ωθούν ένα άλλο πλοίο ή πλοία, ανεξαρτήτως της ύπαρξης φορτίων, με την επιφύλαξη της παροχής επιθαλάσσιας αρωγής.

3. Πλοίο δεν ευρίσκεται σε κοινό κίνδυνο με άλλο πλοίο ή πλοία, εάν αυτό είναι ασφαλές μετά την αποσύνδεσή του από αυτό. Η κοινή ναυτική αποστολή συνεχίζεται, εάν η αποσύνδεση αυτή ή η υποχρεωτική παραμονή σε σύνδεση συνιστά πράξη κοινής αβαρίας.

Άρθρο 214

Υπολογιζόμενες απώλειες, ζημίες ή δαπάνες

1. Στην κοινή αβαρία υπολογίζονται μόνο οι απώλειες, ζημίες ή δαπάνες που αποτελούν άμεση συνέπεια πράξης κοινής αβαρίας σύμφωνα με το άρθρο 211.

2. Δεν υπολογίζονται απώλειες, ζημίες ή δαπάνες που πραγματοποιήθηκαν σε σχέση με περιβαλλοντική ζημία ή ως αποτέλεσμα διαφυγής ή απόρριψης ρυπογόνων ουσιών από την περιουσία που εμπλέκεται στην κοινή ναυτική αποστολή.

3. Δεν υπολογίζονται αποζημιώσεις υπεραναμονής, αγοραίες απομειώσεις και κάθε απώλεια ή ζημία ή δαπάνες που καταβλήθηκαν εξαιτίας καθυστέρησης είτε κατά τη διάρκεια του ταξιδιού ή μεταγενέστερα, καθώς και οποιαδήποτε άλλη έμμεση ζημία.

CHAPTER III

GENERAL AVERAGE

Article 211

General average - Definition

There is a general average act when, and only when, any extraordinary sacrifice or expenditure is intentionally and reasonably made or incurred for the purpose of preserving the ship and cargo from perils of the sea occurring during a common maritime adventure.

Article 212

Application of provisions

General average sacrifices and expenditures sustained by the interests in the ship, the cargo and the freight contributing to the general average shall be borne by those interests, in accordance with this Chapter.

Article 213

Common maritime adventure

1. There is a common maritime adventure when the ship, the cargo and/or the freight are simultaneously under threat of maritime perils.

2. There is also a common maritime adventure when one or more ships are towing or pushing another ship or ships, irrespective of whether there is cargo, provided that they are not involved in a salvage operation.

3. A ship is not in common peril with another ship or ships if it is safe after disconnecting from that ship or ships. The common maritime adventure shall continue if disconnecting or necessarily remaining in connection constitutes a general average act.

Article 214

Allowance of losses, damages or expenses

1. Only such losses, damages or expenses which are the direct consequence of the general average act in accordance with Article 211 shall be allowed as general average.

2. There shall be no allowance in general average for losses, damage or expenses incurred in respect of damage to the environment or in consequence of the escape or release of pollutant substances from the property involved in the common maritime adventure.

3. Demurrage, loss of market, and any loss or damage sustained or expense incurred by reason of delay, whether on the voyage or subsequently, and any indirect loss whatsoever, shall not be allowed as general average.

Άρθρο 215

Δικαιώματα προς συνεισφορά

1. Τα δικαιώματα προς συνεισφορά στην κοινή αβαρία δεν θίγονται στην περίπτωση που το γεγονός που προκάλεσε τη θυσία ή δαπάνη οφείλεται σε πταίσμα συμμετέχοντος στην κοινή ναυτική αποστολή.

2. Η παρ. 1 δεν θίγει το δικαίωμα αναγωγής κατά του υπαιτίου προσώπου.

Άρθρο 216

Αποδεικτικά στοιχεία

1. Το μέρος εκείνο που ζητά να υπολογισθεί στην κοινή αβαρία η ζημία ή οι δαπάνες που κατέβαλε φέρει το σχετικό βάρος απόδειξης.

2. Εφόσον έχει ορισθεί διακανονιστής αβαριών, τα μέρη που έχουν απαιτήσεις στο πλαίσιο της κοινής αβαρίας, τού παρέχουν εγγράφως στοιχεία σχετικά με την απώλεια ή τη ζημία για την αιτούμενη συνεισφορά τους εντός δώδεκα (12) μηνών από την ολοκλήρωση της κοινής ναυτικής αποστολής.

3. Αν ελλείπει η γνωστοποίηση αυτή ή σε περίπτωση κατά την οποία το οποιοδήποτε μέρος, εντός δώδεκα (12) μηνών από την αίτησή του, δεν παράσχει στοιχεία προς υποστήριξη της υποβληθείσας απαίτησης ή στοιχεία της αξίας της συνεισφοράς, ο διακανονιστής αβαριών έχει τη διακριτική ευχέρεια να υπολογίσει το μέγεθος αυτής ή τη συνεισφερθείσα αξία με βάση τις πληροφορίες που έχει στη διάθεσή του.

4. Ο υπολογισμός αυτός μπορεί να αμφισβητηθεί, μόνον εφόσον αποδειχθεί ότι είναι προδήλως εσφαλμένος.

Άρθρο 217

Συμπληρωματικές δαπάνες

Κάθε συμπληρωματική δαπάνη που καταβλήθηκε προς αποφυγή άλλης, η οποία θα γινόταν αποδεκτή ως κοινή αβαρία, λογίζεται ως τέτοια και γίνεται αποδεκτή, χωρίς να λαμβάνεται υπόψη οτιδήποτε διασώθηκε, έναντι των άλλων συμφερόντων, μόνο μέχρι το ποσό των εξόδων της κοινής αβαρίας που αποφεύχθηκαν.

Άρθρο 218

Διακανονισμός κοινής αβαρίας

1. Ο διακανονισμός της κοινής αβαρίας, τόσο ως προς την απώλεια όσο και ως προς τη συνεισφορά, γίνεται με βάση τις αξίες που ισχύουν κατά τον χρόνο και στον τόπο όπου ολοκληρώνεται η κοινή ναυτική αποστολή.

2. Η παρ. 1 δεν επηρεάζει τον τόπο του διακανονισμού της κοινής αβαρίας όπως προβλέπεται στο άρθρο 220.

Article 215

Rights to contribution

1. Rights to contribution in general average shall not be affected, though the event which gave rise to the sacrifice or expenditure may have been due to the fault of one of the parties to the common maritime adventure.

2. Paragraph 1 shall not prejudice the right of recourse against the party at fault.

Article 216

Evidence

1. The party claiming that the loss sustained or expense incurred be allowable as general average shall bear the burden of proof.

2. Where an average adjuster has been designated, the parties with general average claims shall give notice in writing to the average adjuster of the loss or expense in respect of which they claim contribution within 12 months from the termination of the common maritime adventure.

3. Failing such notification, or if any party does not supply particulars in support of a notified claim or particulars on the value of the contribution within 12 months from their application, the average adjuster shall be at liberty to estimate the extent of the allowance or the contributory value on the basis of the information available to the adjuster.

4. Such estimates may be challenged only if they are proven to be manifestly incorrect.

Article 217

Additional expenses

Any additional expense incurred in place of another expense which would have been allowable as general average shall be deemed to be general average and so allowed without regard to the saving, if any, to other interests, but only up to the amount of the general average expense avoided.

Article 218

General average adjustment

1. General average shall be adjusted as regards both loss and contribution on the basis of values at the time and place when and where the common maritime adventure ends.

2. Paragraph 1 shall not affect the determination of adjustment of the general average, as provided for in Article 220.

Άρθρο 219

Δήλωση για διενέργεια κοινής αβαρίας

Ο διακανονισμός της κοινής αβαρίας προκαλείται με έγγραφη δήλωση του πλοιοκτήτη που απευθύνεται στον διακανονιστή της επιλογής του και στα πρόσωπα που εκπροσωπούν τα συμφέροντα του άρθρου 212. Αν, μετά την παρέλευση ενός (1) μηνός από την υποβολή σε αυτόν σχετικού αιτήματος από πρόσωπο που έχει έννομο συμφέρον να γίνει διακανονισμός, ο πλοιοκτήτης δεν τον ενεργήσει, στην υποβολή της δήλωσης δικαιούται εκείνος που διατύπωσε το αίτημα, ο οποίος θα ορίσει και τον διακανονιστή.

Άρθρο 220

Τόπος διακανονισμού της κοινής αβαρίας

Ο διακανονισμός της κοινής αβαρίας γίνεται στην πραγματική έδρα του πλοιοκτήτη, εκτός αν υπάρχει αντίθετη συμφωνία.

Άρθρο 221

Λοιπές εφαρμοστέες διατάξεις

1. Στην κοινή αβαρία και στη συνεισφορά εφαρμόζονται οι Κανόνες Υόρκης Αμβέρσας του 2016 της Διεθνούς Ναυτικής Επιτροπής, εκτός αν υπάρχει αντίθετη συμφωνία.

2. Με απόφαση του Υπουργού Ναυτιλίας και Νησιωτικής Πολιτικής μπορούν να τίθενται σε εφαρμογή νεότερες εκδοχές των Κανόνων Υόρκης Αμβέρσας.

Article 219

Declaration of preparation of general average [adjustment]

The general average adjustment shall be initiated by means of a written declaration by the owner-operator to the adjuster of its choice and to the persons representing the interests referred to in Article 212. If the owner-operator does not prepare the adjustment after one month has elapsed from the time it received a relevant request from a person with a legitimate interest in the adjustment taking place, the person who submitted the request shall be entitled to submit a declaration and to designate an adjuster.

Article 220

Place of general average adjustment

Unless otherwise agreed upon, the general average adjustment shall be prepared at the actual seat of the owner-operator.

Article 221

Other applicable provisions

1. Unless otherwise agreed upon, the 2016 York-Antwerp Rules of the Comité Maritime International shall apply to general average and contributions.

2. More recent versions of the York-Antwerp Rules may be implemented by a decision of the Minister of Maritime Affairs and Insular Policy.

ΜΕΡΟΣ ΕΝΑΤΟ
ΣΥΝΟΛΙΚΟΣ ΠΕΡΙΟΡΙΣΜΟΣ ΤΗΣ ΕΥΘΥΝΗΣ

ΚΕΦΑΛΑΙΟ Α'
ΟΥΣΙΑΣΤΙΚΕΣ ΔΙΑΤΑΞΕΙΣ

Άρθρο 222
Εφαρμοστέες διατάξεις

1. *Η ευθύνη των προσώπων που αναφέρονται στο άρθρο 223 δύναται να περιοριστεί για απαιτήσεις που απορρέουν από την εκμετάλλευση του πλοίου, σύμφωνα με τη Διεθνή Σύμβαση Λονδίνου του 1976/1996 για τον περιορισμό της ευθύνης για ναυτικές απαιτήσεις, (Διεθνής Σύμβαση Περιορισμού), η οποία κυρώθηκε με τον ν. 1923/1991 (Α' 13), όπως εκάστοτε ισχύει στην Ελλάδα.*

2. *Ο περιορισμός της ευθύνης για απαιτήσεις που εμπίπτουν στο πεδίο εφαρμογής της Διεθνούς Σύμβασης του 1992 αναφορικά με την αστική ευθύνη για ζημίες ρύπανσης από πετρέλαιο, όπως κυρώθηκε με το π.δ. 197/1995 (Α' 106) και εκάστοτε ισχύει στην Ελλάδα (Διεθνής Σύμβαση ευθύνης για ρύπανση από πετρέλαιο) διενεργείται σύμφωνα με τις διατάξεις της Σύμβασης αυτής.*

3. *Ο περιορισμός της ευθύνης για απαιτήσεις που εμπίπτουν στο πεδίο εφαρμογής της Διεθνούς Σύμβασης του 2001 για την αστική ευθύνη για ζημία ρύπανσης από πετρέλαιο κίνησης, όπως κυρώθηκε με τον ν. 3393/2005 (Α' 242) και εκάστοτε ισχύει στην Ελλάδα (Διεθνής Σύμβαση ευθύνης για το πετρέλαιο κίνησης) γίνεται σύμφωνα με την παρ. 1.*

4. *Ο περιορισμός της ευθύνης για απαιτήσεις που εμπίπτουν στο πεδίο εφαρμογής της Διεθνούς Σύμβασης του 2010 για την αστική ευθύνη και αποζημίωση για ζημία σχετική με τη μεταφορά επικίνδυνων και επιβλαβών ουσιών (Διεθνής Σύμβαση ευθύνης για επικίνδυνες και επιβλαβείς ουσίες) διενεργείται σύμφωνα με τις διατάξεις της Σύμβασης αυτής.*

5. *Για τη σύσταση και διανομή του κεφαλαίου περιορισμού και την εν γένει διαδικασία περιορισμού εφαρμόζεται το δεύτερο κεφάλαιο του παρόντος Μέρους.*

PART NINE
GLOBAL LIMITATION OF LIABILITY

CHAPTER I
SUBSTANTIVE PROVISIONS

Article 222
Applicable provisions

1. The liability of the persons referred to in Article 223 may be limited for claims arising in connection with the operation of the ship, in accordance with the 1976/1996 London International Convention on Limitation of Liability for Maritime Claims (International Convention on Limitation of Liability), ratified by Law 1923/1991 (Government Gazette, Series I, Issue 13), as in force in Greece from time to time.

2. Liability for claims falling within the scope of the 1992 International Convention on Civil Liability for Oil Pollution Damage, ratified by Presidential Decree 197/1995 (Government Gazette, Series I, Issue 106) and as in force in Greece from time to time (International Convention on Liability for Oil Pollution Damage) shall be limited in accordance with the provisions of that Convention.

3. Liability for claims falling within the scope of the 2001 International Convention on Civil Liability for Bunker Oil Pollution Damage, ratified by Law 3393/2005 (Government Gazette, Series I, Issue 242) and as in force in Greece from time to time (International Convention on Liability for Bunker Oil Pollution Damage) shall be limited in accordance with paragraph 1.

4. Liability for claims falling within the scope of the 2010 International Convention on Liability and Compensation for Damage in Connection with the Carriage of Hazardous and Noxious Substances by Sea, as in force in Greece at any given time (International Convention on Liability for Damage in Connection with the Carriage of Hazardous and Noxious Substances) shall be limited in accordance with the provisions of that Convention.

5. Chapter II of this Part shall apply to the constitution and distribution of a limitation fund and the limitation procedure in general.

Άρθρο 223

Δικαιούχοι περιορισμού

1. Δικαιούνται να περιορίσουν την ευθύνη τους, σύμφωνα με τη Διεθνή Σύμβαση Περιορισμού, ο πλοιοκτήτης, τα εξομοιούμενα με αυτόν πρόσωπα, το πρόσωπο που παρέχει υπηρεσίες επιθαλάσσιας αρωγής και οι προστηθέντες αυτών. Το ίδιο δικαίωμα έχει και ο ασφαλιστής αστικής ευθύνης για τις κατά νόμο περιορίσιμες απαιτήσεις.

2. Κατά παρέκκλιση του άρθρου 48:

(α) Εξομοιώνονται με τον πλοιοκτήτη, για τους σκοπούς εφαρμογής της Διεθνούς Σύμβασης Περιορισμού, ο κύριος του πλοίου, ο εκμεταλλευόμενος, ο ναυλωτής και ο διαχειριστής αυτού.

(β) Εξομοιώνονται με τον πλοιοκτήτη, για τους σκοπούς εφαρμογής της Διεθνούς Σύμβασης Ευθύνης για το πετρέλαιο κίνησης, ο κύριος του πλοίου, ο εκμεταλλευόμενος αυτό και ο διαχειριστής αυτού.

(γ) Ως πλοιοκτήτης νοείται, για τους σκοπούς της Διεθνούς Σύμβασης ευθύνης για ρύπανση από πετρέλαιο και της Διεθνούς Σύμβασης ευθύνης για επικίνδυνες και επιβλαβείς ουσίες, ο κύριος του πλοίου. Δικαίωμα περιορισμού έχει και ο ασφαλιστής αστικής ευθύνης του κυρίου.

Άρθρο 224

Μη αποδοχή ευθύνης

Η άσκηση του δικαιώματος περιορισμού δεν συνιστά αποδοχή της ευθύνης.

Άρθρο 225

Διαχρονικό δίκαιο

Ο περιορισμός της ευθύνης διενεργείται σύμφωνα με τα όρια των άρθρων 226, 227 και 229 που ισχύουν ή ίσχυαν κατά τον χρόνο επέλευσης του ζημιογόνου περιστατικού.

Άρθρο 226

Εφαρμοζόμενα όρια

1. Τα προβλεπόμενα στη Διεθνή Σύμβαση Περιορισμού όρια ευθύνης εφαρμόζονται σε όλα τα πλοία κατά την έννοια του άρθρου 1 του παρόντος, ανεξάρτητα από τη βάση ευθύνης, με την επιφύλαξη της παρ. 2.

2. Για πλοία ολικής χωρητικότητας μικρότερης των τριακοσίων (300) κόρων, το ανώτατο όριο της παρ. 1(α) του άρθρου 6 της Διεθνούς Σύμβασης Περιορισμού ορίζεται σε ένα εκατομμύριο (1.000.000) μονάδες υπολογισμού, και το ανώτατο όριο της παρ. 1(β) σε πεντακόσιες χιλιάδες (500.000) μονάδες υπολογισμού.

3. Με απόφαση του Υπουργού Ναυτιλίας και Νησιωτικής Πολιτικής μπορούν να τροποποιούνται τα όρια της παρ. 2.

4. Στα πλοία και τις κατηγορίες φορτίων που εμπίπτουν στις Διεθνείς Συμβάσεις που αναφέρονται στις παρ. 2 και 4 του άρθρου 222 εφαρμόζονται τα εκεί προβλεπόμενα όρια περιορισμού.

Article 223

Persons entitled to limitation

1. The owner-operator, persons treated as the owner-operator, the person rendering salvage services and their agents shall be entitled to limitation of their liability in accordance with the International Convention on Limitation of Liability. The civil liability insurer shall have the same entitlement for claims subject by law to limitation.

2. By way of derogation to Article 48:

(a) the owner of the ship, the person operating the ship, the charterer and the manager of the ship shall be treated as the owner-operator for the purposes of the International Convention on Limitation of Liability;

(b) the owner of the ship, the person operating the ship and the manager of the ship shall be treated as the owner-operator for the purposes of the International Convention on Liability for Bunker Oil Pollution Damage;

(c) the owner of the ship shall be treated as the owner-operator for the purposes of the International Convention on Liability for Oil Pollution Damage and the International Convention on Liability for Damage in Connection with the Carriage of Hazardous and Noxious Substances. The civil liability insurer of the owner shall also have an entitlement to limitation.

Article 224

Non-admission of liability

Exercising the right of limitation does not constitute admission of liability.

Article 225

Temporal scope

Liability shall be limited in accordance with the limits laid down in Articles 226, 227 and 229 that are or were in force at the time the harmful event occurred.

Article 226

Applicable limits

1. The limits of liability laid down in the International Convention on Limitation of Liability shall apply to all ships, within the meaning of Article 1 of this Code, irrespective of the basis of liability, without prejudice to paragraph 2.

2. For ships with a gross tonnage not exceeding 300 tons, the maximum limit laid down in Article 6(1) of the International Convention on Limitation of Liability is set at 1,000,000 units of account, and the maximum limit laid down in [Article 6](1)(b) at 500,000 units of account.

3. The limits laid down in paragraph 2 may be amended by a decision of the Minister of Maritime Affairs and Insular Policy.

4. The limits of liability laid down in the International Conventions referred to in Article 222(2) and (4) shall apply to the ships and categories of cargo falling within the scope of those Conventions.

Άρθρο 227
Περιορισμός ευθύνης για ζημίες από στατικά ναυπηγήματα

1. Τα πρόσωπα που αναφέρονται στις παρ. 1 και 2 του άρθρου 219 μπορούν να περιορίσουν την ευθύνη τους για απαιτήσεις που γεννώνται από την εκμετάλλευση στατικών ναυπηγημάτων και εμπίπτουν στις κατηγορίες του άρθρου 2 της Διεθνούς Σύμβασης Περιορισμού.

2. Στα στατικά ναυπηγήματα που διαθέτουν καταμετρηθείσα ολική χωρητικότητα εφαρμόζονται οι παρ. 1 έως 3 του άρθρου 226.

3. Με απόφαση του Υπουργού Ναυτιλίας και Νησιωτικής Πολιτικής καθορίζονται τα όρια περιορισμού για τα στατικά ναυπηγήματα που δεν διαθέτουν καταμετρηθείσα ολική χωρητικότητα.

4. Κατ' εξαίρεση των παρ. 1 και 2, τα όρια περιορισμού δεν εφαρμόζονται σε στατικά ναυπηγήματα που έχουν κατασκευασθεί για τον σκοπό έρευνας ή εκμετάλλευσης των φυσικών πηγών του βυθού ή του υπεδάφους του.

Άρθρο 228
Εμπλεκόμενα πλοία

1. Σε περίπτωση εμπλοκής περισσοτέρων πλοίων στο ίδιο περιστατικό, ο περιορισμός της ευθύνης γίνεται αυτοτελώς για κάθε ένα από αυτά.

2. Περιορισμός ευθύνης δεν χωρεί για ζημίες που έχει υποστεί το ίδιο το πλοίο, με βάση τη χωρητικότητα του οποίου λαμβάνει χώρα ο υπολογισμός των ορίων περιορισμού.

Άρθρο 229
Τροποποιήσεις ορίων περιορισμού

1. Οι τροποποιήσεις των ορίων ευθύνης που προβλέπονται στην παρ. 1 του άρθρου 6 και στην παρ. 1 του άρθρου 7 της Διεθνούς Σύμβασης Περιορισμού τίθενται σε εφαρμογή στην Ελλάδα με τη θέση τους διεθνώς σε ισχύ, με τη διαδικασία σιωπηρής αποδοχής, που προβλέπεται στο άρθρο 8 του Πρωτοκόλλου 1996, το οποίο κυρώθηκε με τον ν. 3743/2009 (Α' 24).

2. Η παρ. 1 εφαρμόζεται και για τις τροποποιήσεις των ορίων ευθύνης που προβλέπονται στην παρ. 1 του άρθρου V της Διεθνούς Σύμβασης για ρύπανση από πετρέλαιο, σύμφωνα με τη διαδικασία του άρθρου 15 του Πρωτοκόλλου του 199**2.**

3. Για τη θέση σε ισχύ των τροποποιήσεων των ορίων ευθύνης που προβλέπονται στις παρ. 1 και 2 εκδίδεται αμελλητί διαπιστωτική πράξη του Υπουργού Ναυτιλίας και Νησιωτικής Πολιτικής.

Άρθρο 230
Επενέργεια κεφαλαίου περιορισμού

1. Κεφάλαιο περιορισμού που έχει συσταθεί σε συμβαλλόμενο στη Διεθνή Σύμβαση Περιορισμού κράτος αναγνωρίζεται στην Ελλάδα, εφόσον στο κράτος αυτό έχει ασκηθεί αγωγή ή άλλο ένδικο βοήθημα για απαιτήσεις που υπόκεινται σε περιορισμό και ισχύουν σε αυτό τα όρια ευθύνης που ισχύουν στην Ελλάδα.

2. Κεφάλαιο περιορισμού που έχει συσταθεί από τον πλοιοκτήτη ή εξομοιούμενα με αυτόν πρόσωπα ή τον ασφαλιστή ισχύει για όλους, συμπεριλαμβανομένων των προστηθέντων τους, εκτός αν πρόκειται για απαιτήσεις που διέπονται από ειδική διεθνή σύμβαση ευθύνης. Ομοίως, το κεφάλαιο που συστήνεται από πρόσωπο που παρέχει υπηρεσίες θαλάσσιας αρωγής ισχύει υπέρ των προστηθέντων του.

Article 227

Limitation of liability for damage caused by stationary floating structures

1. The persons referred to in Article 219(1) and (2) may limit their liability for claims arising from the operation of stationary floating structures and falling within the categories listed in Article 2 of the International Convention on Limitation of Liability.

2. Article 226(1) to (3) shall apply to stationary floating structures with a measured gross tonnage.

3. The limits of liability for stationary floating structures without a measured gross tonnage shall be laid down in a decision issued by the Minister of Maritime Affairs and Insular Policy.

4. By way of exception to paragraphs 1 and 2, the limits of liability shall not apply to stationary floating structures constructed for the purpose of exploring or exploiting the natural resources of the sea-bed or the subsoil thereof.

Article 228

Ships involved

1. Where several ships are involved in the same incident, liability shall be limited separately for each ship.

2. There is no limitation of liability for damage sustained by the ship itself on the basis of whose tonnage the limits of liability are calculated.

Article 229

Amendments to limits of liability

1. Amendments to the limits of liability laid down in Articles 6(1) and 7(1) of the International Convention on Limitation of Liability shall be applied in Greece upon entering into force internationally in accordance with the tacit acceptance procedure laid down for in Article 8 of the 1996 Protocol, ratified by Law 3743/2009 (Government Gazette, Series I, Issue 24).

2. Paragraph 1 shall also apply to amendments to the limits of liability laid down in Article V(1) of the International Convention on Liability for Oil Pollution Damage, in accordance with the procedure laid down in Article 15 of the 1992 Protocol.

3. The Minister of Maritime Affairs and Insular Policy shall promptly issue a decision confirming the entry into force of the amendments to the limits of liability referred to in paragraphs 1 and 2.

Article 230

Effect of limitation fund

1. A limitation fund constituted in a State Party to the International Convention on Limitation of Liability shall be recognised in Greece, provided an action or other form of relief has been filed in that state in regard to claims subject to limitation and the [same] limits of liability in force in Greece are [also] in force in that state.

2. A limitation fund constituted by the owner-operator or the persons treated as the owner-operator or by the insurer shall operate *erga omnes*, including their agents, save in cases of claims governed by a special international convention on liability. Similarly, a fund constituted by a salvor shall operate in favour of its agents.

Άρθρο 231

Έκπτωση από το δικαίωμα περιορισμού

1. Τα αναφερόμενα στο άρθρο 223 πρόσωπα δεν δικαιούνται να περιορίσουν την ευθύνη τους όταν πληρούνται οι προϋποθέσεις του άρθρου 4 της Διεθνούς Σύμβασης Περιορισμού, της παρ. 2 του άρθρου V της Διεθνούς Σύμβασης ευθύνης για ρύπανση από πετρέλαιο και της παρ. 2 του άρθρου 9 της Διεθνούς Σύμβασης ευθύνης για επικίνδυνες και επιβλαβείς ουσίες.

2. Για την έκπτωση από το δικαίωμα περιορισμού απαιτείται προσωπική πράξη ή παράλειψη του δικαιούχου, που τελείται με άμεσο ή ενδεχόμενο δόλο.

3. Για τους σκοπούς του παρόντος, το πταίσμα του πλοιάρχου ή του πληρώματος δεν συνιστά ίδιο πταίσμα του εκμεταλλευόμενου το πλοίο.

Άρθρο 232

Αδρανοποίηση ναυτικών προνομίων

1. Ναυτικά προνόμια δεν λαμβάνονται υπόψη κατά τη διανομή του κεφαλαίου σύμφωνα με την παρ. 1 του άρθρου 12 της Διεθνούς Σύμβασης Περιορισμού.

2. Η παρ. 1 εφαρμόζεται και για τη διανομή του κεφαλαίου σύμφωνα με την παρ. 4 του άρθρου V της Διεθνούς Σύμβασης ευθύνης για ρύπανση από πετρέλαιο και την παρ. 4 του άρθρου 9 της Διεθνούς Σύμβασης ευθύνης για επικίνδυνες και επιβλαβείς ουσίες.

Άρθρο 233

Τόκος και δικαστικές δαπάνες

1. Ο τόκος της παρ. 1 του άρθρου 11 της Διεθνούς Σύμβασης Περιορισμού καθορίζεται με βάση το διατραπεζικό επιτόκιο δανεισμού σε ευρώ (EURIBOR), προσαυξημένο κατά τέσσερις (4) μονάδες, από τον χρόνο του επίδικου περιστατικού έως και τη σύσταση του κεφαλαίου περιορισμού.

2. Οι δικαστικές δαπάνες δεν υπόκεινται σε περιορισμό.

3. Κάθε είδους τέλη, δικαιώματα και πρόστιμα του ελληνικού Δημοσίου ή άλλων φορέων που σχετίζονται με περιορίσιμες απαιτήσεις, υπόκεινται σε περιορισμό σύμφωνα με τη διαδικασία του Κεφαλαίου Β', με εξαίρεση τα πρόστιμα που επιβάλλονται από δημόσιες αρχές για ρύπανση του θαλάσσιου περιβάλλοντος.

ΚΕΦΑΛΑΙΟ Β'

ΔΙΑΔΙΚΑΣΙΑ

Άρθρο 234

Περιορισμός ευθύνης χωρίς σύσταση κεφαλαίου

Το δικαίωμα περιορισμού σύμφωνα με τη Διεθνή Σύμβαση Περιορισμού μπορεί να ασκηθεί και χωρίς σύσταση κεφαλαίου σε κάθε βαθμό δικαιοδοσίας και μέχρι την τελευταία πράξη εκτέλεσης.

Article 231

Loss of entitlement to limitation

1. The persons referred to in Article 223 shall not be entitled to limit their liability where the requirements laid down in Article 4 of the International Convention on Limitation of Liability, Article V(2) of the International Convention on Liability for Oil Pollution Damage and Article 9(2) of the International Convention on Liability for Damage in Connection with the Carriage of Hazardous and Noxious Substances are met.

2. Loss of the right to limitation necessitates a personal act or omission of the beneficiary committed with *dolus directus* or *dolus eventualis*.

3. For the purposes of this Article, fault on the part of the master or the crew shall not in itself constitute a fault on the part of the person operating the ship.

Article 232

Non-application of maritime liens

1. Maritime liens shall not be taken into account when distributing the fund in accordance with Article 12(1) of the International Convention on Limitation of Liability.

2. Paragraph 1 shall also apply to the distribution of the fund in accordance with Article V(4) of the International Convention on Liability for Oil Pollution Damage and Article 9(4) of the International Convention on Liability for Damage in Connection with the Carriage of Hazardous and Noxious Substances.

Article 233

Interest and court costs

1. The interest referred to in Article 11(1) of the International Convention on Limitation of Liability shall be determined on the basis of the Euro Interbank Offered Rate (EURIBOR) plus 4% from the date the incident giving rise to the liability occurred until the date the limitation fund was constituted.

2. Court costs are not subject to limitation.

3. Any and all fees, charges and fines levied by the Greek State or other bodies in relation to claims subject to limitation shall be made subject to limitation in accordance with the procedure laid down in Chapter II, save fines levied by public authorities for pollution of the marine environment.

CHAPTER II

PROCEDURE

Article 234

Limitation of liability without constitution of a [limitation] fund

Entitlement to limitation under the International Convention on Limitation of Liability may be exercised without constitution of a [limitation] fund at every instance up to the final enforcement step.

Άρθρο 235

Δήλωση περί σύστασης κεφαλαίου

1. Τα πρόσωπα του άρθρου 223 που επιθυμούν να προβούν σε περιορισμό ευθύνης με σύσταση κεφαλαίου οφείλουν να το δηλώσουν ενώπιον του γραμματέα του αρμόδιου πρωτοδικείου, με ειδική δήλωση για αυτόν τον σκοπό. Ειδική έκθεση συντάσσεται από τον γραμματέα κάτω από το κείμενο της δήλωσης.

2. Αρμόδιο για τη σύσταση κεφαλαίου με βάση τη Διεθνή Σύμβαση Περιορισμού του 1976, είναι το πρωτοδικείο του Πειραιά.

3. Αρμόδια για τη σύσταση κεφαλαίου, όταν εφαρμόζονται οι παρ. 2, 3 και 4 του άρθρου 222, είναι το πρωτοδικείο του τόπου επέλευσης του ζημιογόνου περιστατικού και συντρεχόντως το πρωτοδικείο του Πειραιά.

Άρθρο 236

Περιεχόμενο δήλωσης

1. Η δήλωση που αναφέρεται στο άρθρο 235 περιέχει τα εξής στοιχεία:

α) Όνομα, σημαία, λιμένα και αριθμό νηολόγησης, αριθμό Διεθνούς Ναυτιλιακού Οργανισμού, διεθνές διακριτικό σήμα και ολική χωρητικότητα του πλοίου,

β) σύντομη περιγραφή του περιστατικού από το οποίο απορρέουν οι απαιτήσεις που υπόκεινται σε περιορισμό και των γνωστών ή πιθανών ζημιών που σχετίζονται με αυτό,

γ) πίνακα με τα στοιχεία των δανειστών με περιορίσιμες απαιτήσεις,

δ) το ύψος του ποσού στο οποίο περιορίζεται η ευθύνη σύμφωνα με τα εκάστοτε εφαρμοζόμενα όρια,

ε) διορισμό αντικλήτου για την επίδοση όλων των δικογράφων, αποφάσεων και εγγράφων που αφορούν στη διαδικασία του περιορισμού,

στ) τον τρόπο με τον οποίο θα συσταθεί το κεφάλαιο περιορισμού, κατά το άρθρο 237.

2. Στη δήλωση επισυνάπτονται από τον υποβάλλοντα, με ποινή απαραδέκτου, τα ακόλουθα έγγραφα:

α) Επικυρωμένο αντίγραφο του διεθνούς πιστοποιητικού καταμέτρησης ή, ανάλογα με την περίπτωση, του πιστοποιητικού καταμέτρησης του πλοίου σύμφωνα με την εθνική νομοθεσία,

β) βεβαίωση της Τράπεζας της Ελλάδας για την ισοτιμία σε ευρώ του Ειδικού Τραβηκτικού Δικαιώματος, κατά την ημερομηνία σύστασης του κεφαλαίου,

γ) αποδεικτικό σύστασης του κεφαλαίου ή την εγγυητική επιστολή που προβλέπονται στο άρθρο 237, και

δ) αποδεικτικό κατάθεσης σε πίστωση ειδικού λογαριασμού πιστωτικού ιδρύματος που λειτουργεί στην Ελλάδα ποσού είκοσι πέντε χιλιάδων (25.000) ευρώ για την κάλυψη των αρχικώς υπολογιζόμενων εξόδων της διαδικασίας και του εκκαθαριστή.

Ο δηλών τον περιορισμό έχει διακριτική ευχέρεια να προσκομίσει κάθε άλλο έγγραφο σχετικό με οποιαδήποτε περιορίσιμη απαίτηση.

Article 235

Fund constitution declaration

1. The persons referred to in Article 223 who wish to limit their liability by constituting a [limitation] fund must declare so to the registrar of the competent court of first instance in a special declaration prepared for that purpose. The registrar shall prepare a special report at the end of the text of the declaration.

2. The Piraeus Court of First Instance shall be competent for the constitution of [limitation] funds on the basis of the 1976 International Convention on Limitation of Liability.

3. Where paragraphs (2), (3) and (4) of Article 222 apply, the court of first instance of the place where the harmful event occurred and the Piraeus Court of First Instance shall have concurrent competence for the constitution of a [limitation] fund.

Article 236

Content of declaration

1. The declaration referred to in Article 235 shall contain the following information:

a) the name, flag, port of registry and registration number, IMO number, international call sign and gross tonnage of the ship;

b) a brief description of the incident giving rise to the claims subject to limitation and the known or possible damage relating to the incident;

c) a table listing the particulars of creditors with claims subject to limitation;

d) the amount to which liability is limited in accordance with the limits applicable from time to time;

e) the appointment of a process agent on whom all procedural documents, decisions, judgments and documentation concerning the limitation procedure are served; [and]

f) the manner in which the limitation fund will be constituted in accordance with Article 237.

2. On penalty of inadmissibility, the following documents shall be attached by the declarant to the declaration:

a) a certified copy of the international tonnage certificate or, as the case may be, the ship measurement certificate issued in accordance with the [applicable] national legislation;

b) an attestation by the Bank of Greece on the EUR - Special Drawing Right exchange rate on the date the fund was constituted;

c) proof of constitution of the fund or the letter of guarantee provided for in Article 237; and

d) proof of deposit of the sum of 25,000 euros into a special account held at a credit institution operating in Greece to cover the initially estimated costs of the procedure and the liquidator.

The limitation declarant shall be at liberty to present any other document concerning any claim subject to limitation.

Άρθρο 237

Σύσταση κεφαλαίου

1. Το κεφάλαιο περιορισμού συστήνεται είτε με την κατάθεση μετρητών του ποσού της περ. (δ) της παρ. 1 του άρθρου 236, σε πίστωση ειδικού λογαριασμού σε πιστωτικό ίδρυμα που λειτουργεί στην Ελλάδα, είτε με την έκδοση εγγυητικής επιστολής πιστωτικού ιδρύματος που λειτουργεί στην Ελλάδα ή αξιόχρεου αλληλασφαλιστικού φορέα.

2. Το πιστωτικό ίδρυμα στο οποίο συστήθηκε το κεφάλαιο είναι υποχρεωμένο να χορηγήσει σε αυτόν που το συνέστησε το αποδεικτικό της περ. (γ) της παρ. 2 του άρθρου 236.

3. Οι τόκοι του ως άνω ειδικού λογαριασμού αποδίδονται σε αυτόν που συνέστησε το κεφάλαιο περιορισμού.

4. Με απόφαση του Υπουργού Ναυτιλίας και Νησιωτικής Πολιτικής καθορίζονται ο τύπος και το ελάχιστο περιεχόμενο της εγγυητικής επιστολής της παρ. 1.

Άρθρο 238

Διορισμός εισηγητή και εκκαθαριστή

1. Ο γραμματέας υποβάλλει τη δήλωση στον προϊστάμενο του πρωτοδικείου χωρίς καθυστέρηση. Ο τελευταίος διορίζει, με πράξη του, εισηγητή και εκκαθαριστή. Με την ίδια διαδικασία γίνεται η αντικατάσταση του εισηγητή.

2. Ο γραμματέας ειδοποιεί τον εκκαθαριστή χωρίς καθυστέρηση. Αν αυτός δεν επιθυμεί τον διορισμό του, οφείλει να το δηλώσει στην γραμματεία εντός τριών (3) ημερών. Σε αντίθετη περίπτωση, θεωρείται ότι τον αποδέχθηκε.

3. Ο εκκαθαριστής μπορεί να ζητήσει από τον εισηγητή την αντικατάστασή του για σοβαρούς λόγους, χωρίς όμως να διακόψει το έργο του μέχρι να αντικατασταθεί από άλλο πρόσωπο. Η πράξη του εισηγητή δεν προσβάλλεται και καταχωρίζεται κάτω από την αίτηση του εκκαθαριστή.

4. Ο εκκαθαριστής μπορεί να αντικατασταθεί με αυτεπάγγελτη πράξη του εισηγητή, κατά της οποίας δικαιούται να ασκήσει ανακοπή, εντός τριών (3) ημερών από την επίδοσή της σε αυτόν, στο μονομελές πρωτοδικείο που δικάζει αμετακλήτως κατά τη διαδικασία της εκούσιας δικαιοδοσίας.

Άρθρο 239

Έλεγχος των τυπικών προϋποθέσεων περιορισμού

1. Η δήλωση του άρθρου 235 υποβάλλεται χωρίς καθυστέρηση στον εισηγητή για να ελέγξει την ορθότητα του υπολογισμού του κεφαλαίου, με βάση τα ισχύοντα ανά περίπτωση όρια και το αξιόχρεο του αλληλασφαλιστικού φορέα που εξέδωσε την εγγυητική επιστολή και εκδίδεται σχετική με αυτά απόφαση. Σε αρνητική περίπτωση ο εισηγητής διατάσσει, με την απόφασή του, ο,τιδήποτε απαιτείται για τη συμμόρφωση, περιλαμβανομένης της συμπλήρωσης του κεφαλαίου μέχρι του επιβαλλόμενου ποσού. Δικαιούται επίσης να διατάξει την καταβολή συμπληρωματικού ποσού για την κάλυψη του κόστους της διαδικασίας.

Article 237

Constitution of the [limitation] fund

1. The limitation fund shall be constituted either by depositing the amount referred to in Article 236(1)(d) in cash into a special account held at a credit institution operating in Greece, or by a credit institution operating in Greece or a solvent mutual insurer issuing a letter of guarantee.

2. The credit institution where the fund was constituted shall be obligated to provide the person who constituted the fund with the proof referred to in Article 236(2)(c).

3. Interest accruing on the aforesaid special account shall be paid to the person who constituted the limitation fund.

4. The form and minimum content of the letter of guarantee referred to in paragraph 1 shall be specified in a decision issued by the Minister of Maritime Affairs and Insular Policy.

Article 238

Appointment of a reporting judge and liquidator

1. The registrar shall submit the declaration to the head of the court of first instance without delay. The latter shall issue a decision appointing a reporting judge and a liquidator. The same procedure shall be followed to replace the reporting judge.

2. The registrar shall notify the liquidator [of their appointment] without delay. If they do not wish to be appointed, they must declare so to the registry within three days; otherwise, they shall be deemed to have accepted their appointment.

3. Where there are serious grounds, the liquidator may submit an application for them to be replaced to the reporting judge, but must continue their work until they are replaced by a different person. The decision issued by the reporting judge may not be contested and shall be recorded at the end of the liquidator's application.

4. The liquidator may be replaced by a decision issued *ex officio* by the reporting judge, against which the liquidator may, within three days from the date the decision is served on the liquidator, file an opposition with the single-member court of first instance, which shall try the matter under non-contentious proceedings and hand down an irrevocable judgment.

Article 239

Examination of formal limitation requirements

1. The declaration referred to in Article 235 shall be submitted without delay to the reporting judge in order to examine the calculation of the [limitation] fund on the basis of the limits applicable in each case and the solvency of the mutual insurer which issued the letter of guarantee, and the reporting judge shall hand down a judgment on the matter. If the requirements are not met, the reporting judge shall order, in their judgment, everything required for compliance, including supplementation of the [limitation] fund up to the required amount. The reporting judge may also order that a supplementary amount be paid to cover the costs of the procedure.

2. Αντίγραφο της απόφασης του εισηγητή κοινοποιείται χωρίς καθυστέρηση από τον γραμματέα σε εκείνον που συνέστησε το κεφάλαιο, στον εκκαθαριστή και, ειδικά στην περίπτωση ζημιών από ρύπανση από πετρέλαιο στη θάλασσα ή ρύπανση από πετρέλαιο κίνησης, και στον Υπουργό Ναυτιλίας και Νησιωτικής Πολιτικής μαζί με την έκθεση του δεύτερου εδαφίου της παρ. 1 του άρθρου 235. Η απόφαση αναρτάται επίσης στον ιστότοπο του πρωτοδικείου Πειραιά.

3. Ανακοπή κατά της απόφασης αυτής επιτρέπεται σε όποιον έχει έννομο συμφέρον, μέσα σε προθεσμία δεκαπέντε (15) ημερών από την κοινοποίησή της στο πρόσωπο που συνέστησε το κεφάλαιο και στον Υπουργό Ναυτιλίας και Νησιωτικής Πολιτικής αντίστοιχα ή από την ανάρτησή της στον ιστότοπο της παρ. 2, για κάθε άλλο πρόσωπο. Οι ανακοπές ασκούνται ενώπιον του πολυμελούς πρωτοδικείου Πειραιά και δικάζονται στην ίδια δικάσιμο, κατά τη διαδικασία της εκούσιας δικαιοδοσίας. Σε παρέμβαση δικαιούται όποιος έχει έννομο συμφέρον. Οι ανακοπές και οι παρεμβάσεις κοινοποιούνται υποχρεωτικά στον εκκαθαριστή.

4. Η ανακοπή και η προθεσμία άσκησης αυτής δεν αναστέλλουν την εκτέλεση της απόφασης του εισηγητή και τη διαδικασία της εκκαθάρισης. Η απόφαση που εκδίδεται επί της ανακοπής δεν υπόκειται σε ένδικα μέσα.

5. Μέσα σε έναν (1) μήνα από την επίδοση της απόφασης του εισηγητή ή από την επίδοση της απόφασης επί της ανακοπής, εκείνος που συνέστησε το κεφάλαιο έχει υποχρέωση να λάβει τα προβλεπόμενα σε αυτές διορθωτικά μέτρα. Αν καθοριστεί ποσό υψηλότερο, υποχρεούται να συμπληρώσει το ποσό που κατατέθηκε, εφαρμόζοντας τη διαδικασία της παρ. 1 του άρθρου 235. Αν καθορισθεί ποσό μικρότερο από αυτό που προσδιορίσθηκε αρχικώς, τότε αποδίδεται σε εκείνον που συνέστησε το κεφάλαιο η διαφορά ή επιτρέπεται σε αυτόν να αντικαταστήσει την εγγυητική επιστολή με την ταυτόχρονη κατάθεση άλλης που ανταποκρίνεται σε ποσό με αυτό που καθορίσθηκε με την απόφαση του εισηγητή ή την απόφαση επί της ανακοπής.

Άρθρο 240

Αμφισβήτηση των ουσιαστικών προϋποθέσεων περιορισμού

1. Αν δανειστής αμφισβητεί τη συνδρομή των ουσιαστικών προϋποθέσεων περιορισμού της ευθύνης, λόγω έκπτωσης του οφειλέτη σύμφωνα με το άρθρο 4 της Διεθνούς Σύμβασης Περιορισμού, την παρ. 2 του άρθρου V της Διεθνούς Σύμβασης Ευθύνης για ρύπανση από πετρέλαιο και το άρθρο 231 του παρόντος, μπορεί να προβάλει τις αντιρρήσεις του με ανακοπή που ασκείται εντός προθεσμίας δύο (2) μηνών από τη δημοσίευση της δήλωσης, απευθύνεται κατά του προσώπου που συνέστησε το κεφάλαιο περιορισμού και εκδικάζεται ενώπιον του πολυμελούς πρωτοδικείου με τη διαδικασία της εκούσιας δικαιοδοσίας. Η παρ. 3 του άρθρου 245 εφαρμόζονται αναλόγως.

2. Η ανακοπή κοινοποιείται στον εκκαθαριστή.

3. Περισσότερες ανακοπές δικάζονται υποχρεωτικά στην ίδια δικάσιμο.

4. Η άσκηση της ανακοπής του παρόντος δεν εμποδίζει τη διαδικασία της εκκαθάρισης, ούτε τη συμμετοχή σε αυτήν του ανακόπτοντα.

5. Η τελεσίδικη αναγνώριση της συνδρομής των ουσιαστικών προϋποθέσεων περιορισμού της ευθύνης του οφειλέτη ισχύει έναντι πάντων. Το ίδιο ισχύει και για την τελεσίδικη αναγνώριση των προϋποθέσεων έκπτωσης. Σε κάθε περίπτωση, η αναγνώριση ενεργεί αναδρομικά.

2. The registrar shall notify a copy of the judgment handed down by the reporting judge without delay to the person who constituted the fund, to the liquidator and, specifically in cases of oil pollution damage or bunker oil pollution damage to the sea, to the Minister of Maritime Affairs and Insular Policy as well, together with the report referred to in the second subparagraph of Article 235(1). The judgment shall also be uploaded to the website of the Piraeus Court of First Instance.

3. An opposition may be filed against this judgment by any person with a legitimate interest, within a deadline of 15 days from the date the judgment was notified to the person who constituted the fund and to the Minister of Maritime Affairs and Insular Policy, respectively, or by any other person from the time the judgment was uploaded to the website referred to in paragraph 2. Oppositions shall be filed with the Piraeus Multi-Member Court of First Instance and tried on the same hearing date under non-contentious proceedings. Any person with a legitimate interest may file an intervention. Oppositions and interventions must necessarily be notified to the liquidator.

4. Filing an opposition and the deadline for filing an opposition shall not stay enforcement of the judgment handed down by the reporting judge and the liquidation process. The judgment handed down on the opposition shall not be subject to legal remedies.

5. The person who constituted the fund shall be obligated to take the corrective measures provided for in the judgment handed down by the reporting judge or the judgment on the opposition within one month from the date either judgment is served. If a higher amount is set, the person who constituted the fund shall be obligated to supplement the amount deposited by following the procedure laid down in Article 235(1). If an amount lower than the one initially determined is set, the person who constituted the fund shall be paid the difference or may replace the letter of guarantee by simultaneously depositing a different letter of guarantee for the amount set in the judgment handed down by the reporting judge or in the judgment on the opposition.

Article 240

Contesting substantive limitation requirements

1. If a creditor contests whether the substantive requirements for limitation of liability are met due to loss of the debtor's entitlement in accordance with Article 4 of the International Convention on Limitation of Liability, Article V(2) of the International Convention on Liability for Oil Pollution Damage and Article 231 of this Code, the creditor may raise their objections in an opposition which shall be filed within a deadline of two months from the date the declaration is published, brought against the person who constituted the limitation fund and adjudicated by the multi-member court of first instance under non-contentious proceedings. Article 245(3) shall apply *mutatis mutandis*.

2. The opposition shall be notified to the liquidator.

3. Where there are several oppositions, they must be tried on the same hearing date.

4. Filing an opposition in accordance with this Article shall not hinder the liquidation procedure from going forward or the opposing party from participating in said procedure.

5. Non-appealable acknowledgement that the substantive conditions for limitation of the debtor's liability are met shall generate effects *erga omnes*. The same shall apply to non-appealable acknowledgement that the conditions for loss of entitlement to liability are met. In all events, acknowledgement shall have retroactive effect.

Άρθρο 241
Αποτελέσματα

Η σύσταση του κεφαλαίου επιφέρει τα παρακάτω αποτελέσματα:

α) Απαγορεύεται η άσκηση ατομικών διωκτικών μέτρων σχετικά με περιορίσιμες απαιτήσεις σε άλλα περιουσιακά στοιχεία προσώπου από το οποίο, ή για λογαριασμό του οποίου, έχει συσταθεί το κεφάλαιο.

β) Δίκες που είναι εκκρεμείς και αφορούν στις ανωτέρω απαιτήσεις διακόπτονται.

γ) Απαγορεύεται κάθε πράξη αναγκαστικής εκτέλεσης ή η λήψη ασφαλιστικών μέτρων για τις ανωτέρω απαιτήσεις.

δ) Ασφαλιστικά μέτρα που έχουν ήδη ληφθεί ανακαλούνται και οι σχετικές ασφάλειες αποδίδονται με απόφαση του δικαστηρίου που τα διέταξε, σύμφωνα με τα προβλεπόμενα στις οικείες διεθνείς συμβάσεις.

ε) Αναγκαστικά μέτρα που έχουν ήδη επιβληθεί ανακαλούνται με διαταγή του εισηγητή, σύμφωνα με τα προβλεπόμενα στις οικείες διεθνείς συμβάσεις.

στ) Οι παραπάνω απαιτήσεις παύουν να είναι τοκοφόρες.

ζ) Το κεφάλαιο αποτελεί χωριστή ομάδα περιουσίας και διατίθεται αποκλειστικά για την ικανοποίηση των απαιτήσεων για τις οποίες συστάθηκε.

η) Πτώχευση του οφειλέτη ή τρίτου που συνέστησε το κεφάλαιο δεν έχει επίδραση στη διαδικασία της εκκαθάρισης και το κεφάλαιο δεν περιλαμβάνεται στην πτωχευτική περιουσία.

Άρθρο 242
Χρόνος επέλευσης των αποτελεσμάτων

Τα αποτελέσματα του άρθρου 241 επέρχονται από τον χρόνο της δήλωσης.

Άρθρο 243
Διαδικασία αναγγελίας απαιτήσεων

1. Ο εκκαθαριστής καλεί χωρίς καθυστέρηση τους δανειστές περιορίσιμων απαιτήσεων να αναγγείλουν την απαίτησή τους εντός έξι (6) μηνών από την τελευταία δημοσίευση σχετικής πρόσκλησης στον ιστότοπο του πρωτοδικείου του Πειραιά και σε μία καθημερινή εφημερίδα μεγάλης κυκλοφορίας. Η αναγγελία πρέπει να περιέχει τον διορισμό αντικλήτου. Ειδικά για τις αξιώσεις από θαλάσσια ρύπανση ή τις αξιώσεις του άρθρου 71, η πρόσκληση δημοσιεύεται και σε μία τοπική εφημερίδα του τόπου όπου προκλήθηκαν κυρίως οι ζημίες και τοιχοκολλάται στο τοπικό δημοτικό κατάστημα.

2. Η αναγγελία γίνεται με δικόγραφο που κατατίθεται στον γραμματέα και συντάσσεται σχετική έκθεση. Ακριβές αντίγραφο εγχειρίζεται στον εκκαθαριστή μαζί με τα έγγραφα που αποδεικνύουν την απαίτηση.

3. Η αναγγελία περιέχει τα στοιχεία του άρθρου 216 του Κώδικα Πολιτικής Δικονομίας (π.δ. 503/1985, Α' 182). Αν κατά την ημερομηνία της αναγγελίας δεν είναι με ακρίβεια γνωστό το ύψος της απαίτησης, η αναγγελία μπορεί να προσδιορίζει κατά προσέγγιση το ύψος του ποσού μέχρι το οποίο μπορεί να φθάσει. Σε κάθε περίπτωση, ο οριστικός προσδιορισμός του ποσού μπορεί να γίνει το αργότερο εντός δέκα (10) ημερών από τη σχετική ειδοποίηση του εκκαθαριστή προς τον αναγγελθέντα.

4. Εκπρόθεσμη αναγγελία είναι δυνατή, εφόσον το επιτρέψει ο εισηγητής μετά από αίτηση που δικάζεται κατά τη διαδικασία των ασφαλιστικών μέτρων και απευθύνεται προς τον εκκαθαριστή, και υπό την προϋπόθεση ότι δεν έχει ολοκληρωθεί ο έλεγχος των απαιτήσεων και το εκπρόθεσμο οφείλεται σε άγνοια της πρόσκλησης ή σε άλλη αιτία που δεν οφείλεται σε υπαιτιότητα του αιτούντα.

5. Η αναγγελία απαιτήσεων διακόπτει την παραγραφή.

Article 241
Effects

Constitution of the [limitation] fund shall generate the following effects:

a) individual prosecution steps may not be taken in regard to claims subject to limitation concerning other assets of a person by whom or on whose behalf the fund was constituted;

b) pending proceedings concerning the aforesaid claims shall be stayed;

c) no compulsory enforcement steps or interim measures may be taken in regard to the aforesaid claims;

d) interim measures already taken and the relevant security shall be paid, pursuant to a judgment by the court which ordered them, in accordance with the provisions of the applicable international conventions;

e) compulsory measures already imposed shall be revoked by order of the reporting judge, in accordance with the provisions of the applicable international conventions;

f) the aforesaid claims shall cease to accrue interest;

g) the fund shall constitute a separate pool of assets and shall be used exclusively to satisfy the claims for which it was constituted;

h) any bankruptcy of the debtor or third party who constituted the fund shall not affect the liquidation procedure, and the fund shall not be included in the bankruptcy estate.

Article 242
When effects occur

The effects referred to in Article 241 shall occur from the time the declaration [was submitted].

Article 243
Claim lodgement procedure

1. The liquidator shall, without delay, call upon the creditors of claims liable to limitation to lodge their claim within six months from the last publication of a relevant notice on the website of the Piraeus Court of First Instance and in one widely circulated daily newspaper. The lodgement must refer to the appointment of a process agent. With specific regard to claims arising from marine pollution or the claims referred to in Article 71, the notice shall also be published in a local newspaper [circulated] at the place where the damage mainly occurred and shall be posted at a local town hall.

2. Lodgement shall take the form of a procedural document filed with the registrar, and a relevant report shall be prepared. An exact copy shall be delivered to the liquidator, together with the documents proving the claim.

3. The lodgement shall contain the information required under Article 216 of the Code of Civil Procedure (Presidential Decree 503/1985, Government Gazette, Series I, Issue 182). If the amount of the claim is not precisely known on the date of the lodgment, the lodgement may approximately specify the amount which the claim may reach. In all events, the amount may be definitively determined no later than 10 days from the date the relevant notification was sent by the liquidator to the creditor lodging the claim.

4. Late lodgements may be submitted, if permitted by the reporting judge following an application tried under interim measures proceedings and addressed to the liquidator, on the condition that the examination of claims has not been completed and the lateness is due to unawareness of the notice or other cause for which the applicant is not at fault.

5. Lodgement of claims shall suspend the time-barring period.

Άρθρο 244

Έλεγχος των αναγγελθεισών απαιτήσεων

1. Ο έλεγχος των απαιτήσεων γίνεται από τον εκκαθαριστή, υπό την εποπτεία του εισηγητή και συντάσσεται έκθεση από τον γραμματέα. Ο εκκαθαριστής καλεί με οποιονδήποτε πρόσφορο τρόπο, έγγραφο ή ηλεκτρονικό, τους δανειστές που αναγγέλθηκαν και εκείνον που συνέστησε το κεφάλαιο, να παραστούν κατά τον έλεγχο των απαιτήσεων, γνωστοποιώντας συγχρόνως τα πρόσωπα των αναγγελθέντων και το ύψος των απαιτήσεών τους.

2. Ο έλεγχος των απαιτήσεων μπορεί να γίνει σε μία συνεδρίαση ή σε περισσότερες κατόπιν απόφασης του εισηγητή περί αναβολής και ορισμού νέου χρόνου συνέχισης του ελέγχου χωρίς νέα ειδοποίηση των ενδιαφερομένων μερών, τα οποία πάντως δικαιούνται να παρίστανται σε οποιαδήποτε συνεδρίαση και να προβάλλουν παρατηρήσεις για κάθε άλλη υπό έλεγχο απαίτηση.

3. Ο γραμματέας και ο εκκαθαριστής χορηγούν αντίγραφα της αναγγελίας και των αποδεικτικών εγγράφων, αντιστοίχως, σε οποιονδήποτε έχει έννομο συμφέρον, με δαπάνη του τελευταίου.

4. Κατά τον έλεγχο των απαιτήσεων ο εκκαθαριστής δικαιούται αιτιολογημένα να ζητήσει πρόσθετα αποδεικτικά έγγραφα. Σε περίπτωση μη συμμόρφωσης του δανειστή, ο εκκαθαριστής έχει το δικαίωμα να απορρίψει την απαίτηση ή μέρος αυτής.

5. Μετά το τέλος του ελέγχου ο εκκαθαριστής καταθέτει στον γραμματέα πίνακα των απαιτήσεων που έγιναν προσωρινά δεκτές, καθώς και εκείνων που απορρίφθηκαν, στον οποίο θεωρούνται ενσωματωμένες οι εκθέσεις της παρ. 1, και ειδοποιεί χωρίς καθυστέρηση με οποιοδήποτε πρόσφορο τρόπο, έγγραφο ή ηλεκτρονικό, τους δανειστές που αναγγέλθηκαν και εκείνον που συνέστησε το κεφάλαιο.

Άρθρο 245

Άσκηση ανακοπών

1. Μέσα σε προθεσμία τριάντα (30) ημερών από την κατάθεση του προσωρινού πίνακα, κάθε δανειστής που αναγγέλθηκε και εκείνος που συνέστησε το κεφάλαιο μπορούν να ασκήσουν ανακοπή κατά της απόφασης του εκκαθαριστή για την αποδοχή ή μη της απαίτησης του, καθώς και οποιασδήποτε άλλης απαίτησης τρίτου εφόσον έχει έννομο συμφέρον.

2. Η ανακοπή ασκείται με δικόγραφο που απευθύνεται κατά του εκκαθαριστή. Σε περίπτωση που η ανακοπή στρέφεται εναντίον της αποδοχής απαίτησης άλλου δανειστή, το δικόγραφο απευθύνεται και κατά του τρίτου.

3. Η ανακοπή ασκείται ενώπιον του πολυμελούς πρωτοδικείου, εφαρμοζομένων των διατάξεων της εκούσιας δικαιοδοσίας, πλην των άρθρων 763, 765 και 773 έως 775 του Κώδικα Πολιτικής Δικονομίας. Η άσκηση τριτανακοπής δεν επιτρέπεται.

4. Κατά την κατάθεση των ανακοπών δεν ορίζεται δικάσιμος. Ο εκκαθαριστής υποχρεούται μετά τη λήξη της προθεσμίας της παρ. 1 να επισπεύσει τη συζήτηση των ανακοπών κατά την ίδια υποχρεωτικά δικάσιμο, καλώντας σε αυτή τους διαδίκους τριάντα (30) ημέρες νωρίτερα.

5. Παρέμβαση ασκείται με ποινή απαραδέκτου το αργότερο δέκα (10) ημέρες πριν από την ημερομηνία της συζήτησης των ανακοπών και προσδιορίζεται υποχρεωτικά για συζήτηση κατά την ίδια δικάσιμο.

6. Το δικαστήριο έχει δικαίωμα να διατάξει τη συνεκδίκαση ή τον χωρισμό των ανακοπών.

Article 244
Examination of lodged claims

1. Claims shall be examined by the liquidator, under the oversight of the reporting judge, and the registrar shall prepare a report. The liquidator shall use any expedient means, whether written or electronic, to call upon the creditors who lodged claims and the person who constituted the fund to attend the examination of the claims, simultaneously identifying the creditors who lodged claims and the level of their claims.

2. The claims may be examined during a single session or several sessions, following a decision by the reporting judge on adjournment and designation of a new time to resume the examination, with no subsequent notice being sent to the stakeholders, who shall nevertheless be entitled to attend any session and submit observations concerning any other claim being examined.

3. The registrar and the liquidator shall issue copies of the lodgement and documentary evidence, respectively, to any person with a legitimate interest, and the cost shall be borne by the latter.

4. When examining the claims, the liquidator shall be entitled to request additional documentary evidence, and shall provide reasons for this request. If the creditor fails to comply, the liquidator shall have the right to deny the claim or part of the claim.

5. After the examination has been completed, the liquidator shall submit a table of provisionally accepted claims and denied claims to the registrar, with the reports referred to in paragraph 1 incorporated in said table, and shall, without delay, use any expedient means, whether written or electronic, to notify the creditors who lodged claims and the person who constituted the fund.

Article 245
Filing of oppositions

1. Within a deadline of 30 days from the date the provisional table is filed, any creditor who lodged a claim and the person who constituted the fund may file an opposition against the liquidator's decision on accepting or denying their claim, as well as any other claim of a third party, provided said third party has a legitimate interest.

2. Oppositions are filed by means of a procedural document brought against the liquidator. Where the opposition is brought against the acceptance of a different creditor's claim, the procedural document shall also be brought against that [creditor].

3. Oppositions are filed with the multi-member court of first instance, and the provisions on non-contentious proceedings shall apply, save Articles 763, 765, 773 to 775 of the Code of Civil Procedure. Third-party proceedings may not be brought.

4. When oppositions are filed, no hearing date shall be set. After the deadline laid down in paragraph 1 has elapsed, the liquidator shall be obligated to initiate the hearing of the oppositions, which must necessarily be heard on the same hearing date, and to summon the parties in the proceedings to that hearing 30 days beforehand.

5. On penalty of inadmissibility, interventions must be filed no later than 10 days prior to the hearing date for the oppositions, and must necessarily be set for a hearing on the same hearing date.

6. The court shall have the right to order joinder or splitting of oppositions.

Άρθρο 246

Οριστικός πίνακας

1. Εάν δεν ασκηθεί εμπρόθεσμα ανακοπή κατά του προσωρινού πίνακα, αυτός καθίσταται οριστικός.

2. Μετά το αμετάκλητο των αποφάσεων επί των ανακοπών καταρτίζεται από τον εκκαθαριστή ο οριστικός πίνακας, που κατατίθεται στον γραμματέα και γνωστοποιείται στον εισηγητή. Κατά του πίνακα επιτρέπεται μόνο αίτηση διόρθωσης για λογιστικά λάθη που απευθύνεται κατά του εκκαθαριστή και ασκείται ενώπιον του εισηγητή κατά τη διαδικασία των ασφαλιστικών μέτρων και μέσα σε αποσβεστική προθεσμία δεκαπέντε (15) ημερών από την κατάθεση του πίνακα στον γραμματέα.

3. Όταν παρέλθει άπρακτη η προθεσμία του δεύτερου εδαφίου της παρ. 2 του άρθρου 245, αρχίζει η καταβολή σε κάθε δανειστή του ποσού για το οποίο κατατάχθηκε αυτός στον πίνακα διανομής.

4. Με την καταβολή σε κάθε δανειστή του ποσού που του ανήκει σύμφωνα με τον οριστικό πίνακα διανομής και των τυχόν συμπληρωματικών πινάκων, επέρχεται απόσβεση της αντίστοιχης αξίωσης.

5. Προσωρινές καταβολές στους δανειστές επιτρέπονται ακόμη και πριν κριθεί ο πίνακας οριστικός, εφόσον εγκρίνει τούτο ο εισηγητής, μετά από πρόταση του εκκαθαριστή. Ο εισηγητής δικαιούται να διατάξει την επανεισαγωγή προσωρινών καταβολών στο συσταθέν κεφάλαιο σε κάθε περίπτωση, εφαρμοζόμενης αναλογικά της παρ. 6.

6. Με αίτηση του εκκαθαριστή που εκδικάζεται κατά τη διαδικασία των ασφαλιστικών μέτρων ο εισηγητής δικαιούται να διατάξει επίσης τον προσωρινό αποχωρισμό από το κεφάλαιο ποσού για την κάλυψη των εξόδων της διαδικασίας και αμοιβής του εκκαθαριστή, σε περίπτωση που το ποσό της περ. (δ) της παρ. 2 του άρθρου 236 αποδειχθεί ανεπαρκές.

7. Με αίτηση του εκκαθαριστή που εκδικάζεται κατά τη διαδικασία των ασφαλιστικών μέτρων ο εισηγητής μπορεί να διατάξει την ολική ή μερική επανεισαγωγή στο κεφάλαιο κάθε ποσού που αποχωρίσθηκε από αυτό για την εφαρμογή της παρ. 6 και δεν έχει ήδη διατεθεί.

Άρθρο 247

Διανομή κεφαλαίου

1. Οι καταβολές προς τους δανειστές και τον εκκαθαριστή γίνονται με ένταλμα στο πιστωτικό ίδρυμα όπου τηρούνται οι ειδικοί λογαριασμοί της παρ. 1 των άρθρου 237 και της περ. (δ) της παρ. 2 του άρθρου 236 αντίστοιχα ή στο πιστωτικό ίδρυμα ή στον αλληλασφαλιστικό οργανισμό που εξέδωσε την εγγυητική επιστολή, σύμφωνα με την παρ. 1 του άρθρου 23**7.** Το ένταλμα εκδίδεται από τον εκκαθαριστή και θεωρείται από τον εισηγητή.

2. Με το πρώτο ένταλμα ο εκκαθαριστής οφείλει να παραδώσει στο ανωτέρω πιστωτικό ίδρυμα ή αλληλασφαλιστικό οργανισμό βεβαίωση του γραμματέα, θεωρημένη από τον προϊστάμενο του πρωτοδικείου, από την οποία να προκύπτει η ταυτότητα του εκκαθαριστή και του εισηγητή του συγκεκριμένου κεφαλαίου κατά τον χρόνο έκδοσης του εντάλματος. Η βεβαίωση παραμένει στο πιστωτικό ίδρυμα ή στον αλληλοασφαλιστικό οργανισμό και ισχύει μέχρι να παραδοθεί σε αυτούς από τον εκκαθαριστή νεότερη με διαφορετικό περιεχόμενο.

Article 246

Final table

1. If no opposition against the provisional table is filed in good time, the table shall become final.

2. Once the judgments handed down on the oppositions have become irrevocable, the liquidator shall compile the final table, which shall be filed with the registrar and notified to the reporting judge. Only applications for correction of mathematical errors may be filed against the table and shall be brought against the liquidator and filed with the reporting judge under interim measures proceedings and within a fixed deadline of 15 days from the date the table is filed with the registrar.

3. Once the deadline laid down in the second subparagraph of Article 245(2) has lapsed without the relevant steps having been taken, the amount for which the creditors were ranked in the distribution table shall begin to be paid to each creditor.

4. Once each creditor has been paid the amount due to them in accordance with the final distribution table and any supplementary tables, the corresponding claim shall be extinguished.

5. Subject to approval by the reporting judge, on a proposal from the liquidator, temporary payments to creditors shall be permitted even before the table is finalised. In all events, the reporting judge shall be entitled to order that provisional payments be paid back into the fund constituted, and paragraph 6 shall apply *mutatis mutandis*.

6. Where the amount referred to in Article 236(2)(d) proves insufficient and following an application filed by the liquidator and tried under interim measures proceedings, the reporting judge shall also be entitled to order that an amount from the fund be temporarily earmarked to cover the costs of the procedure and the liquidator's fee.

7. Following an application filed by the liquidator and tried under interim measures proceedings, the reporting judge may order that any amount from the fund earmarked for the purposes of application of paragraph 6 and not already used be paid back into the fund, whether in whole or in part.

Article 247

Distribution of the fund

1. Payments to the creditors and the liquidator shall be effected by means of a payment order sent to the credit institution where the special accounts referred to in Articles 237(1) and 236(2)(d) are held, respectively, or to the credit institution or mutual insurer which issued the letter of guarantee, in accordance with Article 237(1). The payment order shall be issued by the liquidator and certified by the reporting judge.

2. Together with the first payment order, the liquidator must provide the aforesaid credit institution or mutual insurer with a certificate, issued by the registrar and certified by the head of the court of first instance, establishing the identity of the liquidator and the reporting judge for the fund in question at the time the payment order is issued. The certificate shall remain in the possession of the credit institution or mutual insurer and in effect until the liquidator issues the foregoing parties a more recent certificate with different contents.

Άρθρο 248

Πέρας διαδικασίας περιορισμού

1. Η διαδικασία περιορισμού θεωρείται περατωθείσα με τη σύνταξη του πρακτικού της παρ. 3.

2. Ο εκκαθαριστής λογοδοτεί ενώπιον του εισηγητή, στο πρόσωπο που συνέστησε το κεφάλαιο και στους δανειστές, καλώντας τους με οποιοδήποτε πρόσφορο τρόπο, έγγραφο ή ηλεκτρονικό, μέσα σε προθεσμία είκοσι (20) ημερών από το τέλος της εκκαθάρισης.

3. Με τη λογοδοσία του εκκαθαριστή ο εισηγητής κηρύσσει την εκκαθάριση οριστικά τελειωμένη, καθορίζει το τυχόν υπόλοιπο της αμοιβής του εκκαθαριστή και, αφού μνημονευθούν όλα τα σχετικά στο οικείο πρακτικό, διατάσσει την επιστροφή του υπολοίπου μη διανεμηθέντος κεφαλαίου σε αυτόν που το συνέστησε. Σε περίπτωση σύστασης του κεφαλαίου με εγγυητική επιστολή, ο εισηγητής μεριμνά για την επιστροφή του πρωτοτύπου αυτής.

ΚΕΦΑΛΑΙΟ Γ'

ΔΙΑΔΙΚΑΣΙΑ ΕΚΔΙΚΑΣΗΣ ΔΙΕΘΝΩΝ ΔΙΑΦΟΡΩΝ ΑΠΟ ΡΥΠΑΝΣΗ ΠΕΤΡΕΛΑΙΟΥ

Άρθρο 249

Ικανότητα παράστασης και εκπροσώπησης του Διεθνούς Κεφαλαίου

1. Το Διεθνές Κεφάλαιο Αποζημίωσης Ζημιών Ρύπανσης από Πετρέλαιο του 1992 (Διεθνές Κεφάλαιο) αναγνωρίζεται στην Ελλάδα ως νομικό πρόσωπο, ικανό να αναλαμβάνει δικαιώματα και υποχρεώσεις και να παρίσταται στο δικαστήριο ως διάδικος με δικό του όνομα, για όλες τις έννομες σχέσεις και τις δίκες που προβλέπονται από τη Διεθνή Σύμβαση για την ίδρυση διεθνούς κεφαλαίου αποζημίωσης ζημιών ρύπανσης από πετρέλαιο, όπως κυρώθηκε με το άρθρο μόνο του π.δ. 270/1995 (Α' 151) και εκάστοτε ισχύει στην Ελλάδα (Σύμβαση Διεθνούς Κεφαλαίου).

2. Το Διεθνές Κεφάλαιο εκπροσωπείται από τον Διευθυντή του άρθρου 29 της Σύμβασης Διεθνούς Κεφαλαίου.

3. Η παρ. 1 εφαρμόζεται και για το Διεθνές Κεφάλαιο για Επικίνδυνες και Επιβλαβείς Ουσίες που προβλέπεται στο τρίτο Κεφάλαιο της Διεθνούς Σύμβασης ευθύνης για επικίνδυνες και επιβλαβείς ουσίες.

Άρθρο 250

Αρμοδιότητα

1. Αρμόδιο δικαστήριο να δικάσει τις διαφορές που αναφέρονται στο άρθρο 7 της Σύμβασης Διεθνούς Κεφαλαίου είναι το πολυμελές πρωτοδικείο στην περιφέρεια του οποίου έλαβε χώρα το συμβάν που προκάλεσε τη ρύπανση κατά τη διαδικασία των περιουσιακών διαφορών. Συντρέχουσα κατά τόπον αρμοδιότητα έχει το πολυμελές πρωτοδικείο Πειραιά.

2. Αρμόδιο να δικάσει τις διαφορές που αναφέρονται στα άρθρα 10 έως 13 της Σύμβασης Διεθνούς Κεφαλαίου είναι, σύμφωνα με τις διατάξεις του Κώδικα Πολιτικής Δικονομίας περί αρμοδιότητας των δικαστηρίων, το πολυμελές ή μονομελές πρωτοδικείο Πειραιά, δικάζον κατά τη διαδικασία των περιουσιακών διαφορών, ανεξάρτητα από το εάν ο εναγόμενος έχει την κατοικία ή την έδρα του στην Ελλάδα.

Article 248

Completion of limitation procedure

1. The limitation procedure shall be deemed completed once the report referred to in paragraph 3 has been prepared.

2. The liquidator shall render account to the reporting judge, the person who constituted the fund and the creditors, using any expedient means, whether written or electronic, to call upon them within a deadline of 20 days from the end of the liquidation.

3. Once the liquidator has rendered account, the reporting judge shall declare the liquidation definitively completed, specify any balance of the liquidator's fee and, having recorded all relevant information in a report, order that the balance of any non-distributed fund amounts be returned to the person who constituted the fund. Where the fund was constituted by means of a letter of guarantee, the reporting judge shall return the original letter.

CHAPTER III

PROCEDURE FOR THE ADJUDICATION OF INTERNATIONAL DISPUTES ARISING IN CONNECTION WITH OIL POLLUTION

Article 249

Legal standing and representation of the International Fund

1. The 1992 International Oil Pollution Compensation Fund (International Fund) is recognised in Greece as a legal person able to assume rights and obligations and appear in court as a party in the proceedings in its own name in regard to all legal relationships and proceedings provided for in the International Convention on the Establishment of an International Fund for Compensation for Oil Pollution Damage, ratified by the sole Article of Presidential Decree 270/1995 (Government Gazette, Series I, Issue 151) and in force in Greece from time to time (International Fund Convention).

2. The International Fund shall be represented by the Director referred to in Article 29 of the International Fund Convention.

3. Paragraph 1 shall also apply to the International Hazardous and Noxious Substances Fund provided for in Chapter III of the International Convention on Liability for Damage in Connection with the Carriage of Hazardous and Noxious Substances.

Article 250

Competence

1. The multi-member court of first instance in whose district the incident which caused the pollution occurred shall be competent to try the disputes referred to in Article 7 of the International Fund Convention, trying the matter under the procedure on property disputes. The Piraeus Multi-Member Court of First Instance shall have concurrent jurisdiction *ratione loci*.

2. In accordance with the provisions of the Code of Civil Procedure on the jurisdiction of courts, the Piraeus Multi-Member or Single-Member Court of First Instance shall be competent to try the disputes referred to in Articles 10 to 13 of the International Fund Convention, trying the matter under the procedure on property disputes, irrespective of whether or not the defendant has its place of domicile or registered offices in Greece.

Άρθρο 251

Αγωγή κατά του Διεθνούς Κεφαλαίου

1. Εάν έχει συσταθεί κεφάλαιο περιορισμού της ευθύνης για ζημίες από ρύπανση κατά το άρθρο 237, αγωγή κατά του Διεθνούς Κεφαλαίου σύμφωνα με το άρθρο 7 της Σύμβασης Διεθνούς Κεφαλαίου απορρίπτεται ως απαράδεκτη εάν δεν έχει υποβληθεί σχετική αναγγελία στον εκκαθαριστή σύμφωνα με το άρθρο 243.

2. Εάν ασκηθεί αναγγελία στον εκκαθαριστή, το δικαστήριο που επιλαμβάνεται της αγωγής κατά του Κεφαλαίου, σύμφωνα με το άρθρο 7 της Σύμβασης Διεθνούς Κεφαλαίου, αναβάλλει την έκδοση οριστικής απόφασης μέχρι τη σύνταξη του οριστικού πίνακα διανομής του άρθρου 246.

Article 251

Actions against the International Fund

1. If a limitation fund concerning liability for pollution damage has been constituted in accordance with Article 237, any action against the International Fund in accordance with Article 7 of the International Fund Convention shall be dismissed as inadmissible if a relevant claim has not been lodged with the liquidator in accordance with Article 243.

2. If a claim is lodged with the liquidator, the court seised of the action brought against the Fund, in accordance with Article 7 of the International Fund Convention, shall stay the handing down of a final judgment until the final distribution table referred to in Article 246 has been prepared.

ΜΕΡΟΣ ΔΕΚΑΤΟ
ΘΑΛΑΣΣΙΑ ΑΣΦΑΛΙΣΗ

ΚΕΦΑΛΑΙΟ Α'
ΕΦΑΡΜΟΖΟΜΕΝΕΣ ΔΙΑΤΑΞΕΙΣ ΚΑΙ ΑΝΤΙΚΕΙΜΕΝΟ ΤΗΣ ΘΑΛΑΣΣΙΑΣ ΑΣΦΑΛΙΣΗΣ

Άρθρο 252
Εφαρμοζόμενες διατάξεις

__1.__ Στη θαλάσσια ασφάλιση εφαρμόζεται το παρόν Μέρος και συμπληρωματικώς ο ν. 2496/1997 (Α' 87), στο μέτρο που οι διατάξεις του δεν είναι ασυμβίβαστες με την ασφάλιση αυτή και δεν τροποποιούνται από το παρόν.

__2.__ Με την επιφύλαξη του άρθρου 253, της παρ. 3 του άρθρου 265, των παρ. 1 και 2 του άρθρου 269 και του άρθρου 270, το παρόν Μέρος ισχύει, εφόσον δεν υπάρχει αντίθετη συμφωνία των συμβαλλομένων.

Άρθρο 253
Αντικείμενο της θαλάσσιας ασφάλισης

__1.__ Στη θαλάσσια ασφάλιση ο λήπτης της ασφάλισης μπορεί να ασφαλίσει κάθε περιουσία για τη διατήρηση της οποίας έχει έννομο συμφέρον και η οποία εκτίθεται σε κίνδυνο στη θάλασσα (θαλάσσιος κίνδυνος).

__2.__ Στη θαλάσσια ασφάλιση το ασφάλισμα συνίσταται στην αποκατάσταση της ζημίας της περιουσίας που συμφωνήθηκε ότι θα καλύπτεται (ασφαλισμένη περιουσία), όταν επέλθει η ασφαλιστική περίπτωση (ασφαλιστική ζημία).

__3.__ Η ζημία της ασφαλισμένης περιουσίας μπορεί να συνίσταται στη βλάβη ή στην απώλεια αγαθών, όπως ιδίως του πλοίου, του φορτίου και του ναύλου, απαιτήσεων και κερδών συμπεριλαμβανομένου του ελπιζόμενου κέρδους, καθώς και στις δαπάνες απόκρουσης και ικανοποίησης απαιτήσεων τρίτων.

Άρθρο 254
Περιεχόμενο του ασφαλιστηρίου

Το ασφαλιστήριο πρέπει να αναγράφει:

(α) Τον τόπο και χρόνο έκδοσής του,

(β) τα στοιχεία των συμβαλλομένων, του ασφαλισμένου και του δικαιούχου του ασφαλίσματος, αν αυτοί είναι διαφορετικά πρόσωπα,

(γ) τη διάρκεια της ασφαλιστικής κάλυψης,

(δ) την περιουσία που εκτίθεται σε θαλάσσιους κίνδυνους ή σχετίζεται με την επέλευσή τους και τη χρηματική αξία της,

(ε) τους καλυπτόμενους θαλάσσιους κινδύνους,

(στ) το ανώτατο όριο ευθύνης του ασφαλιστή (ασφαλιστικό ποσό),

(ζ) τις τυχόν εξαιρέσεις κάλυψης,

(η) το ασφάλιστρο,

(ι) το όνομα, την εθνικότητα, τον λιμένα νηολόγησης, και τον αριθμό νηολογίου του πλοίου, καθώς και τον αριθμό του Διεθνούς Ναυτιλιακού Οργανισμού που φέρει το πλοίο.

PART TEN
MARINE INSURANCE

CHAPTER I
APPLICABLE PROVISIONS AND SCOPE OF MARINE INSURANCE

Article 252
Applicable provisions

1. This Part and, on a supplementary basis, Law 2496/1997 (Government Gazette, Series I, Issue 87) shall apply to marine insurance, insofar as its provisions are not incompatible with such insurance and are not amended by this Code.

2. Without prejudice to Articles 253, 265(3), 269(1) and (2) and 270, this Part shall apply provided the contracting parties have not agreed otherwise.

Article 253
Scope of marine insurance

1. In marine insurance, the policyholder may insure any property in whose preservation they have a legitimate interest and which is exposed to risks at sea (marine risks).

2. In marine insurance, the indemnity concerns indemnification of the property loss agreed to be covered (insured property) when the contingency occurs (claim).

3. Loss of insured property may concern damage to or loss of goods, such as, in particular, the ship, the cargo and the freight, receivables and profits, including anticipated profits, as well as the expenditure for rebutting and satisfying third-party claims.

Article 254
Content of insurance policies

The insurance policy must indicate:

(a) the place and time at which it was issued;

(b) the particulars of the contracting parties, the assured and the insurance beneficiary, where they are different persons;

(c) the duration of insurance coverage;

(d) the property exposed to marine risks or connected with their occurrence, as well as its monetary value;

(e) the marine risks covered;

(f) the maximum limit of liability of the insurer (sum insured);

(g) any exclusions from coverage;

(h) the premium;

(i) the name, nationality, port of registry and ship registry number, as well as the ship's IMO number.

ΚΕΦΑΛΑΙΟ Β'
ΔΙΑΡΚΕΙΑ ΤΗΣ ΘΑΛΑΣΣΙΑΣ ΑΣΦΑΛΙΣΗΣ

Άρθρο 255
Θαλάσσια ασφάλιση πλοίου ορισμένου χρόνου

1. Στη θαλάσσια ασφάλιση πλοίου ορισμένου χρόνου η ασφαλιστική κάλυψη αρχίζει από την ημερομηνία του ασφαλιστηρίου. Οι κίνδυνοι της πρώτης και της τελευταίας ημέρας παραμένουν σε βάρος του ασφαλιστή. Η ημέρα υπολογίζεται από μεσονύκτιο σε μεσονύκτιο στον τόπο έκδοσης του ασφαλιστηρίου.
2. Εάν ο χρόνος της ασφάλισης λήξει κατά τη διάρκεια του πλου, η ασφαλιστική κάλυψη παρατείνεται και λήγει την επομένη της ημέρας κατά την οποία το πλοίο αγκυροβόλησε στον πρώτο λιμένα, εφόσον ο λήπτης της ασφάλισης ζήτησε εγγράφως από τον ασφαλιστή την παράταση της κάλυψης πριν από τη λήξη του χρόνου ασφάλισης. Στην περίπτωση αυτή, ο ασφαλιστής δικαιούται πρόσθετο ανάλογο ασφάλιστρο.

Άρθρο 256
Θαλάσσια ασφάλιση πλοίου κατά ταξίδι

1. Στη θαλάσσια ασφάλιση πλοίου κατά ταξίδι η ασφαλιστική κάλυψη αρχίζει από την έναρξη του συμφωνημένου στο ασφαλιστήριο ταξιδιού και λήγει με το πέρας του ταξιδιού.
2. Εάν ακολουθήσει νέα ασφάλιση κατά ταξίδι, η ασφαλιστική κάλυψη για το προηγούμενο λήγει με την έναρξη της ασφάλισης για το νέο ταξίδι.

Άρθρο 257
Θαλάσσια ασφάλιση φορτίου

Στη θαλάσσια ασφάλιση φορτίου η ασφαλιστική κάλυψη αρχίζει με την εκ μέρους του θαλάσσιου μεταφορέα παραλαβή αυτού με σκοπό τη μεταφορά και λήγει τη στιγμή της προσήκουσας παράδοσης του φορτίου στον δικαιούχο, σε κάθε περίπτωση δε τριάντα (30) ημέρες από την εκφόρτωση του φορτίου στον λιμένα προορισμού.

Άρθρο 258
Διαδοχή στην ασφαλιστική σχέση

1. Η θαλάσσια ασφάλιση λήγει, αν τον λήπτη της ασφάλισης ή τον ασφαλισμένο διαδεχθεί άλλος στην ασφαλιστική σχέση.
2. Η παρ. 1 ισχύει και στην ασφάλιση φορτίου, εφόσον δεν έχει εκδοθεί ασφαλιστήριο σε διαταγή ή στον κομιστή.

ΚΕΦΑΛΑΙΟ Γ'
ΑΣΦΑΛΙΣΤΙΚΟΣ ΚΙΝΔΥΝΟΣ - ΛΕΙΤΟΥΡΓΙΑ ΤΗΣ ΣΥΜΒΑΣΗΣ ΘΑΛΑΣΣΙΑΣ ΑΣΦΑΛΙΣΗΣ

Άρθρο 259
Καθολικότητα των ασφαλισμένων κινδύνων

1. Με την επιφύλαξη των περ. (ε) και (ζ) του άρθρου 254 και του άρθρου 260, στη θαλάσσια ασφάλιση ο ασφαλιστής ευθύνεται για τις ζημίες που προκαλούνται από οποιοδήποτε γεγονός επέρχεται κατά τη διάρκεια του πλου.

CHAPTER II
DURATION OF MARINE INSURANCE

Article 255
Fixed-term marine insurance of ships

1. In fixed-term marine insurance of ships, insurance coverage begins on the date of the insurance policy. Risks occurring on the first and on the final day shall be borne by the insurer. A day is considered to last from midnight to midnight at the place where the insurance policy was issued.

2. If the insurance term expires during a voyage, insurance coverage shall be extended and expire on the day following the date on which the ship drops anchor at the first port, provided the policyholder submitted a coverage extension request to the insurer in writing before the insurance term expired. In this case, the insurer shall be entitled to an additional pro rata premium.

Article 256
Voyage policy

1. In cases of a voyage policy, insurance coverage begins when the voyage agreed upon in the insurance policy commences and expires when the voyage ends.

2. If a new voyage policy is taken out, the insurance coverage concerning the previous voyage shall end when the insurance concerning the new voyage commences.

Article 257
Cargo policy

In cases of a cargo policy, insurance coverage begins when the carrier by sea takes receipt of the cargo for the purpose of carriage and expires when the cargo is duly delivered to the person entitled to the cargo and, in all events, 30 days after the cargo was discharged at the port of destination.

Article 258
Succession in insurance relationships

1. Marine insurance shall expire if the policyholder or the assured is succeeded in the insurance relationship by a different person.

2. Paragraph 1 shall also apply to cargo policies, provided an insurance policy has not been issued to order or to bearer.

CHAPTER III
INSURANCE RISK - FUNCTION OF MARINE INSURANCE CONTRACTS

Article 259
Universal nature of insured risks

1. Without prejudice to Articles 254(e) & (g) and 260, under marine insurance, the insurer is liable for losses caused by any event occurring during the voyage.

2. Στην ασφάλιση πλοίου, σε περίπτωση σύγκρουσης ο ασφαλιστής ευθύνεται επίσης για τις ζημίες που το πλοίο προκάλεσε σε τρίτους, με εξαίρεση ζημίες λόγω θανάτου, σωματικής βλάβης ή ασθένειας.
3. Ο ασφαλιστής δεν ευθύνεται για τα έξοδα ναυσιπλοΐας, ελλιμενισμού, ναυλοχίας, καθαρισμού ούτε για τα κάθε είδους τέλη και δικαιώματα που αφορούν στο πλοίο ή το φορτίο.

Άρθρο 260
Εξαίρεση των πολεμικών κινδύνων από την κάλυψη

1. Εκτός αν ρητώς συμφωνηθεί διαφορετικά στο ασφαλιστήριο, δεν παρέχεται ασφαλιστική κάλυψη στο μέτρο που η πραγματοποίηση του ασφαλιστικού κινδύνου προέρχεται από πολεμικούς κινδύνους.
2. Πολεμικοί κίνδυνοι είναι πολεμικά γεγονότα ή πολεμικές ενέργειες, καθώς και γεγονότα που επήλθαν μετά τη λήξη του πολέμου αλλά εξαιτίας αυτού. Με τους πολεμικούς κινδύνους εξομοιώνονται οι κίνδυνοι από εμφύλιο πόλεμο, στάση ή λαϊκές ταραχές.
3. Σε περίπτωση αμφιβολίας, η ζημία θεωρείται ότι επήλθε από θαλάσσιο κίνδυνο.

Άρθρο 261
Ασφάλιστρο

1. Το ασφάλιστρο οφείλεται εφόσον άρχισε η ασφαλιστική κάλυψη. Σε περίπτωση ματαίωσης του ασφαλιστικού κινδύνου η σύμβαση λύεται αυτοδικαίως.
2. Σε περίπτωση λύσης της ασφαλιστικής σύμβασης ο ασφαλιστής δικαιούται το δεδουλευμένο ασφάλιστρο. ΑV ο ασφαλιστικός κίνδυνος επήλθε πριν από τη λύση της σύμβασης, το ασφάλιστρο οφείλεται πλήρες, εφόσον άρχισε η ασφαλιστική κάλυψη.

Άρθρο 262
Ευθύνη του ασφαλιστή φορτίου σε περίπτωση μεταφόρτωσης

Εάν εξαιτίας ανικανότητας του πλοίου να συνεχίσει τον πλου κατέστη αναγκαία η μεταφόρτωση του ασφαλισμένου φορτίου, ο ασφαλιστής ευθύνεται και για τα έξοδα μεταφόρτωσης, εναπόθεσης και φύλαξης, τον πρόσθετο ναύλο και τα τυχόν έξοδα διάσωσης, όχι όμως πέραν του ασφαλιστικού ποσού.

Άρθρο 263
Επίταση του κινδύνου

1. Ο λήπτης της ασφάλισης οφείλει να δηλώσει χωρίς υπαίτια βραδύτητα στον ασφαλιστή κάθε στοιχείο ή περιστατικό, το οποίο μπορεί να επιφέρει σημαντική επίταση του κινδύνου, σε βαθμό, που αν ο ασφαλιστής το γνώριζε, δεν θα είχε συνάψει την ασφάλιση ή δεν θα την είχε συνάψει με τους ίδιους όρους. Όταν ο ασφαλιστής λάβει γνώση της επίτασης του κινδύνου, εφαρμόζεται η παρ. 2 του άρθρου 4 του ν. 2496/1997 (Α' 87).
2. Αν από πράξη του λήπτη της ασφάλισης ή του ασφαλισμένου προκληθεί αλλαγή ταξιδιού ή αλλαγή πλοίου, ο ασφαλιστής παύει να ευθύνεται από τη στιγμή της αλλαγής, διατηρώντας την αξίωσή του στο ασφάλιστρο.

2. In the event of collision of an insured ship, the insurer is also liable for any losses the ship caused to third parties, excluding losses due to death, personal injury or sickness.
3. The insurer is not liable for the costs of navigation, entering port, lying in port and cleaning, or any type of fees and charges concerning the ship or the cargo.

Article 260

Exclusion of war risks from coverage

1. Unless expressly agreed upon otherwise in the insurance policy, insurance coverage shall not be provided insofar as the insured risk materialises due to war risks.
2. War risks [means] wartime events or acts of war, as well as events that occurred after the war has ended but due to the war. Risks arising from civil war, riot or civil unrest shall be treated as war risks.
3. In case of doubt, the loss shall be considered to have occurred due to marine risks.

Article 261

Insurance premium

1. The insurance premium shall be owed, provided insurance coverage began. If the insured risk no longer applies, the contract shall end automatically.
2. If the insurance contract ends, the insurer shall be entitled to earned premiums. If the insured risk occurred before the contract ended, the premium shall be due in full, provided insurance coverage had begun.

Article 262

Liability of cargo insurers in case of transhipment

If the ship becomes unseaworthy, necessitating transhipment of the insured cargo, the insurer shall also be liable for the costs of transhipment, storage and guarding, excess freight and any salvage costs, but not beyond the sum insured.

Article 263

Risk intensification

1. The policyholder must, without undue delay, declare to the insurer any information or event which could significantly intensify the risk to the extent where, had the insurer been aware of such information or event, it would not have entered into the insurance contract at all or would not have entered into it under the same terms. Where the insurer is made aware of an intensification in risk, Article 4(2) of Law 2496/1997 (Government Gazette, Series I, Issue 87) shall apply.
2. If an act of the policyholder or the assured causes a change in voyage or ship, the insurer shall cease to be liable from the moment the change occurs, and the insurer shall remain entitled to claim the premium.

3. Αν από πράξη του λήπτη της ασφάλισης ή του ασφαλισμένου προκληθεί μη αναγκαία παρέκκλιση, ο ασφαλιστής δεν ευθύνεται για όσο διάστημα διαρκεί η παρέκκλιση, διατηρώντας την αξίωσή του στο ασφάλιστρο.
4. Σε περίπτωση αντικατάστασης του πλοιάρχου, ο ασφαλιστής παύει να ευθύνεται από τη στιγμή της αντικατάστασης, αν αυτή επιφέρει σημαντική επίταση του κινδύνου, διατηρώντας την αξίωσή του στο ασφάλιστρο.

Άρθρο 264
Πραγματοποίηση του κινδύνου

1. Με την πραγματοποίηση του κινδύνου, ο λήπτης της ασφάλισης οφείλει να γνωστοποιεί χωρίς υπαίτια βραδύτητα στον ασφαλιστή όλες τις αναγκαίες πληροφορίες και τα στοιχεία που σχετίζονται με τις περιστάσεις και τις συνέπειες της πραγματοποίησης του κινδύνου.
2. Ο λήπτης της ασφάλισης οφείλει να λάβει κάθε εύλογο μέτρο για την αποτροπή ή μείωση της ζημίας.
3. Η υπαίτια παράβαση από τον λήπτη της ασφάλισης των υποχρεώσεων των παρ. 1 και 2 παρέχει το δικαίωμα στον ασφαλιστή να ζητήσει την αποκατάσταση της ζημίας του.
4. Ο ασφαλιστής δεν απαλλάσσεται της υποχρέωσης προς καταβολή του ασφαλίσματος από μόνο το γεγονός ότι η απώλεια ή ζημία οφείλεται σε υπαιτιότητα του πλοιάρχου, του πληρώματος ή του πλοηγού.

Άρθρο 265
Υπολογισμός του ασφαλίσματος

1. Βάση υπολογισμού του ασφαλίσματος είναι η αξία την οποία είχε η ασφαλισμένη περιουσία κατά τον χρόνο έναρξης της ασφαλιστικής κάλυψης (αρχική ασφαλιστική αξία).
2. Στην αξία του φορτίου προστίθενται τα έξοδα φόρτωσης και εκφόρτωσης, ο ναύλος και το ασφάλιστρο.
3. Η αξία της ασφαλισμένης περιουσίας μπορεί να αποτιμηθεί με έγγραφη συμφωνία των συμβαλλομένων μερών. Η προσβολή της συμφωνίας αποτίμησης λόγω πλάνης αποκλείεται. Η αξία αποτίμησης μπορεί να υπερβαίνει την αρχική ασφαλιστική αξία μόνο αν τούτο δικαιολογείται από εύλογους επιχειρηματικούς λόγους, οι οποίοι αναφέρονται ρητά στη συμφωνία, όχι όμως σε ποσοστό άνω του είκοσι τοις εκατό (20%).

Άρθρο 266
Νομιμοποίηση στην θαλάσσια ασφάλιση φορτίου

Στη θαλάσσια ασφάλιση φορτίου η νόμιμη κατοχή του ασφαλιστηρίου και της φορτωτικής ή άλλου ισοδυνάμου εγγράφου μεταφοράς αρκεί για τη νομιμοποίηση του κατόχου προς είσπραξη του ασφαλίσματος.

ΚΕΦΑΛΑΙΟ Δ'
ΕΓΚΑΤΑΛΕΙΨΗ

Άρθρο 267
Δικαίωμα εγκατάλειψης

Ο ασφαλισμένος δικαιούται να εγκαταλείψει στον ασφαλιστή το ασφαλισθέν πλοίο, φορτίο και τον ασφαλισθέντα ναύλο και να απαιτήσει το οφειλόμενο επί ολικής απώλειας ασφάλισμα, στις περιπτώσεις και υπό τους όρους των άρθρων 268 έως 271.

3. If an act of the policyholder or the assured causes an unnecessary deviation, the insurer shall cease to be liable for the duration of the deviation, and the insurer shall remain entitled to claim the premium.
4. If the master is replaced, the insurer shall cease to be liable from the moment the replacement occurs, where it entails a significant intensification in risk, and the insurer shall remain entitled to claim the premium.

Article 264
Materialisation of risk

1. If the risk materialises, the policyholder must, without undue delay, notify the insurer of all necessary information concerning the circumstances and consequences of materialisation of the risk.
2. The policyholder must take all reasonable steps to prevent or minimise losses.
3. Culpable breach of the obligations laid down in paragraphs 1 and 2 by the policyholder shall entitle the insurer to request that its losses be made good.
4. The insurer shall not be released from its obligation to pay the indemnity due to the fact alone that the loss or damage is due to fault of the master, the crew or the pilot.

Article 265
Calculation of indemnity

1. The basis for calculating the indemnity is the value of the insured property at the time insurance coverage began (initial insurance value).
2. The loading and discharge costs, the freight and the insurance premium are added to the value of the cargo.
3. The insured property may be valued following an agreement between the contracting parties in writing. The valuation agreement may not be contested on grounds of mistake. The valuation amount may exceed the initial insurance value solely if justified on reasonable business grounds, which must be expressly set forth in the agreement, but by no more than 20%.

Article 266
Entitlement in cargo policies

In cases of a cargo policy, lawful possession of the insurance policy and the bill of lading or other equivalent transport document shall suffice to entitle the holder to collect the indemnity.

CHAPTER IV
ABANDONMENT

Article 267
Right to abandonment

The assured shall be entitled to abandon the insured ship, cargo and freight to the insurer and to claim the indemnity owed for the total loss, in the cases provided for and under the terms laid down in Articles 268 to 271.

Άρθρο 268

Περιπτώσεις εγκατάλειψης

1. Η εγκατάλειψη του πλοίου και του ναύλου επιτρέπεται εφόσον:

α) το πλοίο, συνεπεία καλυπτόμενου ασφαλιστικού κινδύνου, απωλέσθηκε ή κατέστη ανίκανο προς πλου και δεν είναι αντικειμενικώς δυνατή η επισκευή του, ή

β) τα έξοδα για την ανέλκυση, τη ρυμούλκηση, την επισκευή και την επαναφορά του βλαβέντος πλοίου σε κατάσταση, ώστε το πλοίο να ανακτήσει την κλάση, την οποία είχε πριν την επέλευση του ασφαλιστικού κινδύνου, υπερβαίνουν τα τρία τέταρτα (3/4) της ασφαλιστικής αξίας ή όταν η επισκευή δεν είναι εφικτή στον τόπο όπου επήλθε ο ασφαλιστικός κίνδυνος ούτε είναι δυνατή η μεταφορά των μέσων της επισκευής στον τόπο αυτό ή η ρυμούλκηση του πλοίου σε λιμένα όπου είναι δυνατόν να επισκευαστεί, ή

γ) από την τελευταία είδηση για το πλοίο παρήλθε χρονικό διάστημα είκοσι μίας (21) ημερών, οπότε ο κίνδυνος θεωρείται ότι επήλθε την επομένη της ημέρας, στην οποία ανάγεται η τελευταία είδηση, ή

δ) το πλοίο αλωθεί ή εμποδισθεί κατά διαταγή ξένης δύναμης, για διάστημα τουλάχιστον δώδεκα (12) μηνών, εφόσον η ασφάλιση καλύπτει τους κινδύνους πολέμου ή πειρατείας.

2. Η εγκατάλειψη του φορτίου επιτρέπεται εφόσον:

α) επιτρέπεται η εγκατάλειψη του πλοίου που μεταφέρει το φορτίο σύμφωνα με την παρ. 1 και υπό τον όρο ότι η μεταφόρτωση και επαναπροώθηση του φορτίου στον τόπο προορισμού δεν είναι εφικτή ή τα έξοδα μεταφόρτωσης και επαναπροώθησής του στον τόπο προορισμού, εφόσον επιβαρύνουν τον ασφαλισμένο, υπερβαίνουν την αξία του φορτίου στον λιμένα προορισμού ή

β) τα έξοδα αποκατάστασης της ζημίας του φορτίου, συμπεριλαμβανομένων και των εξόδων μεταφόρτωσης και επαναπροώθησής του στον τόπο προορισμού, εφόσον τα τελευταία επιβαρύνουν τον ασφαλισμένο, υπερβαίνουν την αξία του φορτίου στον λιμένα προορισμού ή

γ) το φορτίο αλωθεί ή εμποδισθεί κατά διαταγή ξένης δύναμης, για διάστημα τουλάχιστον τριών (3) μηνών, εφόσον η ασφάλιση καλύπτει τους κινδύνους πολέμου ή πειρατείας.

Άρθρο 269

Άσκηση του δικαιώματος εγκατάλειψης

1. Το δικαίωμα εγκατάλειψης ασκείται με έγγραφη δήλωση που κοινοποιείται στον ασφαλιστή. Εφόσον πρόκειται για εγκατάλειψη πλοίου, η δήλωση του πρώτου εδαφίου καταχωρίζεται στη μερίδα του πλοίου στο νηολόγιο ή στο ειδικό δημόσιο βιβλίο του άρθρου 4 με επιμέλεια του ασφαλισμένου.

2. Η προθεσμία άσκησης του δικαιώματος εγκατάλειψης σύμφωνα με την παρ. 1 είναι τέσσερις (4) μήνες και αρχίζει από την επόμενη της ημέρας κατά την οποία επήλθε ο ασφαλιστικός κίνδυνος ή συμπληρώθηκε η προθεσμία στις περ. γ' και δ' της παρ. 1 του άρθρου 268 και στην περ. γ' της παρ. 2 του άρθρου 268 ή θεμελιώνεται δικαίωμα εγκατάλειψης του πλοίου στην περ. α' της παρ. 2 του άρθρου 268.

3. Ο ασφαλιστής μπορεί να τάξει εύλογη προθεσμία στον ασφαλισμένο για να ασκήσει το δικαίωμα εγκατάλειψης. Με την άπρακτη πάροδο της ταχθείσης προθεσμίας, ο ασφαλισμένος στερείται του δικαιώματος της εγκατάλειψης.

Article 268

Cases of abandonment

1. Abandonment of the ship and freight shall be permitted if:

a) the ship, due to a risk insured against, was lost or rendered unseaworthy and its repair is objectively impossible; or

b) the costs of removing, towing, repairing and restoring the damaged ship to its class prior to occurrence of the risk insured against exceed 3/4 of the insurance value, or where the repair is not feasible at the place where the risk insured against occurred nor can the repair equipment be transported to that place or the ship be towed to a port where it can be repaired; or

c) 21 days have elapsed from the last time news concerning the ship was received, in which case the risk shall be considered to have occurred the day after the date on which the last news was received; or

d) the ship is captured or detained by order of any foreign power for a period of at least 12 months, provided the insurance covers war or piracy risks.

2. Abandonment of cargo shall be permitted if:

a) the ship carrying the cargo may be abandoned in accordance with paragraph 1 and on the condition that transhipment and re-dispatch of the cargo to its destination is not possible or the costs of transhipment and re-dispatch to the destination, where borne by the assured, exceed the value of the cargo at the port of destination; or

b) the costs of remedying the damage to the cargo, including the costs of transhipment and re-dispatch to its destination, where the latter are borne by the assured, exceed the value of the cargo at the port of destination; or

c) the cargo is captured or detained by order of any foreign power for a period of at least three months, where the insurance covers war or piracy risks.

Article 269

Exercising the right of abandonment

1. The right of abandonment shall be exercised by means of a written declaration communicated to the insurer. In the event of abandonment of a ship, the declaration referred to in the first subparagraph shall be entered by the assured in the [ship registry] account of the ship or in the special public register referred to in Article 4.

2. The deadline for exercising the right of abandonment in accordance with paragraph 1 is four months, starting on the day after the date on which the risk insured against occurred or the deadline laid down in Article 268(1)(c) and (d) and Article 268(2)(c) lapses or a right of abandonment of the ship arises on the basis of Article 268(2)(a).

3. The insurer may set a reasonable deadline for the assured to exercise the right of abandonment. Once the deadline set lapses without the relevant steps having been taken, the assured shall forfeit the right of abandonment.

Άρθρο 270
Αποτελέσματα της εγκατάλειψης

1. Η άσκηση του δικαιώματος εγκατάλειψης σύμφωνα με το άρθρο 269, συνεπάγεται τη μεταβίβαση στον ασφαλιστή των δικαιωμάτων επί του πλοίου ή του φορτίου ή του ναύλου σύμφωνα με τους όρους των παρ. 2 και 3.

2. Η μεταβίβαση σύμφωνα με την παρ. 1 επέρχεται, αν ο ασφαλιστής δεν αμφισβητήσει το δικαίωμα της εγκατάλειψης εντός εξήντα (60) ημερών από την άσκησή του με έγγραφη δήλωση, η οποία κοινοποιείται στον ασφαλισμένο και, εφόσον πρόκειται για εγκατάλειψη πλοίου, εγγράφεται υποχρεωτικά στη μερίδα του πλοίου στο νηολόγιο ή στο ειδικό βιβλίο του άρθρου 4. Η μεταβίβαση θεωρείται συντελεσθείσα από την άσκηση του δικαιώματος εγκατάλειψης σύμφωνα με το άρθρο 269.

3. Σε περίπτωση αμφισβήτησης από τον ασφαλιστή, η μεταβίβαση θεωρείται συντελεσθείσα από την άσκηση του δικαιώματος εγκατάλειψης σύμφωνα με το άρθρο 269, εφόσον το δικαίωμα εγκατάλειψης αναγνωριστεί με τελεσίδικη δικαστική απόφαση, που εκδίδεται κατά τη διαδικασία των ασφαλιστικών μέτρων και δημοσιεύεται στο νηολόγιο ή στο ειδικό βιβλίο του άρθρου 4. Στην περίπτωση αυτή ο ασφαλισμένος έχει κατά του ασφαλιστή αξίωση σύμφωνα με τις διατάξεις του Αστικού Κώδικα για τη διοίκηση αλλοτρίων.

4. Ο ασφαλισμένος υποχρεούται να παράσχει στον ασφαλιστή κάθε πληροφορία σχετικά με το εγκαταλειφθέν πλοίο ή φορτίο ή τον εγκαταλειφθέντα ναύλο και να παραδώσει στον ασφαλιστή τα αποδεικτικά έγγραφα που έχει στην κατοχή του.

5. Ο ασφαλιστής του ελπιζόμενου κέρδους δεν αποκτά δικαίωμα από την εγκατάλειψη.

Άρθρο 271
Αποποίηση κυριότητας από τον ασφαλιστή

Ο ασφαλιστής δύναται να αποποιηθεί την κτήση της κυριότητας επί του εγκαταλειφθέντος πλοίου, φορτίου ή ναύλου, με έγγραφη δήλωσή του με την οποία συγχρόνως προσφέρεται χωρίς επιφύλαξη στην καταβολή του οφειλόμενου επί ολικής απώλειας ασφαλίσματος και την οποία υποχρεούται να καταχωρίσει στη μερίδα του πλοίου στο νηολόγιο ή στο ειδικό βιβλίο του άρθρου 4.

Article 270

Effects of abandonment

1. As a result of the right of abandonment being exercised in accordance with Article 269, the insurer shall take over the interest in the ship or cargo or freight, in accordance with the provisions of paragraphs 2 and 3.
2. The transfer referred to in paragraph 1 shall occur if the insurer does not challenge the right of abandonment within 60 days of it being exercised, with said challenge taking the form of a written declaration communicated to the assured and, in cases of abandonment of a ship, necessarily entered in the [ship registry] account of the ship or in the special register referred to in Article 4. The transfer shall be considered complete once the right of abandonment has been exercised in accordance with Article 269.
3. In the event of a challenge by the insurer, the transfer shall be considered complete once the right of abandonment has been exercised in accordance with Article 269, provided the right of abandonment has been acknowledged in a *de jure* non-appealable court judgment handed down under interim measures proceedings and published in the ship registry or special register referred to in Article 4. In this case, the assured shall have a claim against the insurer in accordance with the provisions of the Civil Code on *negotiorum gestio*.
4. The assured shall be obligated to provide the insurer with all information concerning the abandoned ship, cargo or freight, and to hand over any documentary evidence in its possession to the insurer.
5. An insurer of anticipated profits shall acquire no rights from the abandonment.

Article 271

Repudiation of ownership by the insurer

The insurer may repudiate ownership of the abandoned ship, cargo or freight by means of a written declaration in which the insurer unreservedly offers to pay the indemnity owed for total loss and which the insurer must enter in the [ship registry] account of the ship or in the special register referred to in Article 4.

ΜΕΡΟΣ ΕΝΔΕΚΑΤΟ
ΣΥΝΤΗΡΗΤΙΚΗ ΚΑΙ ΑΝΑΓΚΑΣΤΙΚΗ ΚΑΤΑΣΧΕΣΗ

Άρθρο 272
Εφαρμοζόμενες διατάξεις στη συντηρητική κατάσχεση

Για τη συντηρητική κατάσχεση πλοίου εφαρμόζεται, ανάλογα με τη συντρέχουσα περίσταση, η Διεθνής Σύμβαση των Βρυξελλών του 1952 «Περί ενοποιήσεως κανόνων τινών επί συντηρητικής κατασχέσεως θαλασσοπλοούντων πλοίων» που κυρώθηκε με το ν.δ. 4570/1966 (Α' 224), καθώς και ο Κώδικας Πολιτικής Δικονομίας.

Άρθρο 273
Κακόπιστη ακινητοποίηση πλοίου

1. Όποιος, ενεργώντας με κακή πίστη, προκάλεσε με αίτησή του ακινητοποίηση ή απαγόρευση απόπλου πλοίου, μετά από έκδοση δικαστικής προσωρινής διαταγής, η ισχύς της οποίας έπαυσε μεταγενέστερα με δικαστική απόφαση, είναι υπόχρεος σε αποζημίωση.
2. Η αποζημίωση περιλαμβάνει μόνο τις δαπάνες στις οποίες υποβλήθηκε το πλοίο προς τον σκοπό της άρσης του εξασφαλιστικού μέτρου, καθώς και τον ναύλο που θα αποκόμιζε κατά τη συνήθη πορεία των πραγμάτων στην περίοδο ακινητοποίησης.
3. Τα ελληνικά δικαστήρια έχουν συντρέχουσα διεθνή δικαιοδοσία επί διαφορών αποζημίωσης που ανακύπτουν λόγω ακινητοποίησης ή απαγόρευσης απόπλου πλοίου που φέρει ελληνική σημαία, κατόπιν εξασφαλιστικού μέτρου που επιβλήθηκε στην ημεδαπή ή την αλλοδαπή. Η δικαιοδοσία αυτή δεν μπορεί να αποκλειστεί με συμφωνία των μερών.

Άρθρο 274
Εφαρμοζόμενες διατάξεις στην αναγκαστική κατάσχεση

1. Οι διατάξεις του Κώδικα Πολιτικής Δικονομίας για την κατάσχεση ακινήτου εφαρμόζονται και για την κατάσχεση νηολογημένου πλοίου, εκτός αν ορίζεται άλλως στον παρόντα Κώδικα.
2. Οι διατάξεις περί κατασχέσεως ακινήτων του ν.δ. της 17-7/13.8.1923 «περί ειδικών διατάξεων επί ανωνύμων εταιρειών» (Α' 228) δεν εφαρμόζονται στα πλοία.

Άρθρο 275
Αναγκαστική κατάσχεση επί πλοίων

1. Αναγκαστική κατάσχεση πλοίου δεν επιβάλλεται πριν παρέλθουν είκοσι τέσσερις (24) ώρες από την επίδοση της επιταγής προς εκτέλεση.

PART ELEVEN
PREVENTIVE AND COMPULSORY ARREST

Article 272
Provisions applicable to preventive arrest

The 1952 Brussels International Convention for the unification of certain rules relating to arrest of sea-going ships, ratified by Legislative Decree 4570/1966 (Government Gazette, Series I, 224) and the Code of Civil Procedure shall, as appropriate, apply to the preventive arrest of ships.

Article 273
Bad-faith immobilisation of ships

1. Any person who, acting in bad faith, filed an application causing the immobilisation or detention of a ship following a court-issued interim order which subsequently ceased to have effect pursuant to a court judgment, shall be liable to pay compensation.

2. Compensation shall only include the costs incurred by the ship in order to lift the interim measure and the freight that would have been earned in the normal course of events during the immobilisation period.

3. The Greek courts shall have concurrent jurisdiction to try compensation disputes arising due to immobilisation or detention of a ship flying the Greek flag, following an interim measure issued in Greece or abroad. This jurisdiction may not be precluded in an agreement entered into between the parties.

Article 274
Provisions applicable to compulsory arrest

1. Unless otherwise provided for in this Code, the provisions of the Code of Civil Procedure on the attachment of immovables shall also apply to the arrest of registered ships.

2. The provisions on the attachment of immovables contained in the Legislative Decree of 17 July/13 August 1923 on special provisions regarding sociétés anonymes (Government Gazette, Series I, Issue 228) shall not apply to ships.

Article 275
Compulsory arrest of ships

1. Compulsory arrest of a ship shall not be ordered before 24 hours have elapsed from the order for enforcement being served.

2. Η επιταγή μπορεί να επιδοθεί προς τον πλοίαρχο αν η απαίτηση είναι σχετική προς την εκμετάλλευση του πλοίου ή είναι προνομιούχος ή ενυπόθηκη.

3. Αν το πλοίο βρίσκεται υπό την εκμετάλλευση τρίτου, η εκτέλεση ενεργείται κατά του οφειλέτη, αλλά η επιταγή προς εκτέλεση επιδίδεται, με ποινή την ακυρότητα της εκτέλεσης, και προς τον τρίτο ή προς τον πλοίαρχο.

4. Αν στην επιταγή προς εκτέλεση προσδιορίζεται συγκεκριμένο πλοίο, η επίδοση αυτής εμποδίζει τον απόπλου του πλοίου και ο λιμενάρχης, μόλις του επιδοθεί το αντίγραφο της επιταγής, οφείλει να εμποδίσει τον απόπλου. Η κωλυσιπλοΐα μπορεί να αίρεται μετά από έγγραφη συμφωνία δανειστή και οφειλέτη, που επιδίδεται στον λιμενάρχη. Η απαγόρευση απόπλου αίρεται αυτοδίκαια αν δεν επιβληθεί από τον επισπεύδοντα δανειστή αναγκαστική κατάσχεση του πλοίου και δεν επιδοθεί στον λιμενάρχη έως την παρέλευση του πέμπτου (5ου) εικοσιτετραώρου από την επίδοση της επιταγής.

Άρθρο 276

Απαγόρευση διάθεσης ή επιβάρυνσης κατασχεθέντος πλοίου

1. Η διάθεση πλοίου που έγινε μετά την εγγραφή αναγκαστικής κατάσχεσης στο νηολόγιο είναι άκυρη υπέρ εκείνου που επέβαλε την κατάσχεση και υπέρ των δανειστών που αναγγέλθηκαν. Αν πρόκειται για ενυπόθηκο πλοίο είναι άκυρη η διάθεσή του και από τον τρίτο, κύριο ή νομέα. Τα ίδια ισχύουν υπέρ αυτού που επέβαλε συντηρητική κατάσχεση.

2. Αν πριν από την επιβολή κατάσχεσης το πλοίο τελούσε σε ναύλωση κατά το άρθρο 107 από τον οφειλέτη ή τον τρίτο κύριο ή νομέα, ο υπερθεματιστής μπορεί να καταγγείλει τη σύμβαση μέσα σε προθεσμία δεκαπέντε (15) ημερών από την εγγραφή του τίτλου στο νηολόγιο.

3. Το ίδιο ισχύει και για κάθε άλλη έννομη σχέση, δυνάμει της οποίας τρίτος έχει χρήση ή κατοχή στο πλειστηριασθέν πλοίο.

4. Αν ναύλωση γυμνού πλοίου ή άλλη έννομη σχέση συναφθούν μετά την επιβολή κατάσχεσης, ο υπερθεματιστής ασκεί τα δικαιώματα του Κώδικα Πολιτικής Δικονομίας.

Άρθρο 277

Περισσότερες αναγκαστικές κατασχέσεις

1. Υφιστάμενη κατάσχεση πλοίου ή ναυπηγούμενου πλοίου, εφόσον τούτο έχει νηολογηθεί, δεν εμποδίζει την επιβολή άλλης κατάσχεσης.

2. Σε περισσότερες αναγκαστικές κατασχέσεις κάθε ένας από αυτούς που επέβαλαν κατάσχεση εξακολουθεί τις πράξεις της εκτέλεσης μέχρι το πέρας του πλειστηριασμού. Με την κατακύρωση ακυρώνονται αυτοδίκαια όλες οι λοιπές κατασχέσεις, τα δε έξοδα αυτών βαρύνουν αυτούς που επέβαλαν κατάσχεση. Εάν συμπέσουν πλείονες πλειστηριασμοί την ίδια ημέρα, ενεργείται εκείνος που επισπεύδεται με την παλαιότερη κατάσχεση.

3. Αν κατά την ίδια ημέρα έγινε εγγραφή κατάσχεσης και μεταβολής κυριότητας προτιμάται η κατάσχεση.

2. The order may be served on the master if the claim concerns the operation of the ship or is secured by lien or mortgage.

3. Where the ship is being operated by a third party, enforcement shall be done against the debtor, but the order for enforcement must, on penalty of nullity of enforcement, also be served on the third party or on the master.

4. If the order for enforcement names a specific ship, service of the order shall result in the ship being detained and, upon being served a copy of the order, the harbour master must detain the ship. Detention may be lifted following an agreement entered into in writing between the creditor and debtor and served on the harbour master. The detention shall be automatically lifted if it is not imposed by the creditor expediting compulsory arrest of the ship and [the order for enforcement] is not served on the harbour master by the elapse of the fifth 24-hour period from the date the order was served.

Article 276

Prohibition of disposition or encumbrance of an arrested ship

1. Disposition of a ship effected after the entry of its compulsory arrest in the ship registry shall be null and void in relation to the person who obtained an arrest order and creditors who lodged claims. In cases of a mortgaged ship, disposition of the ship by a third party, whether its owner or possessor, shall also be null and void. This shall also apply vis-à-vis the person who obtained a preventive arrest order.

2. If, prior to being arrested, the ship had been chartered in accordance with Article 107 by the debtor or the third-party owner or possessor, the highest bidder may terminate the contract within a deadline of 15 days from the date the title was entered in the ship registry.

3. This shall also apply to all other legal relationships pursuant to which a third party enjoys use or detentorship of the auctioned ship.

4. If a bareboat charter or other legal relationship is entered into after the ship was arrested, the highest bidder may exercise the rights provided for in the Code of Civil Procedure.

Article 277

Several compulsory arrest orders

1. The existence of an arrest order concerning a ship or ship under construction, provided it has been registered, shall not hinder a further arrest order being issued.

2. Where several compulsory arrest orders have been issued, each person who obtained an arrest order shall continue the enforcement steps until the auction has ended. Once the ship has been awarded at auction, all other arrest orders shall be automatically annulled and their costs shall be borne by the persons who obtained them. If several auctions coincide on the same day, [only] the auction initiated by means of the earliest arrest order shall be held.

3. If an arrest is registered on the same day as a transfer of ownership, the arrest shall take precedence.

Άρθρο 278
Αναγκαστική κατάσχεση ελληνικού πλοίου στην αλλοδαπή

1. Για την καταχώριση στο νηολόγιο κατακυρωτικής έκθεσης ή ισοδύναμου προς αυτή τίτλου μετά από πλειστηριασμό στην αλλοδαπή πλοίου με ελληνική σημαία, υποβάλλονται από τον αποκτώντα ή τον κύριο στην αρμόδια λιμενική αρχή τα παρακάτω έγγραφα:

(α) αλλοδαπός τίτλος εκτέλεσης (δικαστική απόφαση ή πράξη αρμοδίου οργάνου εκτέλεσης, σύμφωνα με το δίκαιο του τόπου εκτέλεσης),

(β) βεβαίωση αρμόδιου οργάνου (αλλοδαπής προξενικής αρχής ή ασκούντος δικηγορικό λειτούργημα στον τόπο εκτέλεσης) ότι σύμφωνα με το δίκαιο του τόπου εκτέλεσης ολοκληρώθηκε η διαδικασία του πλειστηριασμού, ότι δεν είναι προσβλητή με ένδικα μέσα και ότι ο υπερθεματιστής απέκτησε το πλοίο ελεύθερο βαρών,

(γ) δημόσιο έγγραφο ότι κατατέθηκε ή συμψηφίστηκε ολικά ή μερικά το εκπλειστηρίασμα.

2. Η καταχώριση στο νηολόγιο του αναφερομένου στην παρ. 1 αλλοδαπού τίτλου επιφέρει τα ίδια έννομα αποτελέσματα με την καταχώριση περίληψης κατακυρωτικής έκθεσης πλειστηριασθέντος στην ημεδαπή ελληνικού πλοίου.

Άρθρο 279
Δικαστική κατακύρωση πλοίου

1. Μετά την επιβολή αναγκαστικής κατάσχεσης στο πλοίο και πριν διεξαχθεί ο πλειστηριασμός ενώπιον του συμβολαιογράφου, ο επισπεύδων, και σε περίπτωση πλειόνων κατασχέσεων οποιοσδήποτε από αυτούς, δύναται να προσφύγει στο μονομελές πρωτοδικείο του τόπου εκτέλεσης ή αυτό του Πειραιά (ναυτικό τμήμα) κατά τη διαδικασία των ασφαλιστικών μέτρων και να ζητήσει την κατακύρωση του πλοίου σε τρίτο.

2. Η διαδικασία ενεργοποιείται με αίτηση του επισπεύδοντος, η οποία επί ποινή απαραδέκτου, περιλαμβάνει τα εξής:

α. αναφορά όλων των αναγκαστικών κατασχέσεων που έχουν επιβληθεί επί του πλοίου και τυχόν υποθηκών που έχουν εγγραφεί επ' αυτού,

β. τον λόγο κατακύρωσης σε τρίτο, ο οποίος στηρίζεται σε ένα ή περισσότερα από τα παρακάτω περιστατικά:

βα. το κατασχεμένο πλοίο εκ της ακινησίας απαξιώνεται με ταχύτατο ρυθμό,

ββ. οι απαιτήσεις του πληρώματος θα ικανοποιηθούν ταχύτερα και αποτελεσματικότερα με την άμεση κατακύρωση,

βγ. άμεσος κίνδυνος ρύπανσης εκ της ακινησίας του πλοίου σε συνδυασμό με το σημείο ελλιμενισμού, το οποίο πρέπει να αποδοθεί ελεύθερο για την εύρυθμη λειτουργία του λιμένα,

βδ. επίτευξη βέλτιστου τιμήματος,

βε. οποιοδήποτε άλλο γεγονός που μπορεί να ενισχύσει την κρίση του δικαστηρίου για το επωφελές της κατακύρωσης.

3. Στην αίτηση επισυνάπτονται υποχρεωτικά:

α. έκθεση από τουλάχιστον δύο (2) εκτιμητές πλοίων διεθνούς κύρους περί της τρέχουσας τιμής εξαγοράς του υπό πλειστηριασμό πλοίου κατά την επίμαχη διαδικασία, ένας (1) τουλάχιστον εκ των οποίων θα καταθέσει υποχρεωτικά ως μάρτυρας κατά την ακροαματική διαδικασία,

β. βεβαίωση από τον συμβολαιογράφο του πλειστηριασμού ότι για το προσφερόμενο από τον τρίτο τίμημα, το οποίο δεν δύναται να υπολείπεται της τιμής πρώτης προσφοράς του επισπευδόμενου πλειστηριασμού, έχει κατατεθεί ισόποση τραπεζική εγγυητική επιστολή σε αυτόν.

Article 278

Compulsory arrest of a Greek ship abroad

1. In order to register an award report or title equivalent thereto in the ship registry after a ship flying the Greek flag has been auctioned abroad, the acquirer or owner shall submit the following documents to the competent port authority:

(a) a foreign enforcement title (court judgment or decision issued by a competent enforcement body, in accordance with the legislation in force at the place of enforcement);

(b) confirmation by a competent body (foreign consular authority or practising attorney at the place of enforcement) that the auction process was completed in accordance with the legislation in force at the place of enforcement, that the process is not subject to legal remedies, and that the highest bidder acquired the ship free of encumbrances;

(c) a public document indicating that the auction price was deposited or offset in whole or in part.

2. Entry of a foreign title in the ship registry in accordance with paragraph 1 shall generate the same legal effects as entry of an award report summary concerning a Greek ship auctioned in Greece.

Article 279

Court-ordered award of a ship

1. After a ship has been placed under compulsory arrest and before the auction is held [by] a notary public, the person seeking enforcement, or any such person where several arrest orders have been issued, may seek recourse to the single-member court of first instance of the place of enforcement or the Piraeus Single-Member Court of First Instance (Maritime [Disputes] Chamber) under interim measures proceedings and request that the ship be awarded to a third party.

2. The procedure shall be initiated by an application filed by the party seeking enforcement which, on penalty of inadmissibility, must contain the following:

a. reference to all compulsory arrest orders issued concerning the ship and any mortgages registered on the ship;

b. the grounds for awarding the ship to a third party, based on one or more of the following:

ba. the arrested ship is rapidly depreciating in value due to its immobilisation;

bb. immediate award of the ship will lead to the claims of the crew being satisfied more quickly and effectively;

bc. immediate danger of pollution due to the ship being immobilised, in conjunction with its berth, which must be vacated in order for the port to operate properly;

bd. achievement of an optimal price; [or]

be. any other fact which could reinforce the court's view that awarding the ship is beneficial.

3. The following must necessarily be attached to the application:

a. a report by at least two internationally reputable ship valuers on the current acquisition price of the ship being auctioned under the procedure in question, of whom at least one must necessarily testify as a witness during the hearing;

b. an attestation prepared by the notary public holding the auction that the third party has deposited a bank-issued letter of guarantee equal in amount to the price offered by said third party, which may not be less than the starting price of the auction being held.

4. Στη διαδικασία κλητεύεται και παρίσταται υποχρεωτικά ο τρίτος, ο οποίος δηλώνει τη βούληση εξαγοράς του κατασχεθέντος πλοίου κατά τους όρους που θα ορίσει το δικαστήριο και με το τίμημα που αναφέρεται στην αίτηση. Επίσης, κλητεύονται οι λοιποί επισπεύδοντες, ο οφειλέτης και οι ενυπόθηκοι δανειστές.

5. Το δικαστήριο αποφαίνεται επί της βασιμότητας της αίτησης εντός πέντε (5) εργάσιμων ημερών και, εφόσον πεισθεί περί αυτής, κατακυρώνει το πλοίο στον τρίτο και διατάσσει την κατάπτωση της εγγυητικής επιστολής, το ποσό της οποίας αποτελεί το πλειστηρίασμα. Απόφαση που αναστέλλει την επίσπευση της διαδικασίας της αναγκαστικής εκτέλεσης εκτιμάται ελεύθερα από το δικαστήριο. Κατά τα λοιπά, εφαρμόζονται οι διατάξεις του Κώδικα Πολιτικής Δικονομίας για την αναγγελία των απαιτήσεων και την κατάταξη αυτών.

6. Η δικαστική απόφαση που διατάζει την κατακύρωση υπόκειται σε έφεση εντός προθεσμίας τριών (3) ημερών από τη δημοσίευσή της. Αν η προθεσμία παρέλθει άπρακτη, η απόφαση που δέχθηκε την αίτηση μαζί με το πιστοποιητικό μη άσκησης ένδικου μέσου υποβάλλονται προς εγγραφή χωρίς υπαίτια βραδύτητα στο νηολόγιο. Επίσης επιδίδονται στον συμβολαιογράφο του πλειστηριασμού. Μετά την εγγραφή το πλοίο είναι ελεύθερο παντός βάρους.

7. Η άσκηση έφεσης και η προθεσμία αυτής έχουν ανασταλτικό αποτέλεσμα. Η συζήτηση της έφεσης ορίζεται εντός πέντε (5) εργάσιμων ημερών από την κατάθεση αυτής, εκδικάζεται κατά την ίδια διαδικασία και εκδίδεται απόφαση εντός πέντε (5) εργάσιμων ημερών. Η απόφαση του δευτεροβάθμιου δικαστηρίου που επικυρώνει την πρωτόδικη, περί κατακύρωσης, απόφαση ή μετά την εξαφάνιση αυτής, δέχεται την αίτηση, εγγράφεται χωρίς υπαίτια βραδύτητα στο νηολόγιο και επιδίδεται στον συμβολαιογράφο. Σε κάθε άλλη περίπτωση η εκδοθείσα απόφαση επιδίδεται στον συμβολαιογράφο, οπότε εξακολουθεί η διαδικασία της αναγκαστικής εκτέλεσης.

8. Με βάση τη δικαστική απόφαση μπορεί να γίνει κατά το άρθρο 943 του Κώδικα Πολιτικής Δικονομίας αναγκαστική εκτέλεση υπέρ του τρίτου, στον οποίο κατακυρώθηκε το πλοίο, και των διαδόχων του και εναντίον εκείνου κατά του οποίου έγινε η εκτέλεση και των διαδόχων του, εφόσον η διαδοχή επέλθει μετά την εγγραφή της κατάσχεσης στο βιβλίο κατασχέσεων του νηολογίου, καθώς και κατά εκείνου που νέμεται ή κατέχει το πράγμα στο όνομα εκείνου κατά του οποίου έγινε η εκτέλεση ή των διαδόχων του, ανεξαρτήτως του αν πρόκειται για σχέση εμπράγματη ή ενοχική. Το άρθρο 947 του Κώδικα Πολιτικής Δικονομίας εφαρμόζεται και εδώ.

9. Με τη δικαστική κατακύρωση ακυρώνονται αυτοδίκαια όλες οι λοιπές κατασχέσεις, τα δε έξοδα αυτών βαρύνουν αυτούς που επέβαλαν κατάσχεση.

4. The third party must necessarily be summonsed to and appear at the proceedings and declare their intention to purchase the arrested ship under the conditions laid down by the court and for the price indicated in the application. The other expediting parties, the debtor and the mortgagees shall also be summonsed.

5. The court shall rule on whether the application is well-founded within five working days and, if convinced, shall award the ship to the third party and order forfeiture of the letter of guarantee, the amount of which constitutes the auction price. Any judgment staying compulsory enforcement shall be weighed up by the court at its unfettered discretion. In all other respects, the provisions of the Code of Civil Procedure on the lodgement and ranking of claims shall apply.

6. The court judgment ordering award [of the ship] shall be subject to appeal, which must be filed within a deadline of three days from the date the judgment is handed down. If the deadline lapses without the relevant steps having been taken, the judgment accepting the application and the certificate that no legal remedies have been filed shall be submitted for entry in the ship registry without undue delay. The foregoing shall also be served on the notary public holding the auction. After the entry has been made, the ship shall be free of all encumbrances.

7. The deadline for filing an appeal and the act of filing an appeal shall have a suspensive effect. The hearing [date] of the appeal shall be set within five working days from the date it is filed, the appeal shall be adjudicated under the same procedure and a judgment shall be handed down within five working days. A second-instance judgment which upholds the first-instance judgment on awarding the ship or which quashes the first-instance judgment and accepts the application shall be entered in the ship registry without undue delay and served on the notary public. In all other cases, the judgment handed down shall be served on the notary public, in which case the compulsory enforcement procedure shall continue.

8. This judgment may serve as a basis for effecting compulsory enforcement under Article 943 of the Code of Civil Procedure for the benefit of the person to whom the ship was awarded and his or her successors and to the detriment of the person against whom enforcement took place and his or her successors, provided succession occurred after the arrest was registered in the arrest register of the ship registry, as well as to the detriment of the person with possession or detentorship of the thing in the name of the person against whom enforcement took place or his or her successors, regardless of whether it concerns an *in rem* or a contractual relationship. Article 947 of the Code of Civil Procedure shall also apply in this case.

9. Once the ship has been awarded by the court, all other arrest orders shall be automatically annulled and their costs shall be borne by the persons who obtained them.

ΜΕΡΟΣ ΔΩΔΕΚΑΤΟ
ΠΑΡΑΓΡΑΦΕΣ

Άρθρο 280
Εφαρμοζόμενες διατάξεις

Με την επιφύλαξη της εφαρμογής διατάξεων υπερνομοθετικής ισχύος, η παραγραφή αξιώσεων που προβλέπονται στον παρόντα διέπεται από το παρόν Μέρος.

Άρθρο 281
Ενιαύσια παραγραφή

Σε ετήσια παραγραφή υπόκεινται:

***1.** Οι αξιώσεις του πλοιάρχου και του πληρώματος για την πληρωμή των μισθών και λοιπών παροχών που πηγάζουν από τη σύμβαση ναυτολόγησης.*

***2.** Οι αξιώσεις του πλοιοκτήτη ή του εφοπλιστή κατά του πλοιάρχου ή του πληρώματος με αιτία τις αδικοπραξίες που τέλεσαν κατά την εκτέλεση της υπηρεσίας τους.*

***3.** Οι αξιώσεις που αιτία έχουν:*

(α) τη χορήγηση υλικών ή τροφίμων και εν γένει τον εφοδιασμό του πλοίου, καθώς και τις δαπάνες πλοιάρχου ή μέλους του πληρώματος για λογαριασμό του πλοίου,

(β) τη διαχείριση πλοίου,

(γ) τη σχέση εφοπλισμού και την ευθύνη του κυρίου του πλοίου,

(δ) τη σύμβαση πρακτορείας πλοίου και φορτίου,

(ε) τη σύμβαση μεταφοράς πραγμάτων,

(στ) τη σύμβαση ναύλωσης, εκτός από τη ναύλωση του πλοίου προς τον σκοπό θαλάσσιας περιήγησης προσώπων σύμφωνα με το άρθρο 164,

(ζ) την κοινή αβαρία.

***4.** Οι αξιώσεις αναγωγής του υπόχρεου προς καταβολή στη μεταφορά πραγμάτων, στη μεταφορά επιβατών, στη σύγκρουση και στην επιθαλάσσια αρωγή.*

Άρθρο 282
Διετής παραγραφή

Σε διετή παραγραφή υπόκεινται οι αξιώσεις με αιτία:

(α) Τη συμπλοιοκτησία.

(β) Τη θαλάσσια ασφάλιση.

(γ) Την επιχείρηση επιθαλάσσιας αρωγής.

(δ) Τη σύγκρουση πλοίων.

(ε) Τη σύμβαση μεταφοράς επιβατών, συμπεριλαμβανομένης και της ναύλωσης του πλοίου προς τον σκοπό θαλάσσιας περιήγησης προσώπων σύμφωνα με το άρθρο 164.

(στ) Τη ναυπήγηση, την επισκευή ή τον εξοπλισμό του πλοίου.

PART TWELVE
TIME-BARRING

Article 280
Applicable provisions

Without prejudice to the application of provisions with superior legal effect, the time-barring of the claims provided for in this Code is governed by this Part.

Article 281
One-year time-barring

The following shall become time-barred after one year:

1. Claims of the master and the crew for payment of wages and other benefits under the employment agreement.

2. Claims of the owner-operator or the operator against the master or the crew for tort committed in the performance of their duties.

3. Claims arising from:

(a) the supply of materials or food and the stocking of the ship in general, as well as the costs incurred by the master or a crew member on behalf of the ship;

(b) management of the ship;

(c) the operation relationship and the liability of the owner of the ship;

(d) the ship and cargo agency contract;

(e) the contract for the carriage of goods;

(f) the charter contract, save chartering of the ship for the purpose of providing cruises to persons in accordance with Article 164; [or]

(g) general average.

4. Actions for recourse by the person liable for payment in cases of carriage of goods, carriage of passengers, collision and salvage.

Article 282
Two-year time-barring

Claims arising from the following shall become time-barred after two years:

(a) joint ship ownership;

(b) marine insurance;

(c) salvage operations;

(d) collision of ships;

(e) the contract of carriage of passengers, including chartering of the ship for the purpose of providing cruises to persons in accordance with Article 164; [or]

(f) construction, repair or fitting-out of the ship.

Άρθρο 283

Απόσβεση δικαιώματος αποζημίωσης από ρύπανση από πετρέλαιο

1. Το δικαίωμα αποζημίωσης κατά του πλοιοκτήτη από ρύπανση από πετρέλαιο, όπως οι όροι αυτοί ορίζονται στη Διεθνή Σύμβαση ευθύνης για ρύπανση από πετρέλαιο και στη Διεθνή Σύμβαση ευθύνης για το πετρέλαιο κίνησης, αποσβέννυται τρία (3) έτη από την ημερομηνία κατά την οποία επήλθε η ζημία σύμφωνα με το άρθρο 8 της Διεθνούς Σύμβασης ευθύνης για ρύπανση από πετρέλαιο και της Διεθνούς Σύμβασης ευθύνης για το πετρέλαιο κίνησης αντίστοιχα. Σε καμιά περίπτωση δεν μπορεί να ασκηθεί αγωγή μετά την παρέλευση έξι (6) ετών από την ημερομηνία που έλαβε χώρα το συμβάν που προκάλεσε τη ζημία. Αν το συμβάν αποτελείται από περισσότερα περιστατικά, η περίοδος των έξι (6) ετών ξεκινά από την ημερομηνία του πρώτου περιστατικού.

2. Το δικαίωμα αποζημίωσης κατά του Διεθνούς Κεφαλαίου, σύμφωνα με τη Διεθνή Σύμβαση Διεθνούς Κεφαλαίου, αποσβέννυται σύμφωνα με τα άρθρα 6 και 7 αυτής. Σε καμιά περίπτωση δεν μπορεί να ασκηθεί αγωγή κατά του Διεθνούς Κεφαλαίου μετά την παρέλευση έξι (6) ετών από την ημερομηνία που έλαβε χώρα το συμβάν που προκάλεσε τη ζημία.

3. Το δικαίωμα αποζημίωσης κατά του Συμπληρωματικού Κεφαλαίου σύμφωνα με το «Πρωτόκολλο του 2003 της Διεθνούς Σύμβασης του 1992 για την ίδρυση Διεθνούς Κεφαλαίου αποζημίωσης ζημιών ρύπανσης από πετρέλαιο», όπως κυρώθηκε με το άρθρο πρώτο του ν. 3482/2006 (Α' 163) αποσβέννυται σύμφωνα με το άρθρο 6 αυτού.

Άρθρο 284

Έναρξη της παραγραφής

1. Αν δεν ορίζεται διαφορετικά στον παρόντα, η παραγραφή των αξιώσεων των άρθρων 281 και 282 αρχίζει μόλις λήξει το έτος, μέσα στο οποίο συμπίπτει η έναρξή της σύμφωνα με τα άρθρα 251 και 252 του Αστικού Κώδικα.

2. Στη χρονοναύλωση, η παραγραφή αρχίζει την επομένη της ημέρας επαναπαράδοσης του πλοίου ή λύσης της σύμβασης. Στη ναύλωση κατά ταξίδι αρχίζει την επόμενη ημέρα από την ολοκλήρωση της εκφόρτωσης ή της λύσης της σύμβασης.

3. Στη σύμβαση μεταφοράς πραγμάτων η παραγραφή αρχίζει από την παράδοση των πραγμάτων ή από την ημερομηνία που θα έπρεπε να είχαν παραδοθεί. Κατά τα λοιπά ισχύουν οι παρ. 6 και 6β του άρθρου 3 των Κανόνων Χάγης-Βίσμπυ, όπως εκάστοτε ισχύουν στην Ελλάδα.

4. Στην επιθαλάσσια αρωγή η παραγραφή αρχίζει από την ημέρα της περάτωσης της επιχείρησης αρωγής.

5. Στη σύγκρουση η παραγραφή αρχίζει από την επέλευση της σύγκρουσης.

6. Στη σύμβαση μεταφοράς επιβάτη, η έναρξη της παραγραφής των αξιώσεων σε περίπτωση σωματικής βλάβης, σε περίπτωση θανάτου που συνέβη κατά τη διάρκεια της μεταφοράς και σε περίπτωση απώλειας ή φθοράς αποσκευών, ρυθμίζεται στο άρθρο 16 της Διεθνούς Σύμβασης Αθηνών. Η παρούσα εφαρμόζεται και επί ναύλωσης του πλοίου σύμφωνα με το άρθρο 164 του παρόντος.

7. Στην κοινή αβαρία η παραγραφή αρχίζει από την κατάθεση του διακανονισμού για την κοινή αβαρία.

8. Στις αξιώσεις αναγωγής της παρ. 4 του άρθρου 281 η παραγραφή αρχίζει από την επομένη της καταβολής.

Article 283

Extinction of the right to compensation for oil pollution damage

1. The right of compensation against the owner-operator for oil pollution damage, as [the relevant requirements] are laid down in the International Convention on Liability for Oil Pollution Damage and the International Convention on Liability for Bunker Oil Pollution Damage, shall be extinguished three years from the date on which the damage occurred, in accordance with Article VIII of the International Convention on Liability for Oil Pollution Damage and the International Convention on Liability for Bunker Oil Pollution Damage, respectively. Under no circumstances shall an action be brought after six years have elapsed from the date of the incident which caused the damage. Where the incident consists of a series of occurrences, the six-year period shall run from the date of the first such occurrence.

2. The right of compensation against the International Fund, in accordance with the International Fund Convention, shall be extinguished in accordance with Articles 6 and 7 of that Convention. Under no circumstances shall an action be brought against the International Fund after six years have elapsed from the date of the incident which caused the damage.

3. The right of compensation against the Supplementary Fund, in accordance with the 2003 Protocol to the 1992 International Convention on the Establishment of an International Fund for Compensation for Oil Pollution Damage, ratified by the first Article of Law 3482/2006 (Government Gazette, Series I, Issue 163), shall be extinguished in accordance with Article 6 of that Protocol.

Article 284

Commencement of time-barring period

1. Unless otherwise provided for in this Code, the time-barring period for the claims referred to in Articles 281 and 282 shall commence at the end of the year during which it would have commenced in accordance with Articles 251 and 252 of the Civil Code.

2. In cases of time charter, the time-barring period shall commence on the day following the date of re-delivery of the ship or dissolution of the agreement. In cases of voyage charter, the time-barring period shall commence on the day following the date of completion of discharge or dissolution of the agreement.

3. In cases of contracts for the carriage of goods, the time-barring period shall commence from the date the goods were or ought to have been delivered. In all other respects, Article III(6) and (6 bis) of the Hague-Visby Rules, as in force in Greece from time to time, shall apply.

4. In cases of salvage, the time-barring period shall commence on the day on which the salvage operations are terminated.

5. In cases of collision, the time-barring period shall commence from occurrence of the collision.

6. In cases of contracts for carriage of passengers, the time-barring period for claims in cases of personal injury, death occurring during the carriage and loss of or damage to luggage is regulated by Article 16 of the Athens Convention. This paragraph shall also apply to the chartering of ships in accordance with Article 164 of this Code.

7. In cases of general average, the time-barring period shall commence upon the filing of the general average adjustment.

8. In cases of actions for recourse under Article 281(4), the time-barring period shall commence on the day following the date of payment.

Άρθρο 285
Διακοπή και αναστολή της παραγραφής

1. Αν δεν ορίζεται διαφορετικά στο παρόν, για τη διακοπή και την αναστολή της παραγραφής εφαρμόζονται οι σχετικές διατάξεις του Αστικού Κώδικα.

2. Με την επιφύλαξη του άρθρου 286, στη σύμβαση μεταφοράς επιβάτη και στη ναύλωση του πλοίου σύμφωνα με το άρθρο 164, δεν επιτρέπεται η άσκηση αγωγής μετά τη λήξη οποιουδήποτε από τα εξής χρονικά διαστήματα:

α) πέντε (5) ετών από την ημερομηνία αποβίβασης του επιβάτη ή από την ημερομηνία κατά την οποία θα έπρεπε να έχει λάβει χώρα η αποβίβαση, ανάλογα με το ποια από τις δύο ημερομηνίες είναι μεταγενέστερη ή, εφόσον το διάστημα της περ. β) εκπνέει νωρίτερα,

β) τριών (3) ετών από την ημερομηνία κατά την οποία ο ενάγων έλαβε γνώση ή όφειλε ευλόγως να έχει λάβει γνώση της σωματικής βλάβης, απώλειας ή φθοράς που προκλήθηκε από το συμβάν.

3. Η έγερση της αγωγής κατά του ασφαλιστή λόγω εγκατάλειψης διακόπτει την παραγραφή και της κατ' αυτού αξίωσης λόγω ζημιών.

Άρθρο 286
Παράταση του χρόνου παραγραφής

Με την επιφύλαξη της εφαρμογής διατάξεων υπερνομοθετικής ισχύος, μετά την έναρξη και πριν τη συμπλήρωση της, η παραγραφή των αξιώσεων των άρθρων 281 και 282 μπορεί να παραταθεί είτε με έγγραφη συμφωνία των μερών είτε με μονομερή δήλωση του οφειλέτη.

Άρθρο 287
Βάση αξιώσεων

Ο χρόνος παραγραφής των αξιώσεων σύμφωνα με τα άρθρα 281 και 282 ισχύει είτε η βάση της αξίωσης είναι συμβατική είτε εξωσυμβατική. Αν η πράξη ή παράλειψη του οφειλέτη συνιστά συνάμα κολάσιμη πράξη που κατά τον ποινικό νόμο υπόκειται σε μακρότερη παραγραφή, αυτή ισχύει και για την αξίωση αποζημίωσης.

Article 285

Interruption and suspension of the time-barring period

1. Unless otherwise provided for in this Code, the relevant provisions of the Civil Code on the interruption and suspension of the time-barring period shall apply.

2. Without prejudice to Article 286, in cases of contracts for the carriage of passengers and ship charter contracts under Article 164, it shall not be permitted to file an action after any of the following periods have elapsed:

a) a period of five years beginning on the date the passenger disembarked or ought to have disembarked, whichever is later, or, if the period provided for in point (b) elapses earlier;

b) a period of three years beginning on the date when the plaintiff knew or ought reasonably to have known of the personal injury, loss or damage caused by the incident.

3. Filing an action against the insurer due to abandonment shall also interrupt the time-barring period for claims against the insurer in respect of losses.

Article 286

Extension of the time-barring period

Without prejudice to the application of provisions with superior legal effect, the time-barring period for the claims referred to in Articles 281 and 282 may, after it has commenced and before it has ended, be extended either by an agreement entered into by the parties in writing or by a unilateral declaration of the debtor.

Article 287

Basis of claims

The time-barring period for the claims referred to in Articles 281 and 282 shall apply whether the basis of the claim is contractual or extra-contractual. If the act or omission of the debtor also constitutes a punishable act which, under criminal law, is subject to a longer time-barring period, that period shall also apply to the claim for compensation.

ΜΕΡΟΣ ΔΕΚΑΤΟ ΤΡΙΤΟ
ΕΞΟΥΣΙΟΔΟΤΙΚΕΣ - ΤΕΛΙΚΕΣ - ΜΕΤΑΒΑΤΙΚΕΣ - ΚΑΤΑΡΓΟΥΜΕΝΕΣ ΔΙΑΤΑΞΕΙΣ

Άρθρο 288
Εξουσιοδοτικές διατάξεις

1. *Με κοινή απόφαση των Υπουργών Ψηφιακής Διακυβέρνησης και Ναυτιλίας και Νησιωτικής Πολιτικής καθορίζονται και τίθενται σε εφαρμογή η τήρηση των βιβλίων, οι πράξεις ή εγγραφές σε αυτά, η υποβολή στην τηρούσα το νηολόγιο και τα λοιπά βιβλία Αρχή εγγράφων κάθε φύσεως, η χορήγηση κάθε είδους πιστοποιητικών, βεβαιώσεων ή άλλων έγγραφων, καθώς και η έκδοση του εγγράφου εθνικότητας με ηλεκτρονικά μέσα, όπως αναφέρονται στα άρθρα 3, 4, 5, 6, 7 και 9, και ορίζονται οι ειδικότερες προϋποθέσεις που πρέπει να πληρούνται, ο τρόπος με τον οποίο γίνεται και αποδεικνύεται η ψηφιακή τήρηση των βιβλίων και οι καταχωριζόμενες σε αυτά πράξεις, η υποβολή εγγράφων και η χορήγηση πιστοποιητικών, βεβαιώσεων ή άλλων έγγραφων με ηλεκτρονικά μέσα, καθώς και κάθε αναγκαία λεπτομέρεια.*

2. *Με κοινή απόφαση των Υπουργών Δικαιοσύνης, Ψηφιακής Διακυβέρνησης και Ναυτιλίας και Νησιωτικής Πολιτικής τίθεται σε εφαρμογή η τήρηση ηλεκτρονικού αρχείου, που προβλέπεται στο άρθρο 10, και ορίζονται οι ειδικότερες προϋποθέσεις που πρέπει να πληρούνται, καθώς και η συγκρότηση, οργάνωση και ασφαλής λειτουργία των απαιτούμενων βάσεων δεδομένων και των αναγκαίων δικτύων επικοινωνίας.*

3. *Με κοινή απόφαση των Υπουργών Ψηφιακής Διακυβέρνησης και Ναυτιλίας και Νησιωτικής Πολιτικής καθορίζονται ειδικότερα:*

α) η διαδικασία για την έκδοση της ηλεκτρονικής φορτωτικής και τη μεταβίβαση αυτής σε νέο κομιστή,

β) οι όροι διασφάλισης της αυθεντικότητας και ακεραιότητας του αρχείου,

γ) τα μέσα απόδειξης της παράδοσης του αρχείου στον κομιστή και της ιδιότητας του τελευταίου και

δ) η διαδικασία επαλήθευσης της έναρξης και παύσης ισχύος του ηλεκτρονικού αρχείου και τυχόν αντικατάστασής του με έγγραφο,

ε) ο τρόπος επιστροφής της ηλεκτρονικής φορτωτικής στον μεταφορέα, σε περίπτωση παράδοσης του φορτίου στον κομιστή και

στ) κάθε άλλη αναγκαία λεπτομέρεια.

Με όμοια απόφαση καθορίζονται περαιτέρω τα υπό α) έως στ) στοιχεία αναφορικά με την ηλεκτρονική διαφορτωτική και τη φορτωτική συνδυασμένης μεταφοράς και τα σχετικά με την ηλεκτρονική έκδοση και διαχείριση δελτίου θαλάσσιας μεταφοράς.

PART THIRTEEN
AUTHORISING/FINAL/TRANSITIONAL/REPEALED PROVISIONS

Article 288
Authorising provisions

1. A joint decision issued by the Minister of Digital Governance and the Minister of Maritime Affairs and Insular Policy shall specify and implement [details concerning] keeping registers, preparing acts or making entries in such registers, submitting any and all documents to the authority responsible for keeping the ship registry and other registers, issuing any and all certificates, attestations or other documents, as well as issuing certificates of nationality using electronic means, as provided for in Articles 3, 4, 5, 6, 7 and 9, and shall lay down [the following:] the specific requirements which must be met [for the foregoing]; the manner in which registers are digitally kept and acts are digitally entered in such registers and proven; the manner in which documents are submitted and certificates, attestations or other documents are issued using electronic means; as well as all other necessary details.

2. A joint decision issued by the Minister of Justice, the Minister of Digital Governance and the Minister of Maritime Affairs and Insular Policy shall roll out the keeping of electronic files, as provided for in Article 10, and lay down the specific requirements which must be met, as well as the establishment, organisation and secure operation of the necessary databases and communication networks.

3. A joint decision issued by the Minister of Digital Governance and the Minister of Maritime Affairs and Insular Policy shall specifically lay down:

a) the procedure for issuing an electronic bill of lading and transferring it to a new bearer;

b) the conditions for ensuring the authenticity and integrity of the files;

c) the means of proving delivery of the file to the bearer and the capacity of the latter;

d) the procedure for verifying the validity start and end dates for electronic files and any replacement of such files by hard-copy files;

e) the manner of returning the electronic bill of lading to the carrier, in cases of delivery of the cargo to the bearer; and

f) all other necessary details.

A similar decision shall further specify details concerning points (a) to (f) with regard to electronic through bills of lading and multimodal transport bills of lading and information concerning the electronic issuance and handling of sea waybills.

4. Με κοινή απόφαση των Υπουργών Ψηφιακής Διακυβέρνησης και Ναυτιλίας και Νησιωτικής Πολιτικής καθορίζεται και τίθεται σε εφαρμογή η τήρηση του ναυτολογίου του πλοίου, οι πράξεις ή εγγραφές σε αυτό, όπως αναφέρονται στην παρ. 3 και 4 του άρθρου 166, και ορίζονται οι ειδικότερες προϋποθέσεις που πρέπει να πληρούνται, ο τρόπος με τον οποίο γίνεται και αποδεικνύεται η ψηφιακή τήρηση του ναυτολογίου του πλοίου και οι καταχωριζόμενες σε αυτό πράξεις και εγγραφές με ηλεκτρονικά μέσα, καθώς και κάθε άλλη αναγκαία λεπτομέρεια.

5. Με απόφαση του Υπουργού Ναυτιλίας και Νησιωτικής Πολιτικής δύνανται να τροποποιούνται οι κατηγορίες πλοίων καθαρής χωρητικότητας κάτω των δέκα (10) κόρων που νηολογούνται κατ' εξαίρεση σύμφωνα με την παρ. 5 του άρθρου 3 και καθορίζεται κάθε αναγκαία λεπτομέρεια.

Άρθρο 289
Τελικές διατάξεις για τον χαρακτηρισμό κινητών πραγμάτων στο πλαίσιο συμβάσεων χρηματοδοτικής μίσθωσης - Τροποποίηση παρ. 3 άρθρου 1 ν. 1665/1986

Στην παρ. 3 του άρθρου 1 του ν. 1665/1986 (Α' 194), περί χαρακτηρισμού κινητών πραγμάτων, στο πλαίσιο συμβάσεων χρηματοδοτικής μίσθωσης, αφαιρείται η εξαίρεση πλοίων και πλωτών ναυπηγημάτων, και η παρ. 3 διαμορφώνεται ως εξής:

«**3.** Στην έννοια των κινητών πραγμάτων της παρ. 1 περιλαμβάνονται τα αεροσκάφη, καθώς και τα ιδιωτικά ή επαγγελματικά πλοία αναψυχής, όπως κάθε φορά αυτά ορίζονται από τις κείμενες διατάξεις, ενώ στην έννοια των ακινήτων πραγμάτων συμπεριλαμβάνονται οι αγροτικές εκτάσεις, οι οριζόντιες και κάθετες ιδιοκτησίες με κτίσματα μετά του ποσοστού του γηπέδου που αναλογεί στα συγκεκριμένα κτίσματα σε σχέση με τη δομήσιμη επιφάνεια του γηπέδου και γενικά τα κτίσματα ή το συγκρότημα κτισμάτων μετά των λοιπών εγκαταστάσεων, συμπεριλαμβανομένου του γηπέδου που αναλογεί στα συγκεκριμένα κτίσματα, σε συνάρτηση με το εμβαδόν του και τη συνολική δομήσιμη επιφάνεια που μπορεί να πραγματοποιηθεί στο γήπεδο και επιπλέον ο ακάλυπτος χώρος που προβλέπεται από τις πολεοδομικές διατάξεις ως χώρος στάθμευσης αυτοκινήτων. Επιτρέπεται η χρηματοδοτική μίσθωση ιδιωτικών και επαγγελματικών πλοίων αναψυχής. Με κοινή απόφαση των Υπουργών Οικονομικών, Ανάπτυξης και Ανταγωνιστικότητας και Ναυτιλίας και Αιγαίου καθορίζονται οι ειδικοί όροι που ρυθμίζουν τη χρηματοδοτική μίσθωση ως προς τα ιδιωτικά και επαγγελματικά πλοία αναψυχής.».

Άρθρο 290
Μεταβατική διάταξη - Περιορισμός ευθύνης για επικίνδυνες και επιβλαβείς ουσίες

Το άρθρο 71, η παρ. 4 του άρθρου 222 και η παρ. 3 του άρθρου 249 τίθενται σε εφαρμογή με τη θέση σε ισχύ και κύρωση της Διεθνούς Σύμβασης Ευθύνης για επικίνδυνες και επιβλαβείς ουσίες.

Άρθρο 291
Μεταβατική διάταξη εφαρμογής άρθρου 4

1. Το άρθρο 4 εφαρμόζεται στις καταχωρίσεις που γίνονται στο ειδικό δημόσιο βιβλίο μετά από την έναρξη ισχύος του, σύμφωνα με την παρ. 2 του άρθρου 306.

2. Τα ενέχυρα που συστήθηκαν σε πλοία του άρθρου 4 ή σε στατικά ναυπηγήματα δεν θίγονται από τον παρόντα.

4. A joint decision issued by the Minister of Digital Governance and the Minister of Maritime Affairs and Insular Policy shall provide for and roll out the keeping of the ship's articles, acts or entries made in the ship's articles, as provided for in Article 166(3) and (4), and lay down [the following:] the specific requirements which must be met; the manner in which the ship's articles are digitally kept and acts are entries are made in the ship's articles using electronic means and are proven; as well as all other necessary details.
5. A decision issued by the Minister of Maritime Affairs and Insular Policy may amend the categories of ships with a net tonnage under 10 tons registered by way of exception in accordance with Article 3(5) and lay down all necessary details.

Article 289

Final provisions on the characterisation of movables in the context of financial leases - Amendment to Article 1(3) of Law 1665/1986

In Article 1(3) of Law 1665/1986 (Government Gazette, Series I, Issue 194) concerning the characterisation of movables in the context of financial leases, the exception of ships and floating craft is removed, and paragraph 3 shall be reformulated as follows:
"3. The concept of movables referred to in paragraph 1 shall include aircraft, as well as private or professional pleasure craft, as defined from time to time in the applicable provisions, while the concept of immovables shall include agricultural land tracts, horizontal and vertical properties with structures thereon, together with the percentage of the lot corresponding to the structures in question in relation to the buildable surface area of the lot and, generally, the structures or complex of structures together with other facilities, including the lot corresponding to the structures in question in relation to the lot area and the total surface area of the lot on which structures may be built and, additionally, the open space provided for in urban planning provisions as a car parking area. The financial leasing of private and professional pleasure craft is permitted. A joint decision of the Minister of Finance, Development and Competitiveness and the Minister of Shipping and the Aegean shall lay down the specific conditions regulating financial leasing in respect of private and professional pleasure craft."

Article 290

Transitional provisions - Limitation of liability for hazardous and noxious substances

Articles 71, 222(4) and 249(3) shall apply when the International Convention on Liability for Damage in Connection with the Carriage of Hazardous and Noxious Substances is ratified and enters into force.

Article 291

Transitional provisions concerning the application of Article 4

1. Article 4 shall apply to entries made in the special public register after the Article enters into force, in accordance with Article 306(2).
2. This Code is without prejudice to pledges established on the ships referred to in Article 4 or stationary floating structures.

Άρθρο 292

Καταργούμενες διατάξεις

Από την έναρξη ισχύος του παρόντος καταργούνται:

(α) Ο ν. 3816/1958 (Α' 32), περί κυρώσεως Κώδικος Ιδιωτικού Ναυτικού Δικαίου.

(β) Το ν.δ. 3899/1958 (Α' 195), περί προτιμώμενης υποθήκης επί πλοίων.

(γ) Ο ν. 762/1978 (Α' 45), περί σύναψης σύμβασης εργασίας με ναυτικούς στην Ελλάδα.

(δ) Το π.δ. 666/1982 (Α' 138), σχετικά με την ίδρυση, διαχείριση και κατανομή του Κεφαλαίου Περιορισμού της Αστικής Ευθύνης του Πλοιοκτήτη για ζημίες ρύπανσης από πετρέλαιο.

(ε) Το π.δ. 98/1990 (Α' 46) για τη διαδικασία εκδίκασης διεθνών διαφορών πετρελαιορύπανσης.

(στ) Η περ. α'της παρ. 6 του άρθρου 77 του ν. 1892/1990 (Α' 101), περί ρύθμισης των ουσιαστικών προϋποθέσεων και την έκταση του περιορισμού της ευθύνης και οφειλής του πλοιοκτήτη.

(ζ) Η παρ. 2 του άρθρου 16 του ν. 4504/2017 (Α' 184) περί τροποποιήσεων των ορίων αστικής ευθύνης που προβλέπονται στο άρθρο 6 της Διεθνούς Σύμβασης για τον περιορισμό της ευθύνης για ναυτικές απαιτήσεις.

(η) Η παρ. 3 του άρθρου 3 του ν. 2844/2000 (Α' 220), περί ενεχύρου χωρίς παράδοση και δημοσιότητας συμβάσεων παροχής ασφάλειας επί κινητών.

Άρθρο 293

Έναρξη ισχύος

1. Η ισχύς του παρόντος αρχίζει από την 1η Μαΐου 2023, με την επιφύλαξη της παρ. 2.

2. Τα άρθρα 4 έως 9 τίθενται σε ισχύ την 1η Νοεμβρίου 2023.

ΜΕΡΟΣ ΔΕΚΑΤΟ ΤΕΤΑΡΤΟ

(Οι διατάξεις των άρθρων 294 έως 308 [Μέρος Δέκατο Τέταρτο] αφορούν μη συναφή ζητήματα και δεν έχουν μεταφραστεί)

ΜΕΡΟΣ ΔΕΚΑΤΟ ΠΕΜΠΤΟ

ΕΝΑΡΞΗ ΙΣΧΥΟΣ

Άρθρο 309

Έναρξη ισχύος

Με την επιφύλαξη του άρθρου 293, η ισχύς του παρόντος αρχίζει από τη δημοσίευσή του στην Εφημερίδα της Κυβερνήσεως.

Παραγγέλλομε τη δημοσίευση του παρόντος στην Εφημερίδα της Κυβερνήσεως και την εκτέλεσή του ως νόμου του Κράτους.

Article 292
Repealed provisions

Upon entry of this Code into force, the following shall be repealed:

(a) Law 3816/1958 (Government Gazette, Series I, Issue 32) ratifying the Code of Private Maritime Law;

(b) Legislative Decree 3899/1958 (Government Gazette, Series I, Issue 195) on preferred mortgages on ships;

(c) Law 762/1978 (Government Gazette, Series I, Issue 45) on the signing of employment contracts with seafarers in Greece;

(d) Presidential Decree 666/1982 (Government Gazette, Series I, Issue 138) on the establishment, management and distribution of the Owner-Operator Civil Liability Limitation Fund for oil pollution damage;

(e) Presidential Decree 98/1990 (Government Gazette, Series I, Issue 46) on the procedure for the adjudication of international oil pollution disputes;

(f) Article 77(6)(a) of Law 1892/1990 (Government Gazette, Series I, Issue 101) regulating the substantive conditions and extent of limitation of the liability and debt of owner-operators;

(g) Article 16(2) of Law 4504/2017 (Government Gazette, Series I, Issue 184) amending the limits of civil liability provided for in Article 6 of the International Convention on Limitation of Liability for Maritime Claims; [and]

(h) Article 3(3) of Law 2844/2000 (Government Gazette, Series I, Issue 220) on pledges without delivery [of the movable] and the disclosure of agreements for the provision of security concerning movables.

Article 293
Entry into force

1. Without prejudice to paragraph 2, this Code shall enter into force on 1 May 2023.

2. Articles 4 to 9 shall enter into force on 1 November 2023.

PART FOURTEEN

(Part Fourteen, consisting of Articles 294 to 308, concerns matters unrelated to the core provisions of the Code of Private Maritime Law, and has been omitted from this translation)

PART FIFTEEN
ENTRY INTO FORCE

Article 309
Entry into force

Without prejudice to Article 293, this Law shall enter into force from its publication in the Government Gazette.

This Law shall be published in the Government Gazette and enforced as a law of the State.

Greek to English Glossary

EL	EN	Notes
Αδικαιολόγητος πλουτισμός	Unjust enrichment	
Αερόστρωμνο όχημα	Air-cushion vehicle	
Αλλαγή σημαίας	Transfer of flag	
Αλληλασφαλιστικός φορέας	Mutual insurer	
Άμεσος δόλος	*Dolus directus*	
Αναγκαστική εκτέλεση	Compulsory enforcement	
Αναγκαστική κατάσχεση	Compulsory arrest	
Ανάλογη εφαρμογή	Application mutatis mutandis	
Αναμονή	Laytime	
Αναξιοπλοΐα	Unseaworthiness	
Αναχώρηση	Departure	
Ανέλκυση	Removal	
Αντίκλητος	Process agent	
Αξιοπλοΐα	Seaworthiness	
Απαγόρευση απόπλου	Detention	
Απλή ναυτική υποθήκη	Simple mortgage	
Αποβίβαση	Disembarkation	
Αποθήκευση	Storage	
Αποκτών	Transferee	
Απονατολόγηση	Leaving service	
Αποποίηση	Repudiation	
Αποσκευές	Luggage	
Αριθμός νηολογίου	Ship registry number	
Ασφάλισμα	Indemnity	
Ασφαλιστήριο	Insurance policy	
Ασφαλιστική ζημία	Claim	
Ασφαλιστική περίπτωση	Contingency	
Ασφάλιστρο	Insurance premium	
Άτακτη καταγγελία	Termination without notice	
Βαθμός	Rank	
Βιβλίο κατασχέσεων	Arrest register	
Δελτίο θαλάσσιας μεταφοράς	Sea waybill	
Διάθεση	Disposition	
Διακανονιστής αβαριών	Average adjuster	

Διακοπή	Interruption
Διαφορτωτική	Through bill of lading
Διαχειριστής (πλοιοκτησίας)	Manager
Διεθνές διακριτικό σήμα	International call sign
Διεθνή ύδατα	International waters
Διεθνής Ναυτιλιακός Οργανισμός (ΔΝΟ)	International Maritime Organisation (IMO)
Διεκδικητική αγωγή	Revendication action
Δικαίωμα αναγωγής	Right of recourse
Δικαστική απόφαση	Court judgment
Δικαστική μεσεγγύηση	Judicial sequestration
Έγγραφο εθνικότητας	Certificate of nationality
Εγκιβωτίωση	Containerisation
Εθνικότητα	Nationality
Ειδικότητα (ναυτικού)	Capacity
Ειδοποίηση ετοιμότητας	Notice of readiness
Εισηγητής	Reporting judge
Εκκαθαριστής	Liquidator
Εκτόπισμα	Displacement
Εκφόρτωση	Unloading
Ελάττωμα	Defect
Εμπορεύματα	Merchandise
Εμπορευματοκιβώτιο	Container
Ενδεχόμενος δόλος	*Dolus eventualis*
Ένταλμα	Payment order
Ενυπόθηκος δανειστής	Mortgagee
Εξάλειψη (υποθήκης)	Extinction
Επαναεριοποίηση	Regasification
Επιβίβαση	Embarkation
Επιθαλάσσια αρωγή	Salvage
Επικαρπία	Usufruct
Επικαρπωτής	Usufructuary
Επίταξη	Requisition
Επιχείρηση επιθαλάσσιας αρωγής	Salvage operation
Εφόδια (πλοίου)	Stores
Εφοπλισμός	Ship operation

Εφοπλιστής	Operator	
Ηλεκτρονική φορτωτική	Electronic bill of lading	
Θαλάσσια ασφάλιση	Marine insurance	
Θαλάσσια μεταφορά	Carriage by sea	
Θαλάσσιες ενδομεταφορές	Maritime cabotage	
Θαλάσσιος κίνδυνος	Marine risk / Peril of the sea	See introduction
Θαλάσσιος μεταφορέας	Carrier by sea	
Καθαρή χωρητικότητα	Net tonnage	
Κεφάλαιο περιορισμού	Limitation fund	
Κοινή αβαρία	General average	
Κοινή ναυτική αποστολή	Common maritime adventure	
Κόρος	Ton	
Κύριος	Owner	
Κυριότητα	Ownership	
Κύτος	Hull	
Κώδικας Ιδιωτικού Ναυτικού Δικαίου	Code of Private Maritime Law	
Λήπτης	Consignee	
Λιμένας εκφόρτωσης	Port of discharge	
Λιμένας νηολόγησης	Port of registry	
Λιμένας προορισμού	Port of destination	
Λιμένας φόρτωσης	Port of loading	
Λιμενική αρχή	Port authority	
Μεσεγγύηση	Detention	
Μεταβιβάζων	Transferor	
Μετανηολόγηση	Transfer of register	
Μετασκευή	Retrofitting	
Μεταφορά στο κατάστρωμα	On-deck carriage	
Μεταφορέας	Carrier	
Μεταφόρτωση	Transhipment	
Μη εκούσια παράδοση	Forced handover	
Μη εμφανές ελάττωμα	Latent defect	
Μη τακτική γραμμή	Tramp service	
Μονάδα υπολογισμού	Unit of account	
Ναυάγιο	Shipwreck	
Ναύλος	Freight	
Ναυλοσύμφωνο	Charter-party	

Ναύλωση	Chartering
Ναύλωση γυμνού πλοίου	Bareboat charter
Ναύλωση κατά χρόνο	Time charter
Ναύλωση-πλαίσιο	Contract of affreightment
Ναυλωτής	Charterer
Ναυπηγείο	Shipyard
Ναυπηγός	Shipbuilder
Ναυπηγούμενο	Ship under construction
Ναυσιπλοΐα	Navigation
Ναυτικό πταίσμα	Nautical fault
Ναυτικός	Seafarer
Ναυτικός πράκτορας	Shipping agent
Ναυτιλιακή εταιρεία	Shipping company
Ναυτολόγηση	Recruitment
Ναυτολόγιο	Ship's articles
Νηολόγηση	Registration
Νηολόγιο	Registry
Ολική χωρητικότητα	Gross tonnage
Ομηρία	Hostage-taking
Ονομαστική φορτωτική	Registered bill of lading
Οπισθογράφηση	Endorsement
Οφειλέτης	Debtor
Παλιννόστηση	Repatriation
Παραγγελιοδόχος θαλάσσιας μεταφοράς	Maritime freight forwarder
Παράρτημα	Accessory
Παροπλισμός	Laying-up
Πεδίο εφαρμογής	Scope
Πιστοποιητικό διαγραφής	Deregistration certificate
Πιστοποιητικό καταμέτρησης	Tonnage certificate
Πιστωτικό ίδρυμα	Credit institution
Πλήρωμα	Crew
Πλοήγηση	Pilotage
Πλοηγός	Pilot
Πλοίαρχος	Master
Πλοίο	Ship
Πλοίο αναψυχής	Pleasure craft

Πλοιοκτήτης	Owner-operator
Πλους	Voyage
Πλους υπό έρμα	Ballast voyage
Πλωτή κατασκευή	Floating construction
Πλωτό ναυπήγημα	Floating craft
Πραγματικός μεταφορέας	Actual carrier
Πρακτορεία	Agency
Πράξη νηολόγησης	Registration decision
Προκυμαία	Quay
Προνομιούχες απαιτήσεις	Preferential claims
Προσύμφωνο ναυτολόγησης	Preliminary employment agreement
Πρόσωπο που παρέχει υπηρεσίες θαλάσσιας αρωγής	Salvor
Προτιμώμενη ναυτική υποθήκη	Preferred mortgage
Προτιμώμενος ενυπόθηκος δανειστής	Preferred mortgagee
Πτώχευση	Bankruptcy
Ρυμούλκηση	Towage
Ρύπανση του θαλάσσιου περιβάλλοντος	Pollution of the marine environment
Στάση	Riot
Στατικό ναυπήγημα	Stationary floating structure
Στοιβασία	Stowage
Σύγκρουση	Collision
Σύμβαση μεταφοράς	Contract of carriage
Σύμβαση ναύλωσης	Charter contract
Σύμβαση ναυπήγησης	Shipbuilding contract
Σύμβαση ναυτολόγησης	Employment agreement
Σύμβαση όγκου	Volume contract
Σύμβαση παραγγελίας	Commission contract
Συμβατικός μεταφορέας	Contracting carrier
Συμβολαιογράφος	Notary public
Συμπλοιοκτησία	Joint ship ownership
Συμπλοιοκτήτης	Joint shipowner
Συντηρητικά μέτρα	Preventive measures
Συντηρητική κατάσχεση	Preventive arrest
Συστατικό	Constituent part
Τακτική γραμμή	Liner service

Τελεσίδικη απόφαση (δικαστηρίου)	*De jure* non-appealable court judgment
Τίτλος κτήσης κυριότητας	Document of title
Τράπεζα της Ελλάδας	Bank of Greece
Υδρογονάνθρακες	Hydrocarbons
Υπεραναμονή	Demurrage
Υποθηκολόγιο	Mortgage register
Υποναύλος	Sub-freight
Υποναύλωση	Sub-chartering
Υποναυλωτής	Sub-charterer
Υπουργείο Ναυτιλίας και Νησιωτικής Πολιτικής	Ministry of Maritime Affairs and Insular Policy
Φορτηγίδα	Lighter
Φόρτωση	Loading
Φορτωτής	Shipper
Φορτωτική	Bill of lading
Φορτωτική ναυλοσυμφώνου	Charter-party bill of lading
Φορτωτική παραλαβής	Received for shipment bill of lading
Φορτωτική σε διαταγή	To order bill of lading
Φορτωτική στον κομιστή	Bearer bill of lading
Φορτωτική συνδυασμένης μεταφοράς	Multimodal transport bill of lading
Φορτωτική φόρτωσης	Shipped bill of lading
Φυσικό αέριο	Natural gas
Χωρητικότητα	Tonnage
Χωρικά ύδατα	Territorial waters

English to Greek Glossary

EN	EL	Notes
Accessory	*Παράρτημα*	
Actual carrier	*Πραγματικός μεταφορέας*	
Agency	*Πρακτορεία*	
Air-cushion vehicle	*Αερόστρωμνο όχημα*	
Application *mutatis mutandis*	*Ανάλογη εφαρμογή*	
Arrest register	*Βιβλίο κατασχέσεων*	
Average adjuster	*Διακανονιστής αβαριών*	
Ballast voyage	*Πλους υπό έρμα*	
Bank of Greece	*Τράπεζα της Ελλάδας*	
Bankruptcy	*Πτώχευση*	
Bareboat charter	*Ναύλωση γυμνού πλοίου*	
Bearer bill of lading	*Φορτωτική στον κομιστή*	
Bill of exchange	*Συναλλαγματική*	
Bill of lading	*Φορτωτική*	
Capacity	*Ειδικότητα (ναυτικού)*	
Carriage by sea	*Θαλάσσια μεταφορά*	
Carrier	*Μεταφορέας*	
Carrier by sea	*Θαλάσσιος μεταφορέας*	
Certificate of nationality	*Έγγραφο εθνικότητας*	
Charter contract	*Σύμβαση ναύλωσης*	
Charterer	*Ναυλωτής*	
Chartering	*Ναύλωση*	
Charter-party	*Ναυλοσύμφωνο*	
Charter-party bill of lading	*Φορτωτική ναυλοσυμφώνου*	
Claim	*Ασφαλιστική ζημία*	
Code of Private Maritime Law	*Κώδικας Ιδιωτικού Ναυτικού Δικαίου*	
Collision	*Σύγκρουση*	
Commission contract	*Σύμβαση παραγγελίας*	
Common maritime adventure	*Κοινή ναυτική αποστολή*	
Compulsory arrest	*Αναγκαστική κατάσχεση*	
Compulsory enforcement	*Αναγκαστική εκτέλεση*	
Consignee	*Λήπτης*	
Constituent part	*Συστατικό*	

Container	*Εμπορευματοκιβώτιο*
Containerisation	*Εγκιβωτίωση*
Contingency	*Ασφαλιστική περίπτωση*
Contract of affreightment	*Ναύλωση-πλαίσιο*
Contract of carriage	*Σύμβαση μεταφοράς*
Contracting carrier	*Συμβατικός μεταφορέας*
Court judgment	*Δικαστική απόφαση*
Credit institution	*Πιστωτικό ίδρυμα*
Crew	*Πλήρωμα*
De jure non-appealable court judgment	*Τελεσίδικη απόφαση (δικαστηρίου)*
Debtor	*Οφειλέτης*
Defect	*Ελάττωμα*
Demurrage	*Υπεραναμονή*
Departure	*Αναχώρηση*
Deregistration certificate	*Πιστοποιητικό διαγραφής*
Detention	*Απαγόρευση απόπλου*
Detention	*Μεσεγγύηση*
Disembarkation	*Αποβίβαση*
Displacement	*Εκτόπισμα*
Disposition	*Διάθεση*
Document of title	*Τίτλος κτήσης κυριότητας*
Dolus directus	*Άμεσος δόλος*
Dolus eventualis	*Ενδεχόμενος δόλος*
Electronic bill of lading	*Ηλεκτρονική φορτωτική*
Embarkation	*Επιβίβαση*
Employment agreement	*Σύμβαση ναυτολόγησης*
Endorsement	*Οπισθογράφηση*
Extinction	*Εξάλειψη (υποθήκης)*
Floating construction	*Πλωτή κατασκευή*
Floating craft	*Πλωτό ναυπήγημα*
Forced handover	*Μη εκούσια παράδοση*
Freight	*Ναύλος*
General average	*Κοινή αβαρία*

Gross tonnage	*Ολική χωρητικότητα*
Hostage-taking	*Ομηρία*
Hull	*Κύτος*
Hydrocarbons	*Υδρογονάνθρακες*
Indemnity	*Ασφάλισμα*
Insurance policy	*Ασφαλιστήριο*
Insurance premium	*Ασφάλιστρο*
International call sign	*Διεθνές διακριτικό σήμα*
International Maritime Organisation (IMO)	*Διεθνής Ναυτιλιακός Οργανισμός (ΔΝΟ)*
International waters	*Διεθνή ύδατα*
Interruption	*Διακοπή*
Joint ship ownership	*Συμπλοιοκτησία*
Joint shipowner	*Συμπλοιοκτήτης*
Judicial sequestration	*Δικαστική μεσεγγύηση*
Latent defect	*Μη εμφανές ελάττωμα*
Laying-up	*Παροπλισμός*
Laytime	*Αναμονή*
Leaving service	*Απoναυτολόγηση*
Lighter	*Φορτηγίδα*
Limitation fund	*Κεφάλαιο περιορισμού*
Liner service	*Τακτική γραμμή*
Liquidator	*Εκκαθαριστής*
Loading	*Φόρτωση*
Luggage	*Αποσκευές*
Manager	*Διαχειριστής (πλοιοκτησίας)*
Marine insurance	*Θαλάσσια ασφάλιση*
Marine risk	*Θαλάσσιος κίνδυνος*
Maritime cabotage	*Θαλάσσιες ενδομεταφορές*
Maritime freight forwarder	*Παραγγελιοδόχος θαλάσσιας μεταφοράς*
Master	*Πλοίαρχος*
Merchandise	*Εμπορεύματα*
Ministry of Maritime Affairs and Insular Policy	*Υπουργείο Ναυτιλίας και Νησιωτικής Πολιτικής*
Mortgage register	*Υποθηκολόγιο*
Mortgagee	*Ενυπόθηκος δανειστής*
Multimodal transport bill of lading	*Φορτωτική συνδυασμένης μεταφοράς*

Mutual insurer	Αλληλασφαλιστικός φορέας
Nationality	Εθνικότητα
Natural gas	Φυσικό αέριο
Nautical fault	Ναυτικό πταίσμα
Navigation	Ναυσιπλοΐα
Net tonnage	Καθαρή χωρητικότητα
Notary public	Συμβολαιογράφος
Notice of readiness	Ειδοποίηση ετοιμότητας
On-deck carriage	Μεταφορά στο κατάστρωμα
Operator	Εφοπλιστής
Owner	Κύριος
Owner-operator	Πλοιοκτήτης
Ownership	Κυριότητα
Payment order	Ένταλμα
Pilot	Πλοηγός
Pilotage	Πλοήγηση
Pleasure craft	Πλοίο αναψυχής
Pollution of the marine environment	Ρύπανση του θαλάσσιου περιβάλλοντος
Port authority	Λιμενική αρχή
Port of destination	Λιμένας προορισμού
Port of discharge	Λιμένας εκφόρτωσης
Port of loading	Λιμένας φόρτωσης
Port of registry	Λιμένας νηολόγησης
Preferential claims	Προνομιούχες απαιτήσεις
Preferred mortgage	Προτιμώμενη ναυτική υποθήκη
Preferred mortgagee	Προτιμώμενος ενυπόθηκος δανειστής
Preliminary employment agreement	Προσύμφωνο ναυτολόγησης
Preventive arrest	Συντηρητική κατάσχεση
Preventive measures	Συντηρητικά μέτρα
Process agent	Αντίκλητος
Quay	Προκυμαία
Raising	Ανέλκυση
Rank	Βαθμός
Received for shipment bill of lading	Φορτωτική παραλαβής
Recruitment	Ναυτολόγηση

Regasification	*Επαναεριοποίηση*
Registered bill of lading	*Ονομαστική φορτωτική*
Registration	*Νηολόγηση*
Registration decision	*Πράξη νηολόγησης*
Registry	*Νηολόγιο*
Repatriation	*Παλιννόστηση*
Reporting judge	*Εισηγητής*
Repudiation	*Αποποίηση*
Requisition	*Επίταξη*
Retrofitting	*Μετασκευή*
Revendication action	*Διεκδικητική αγωγή*
Right of recourse	*Δικαίωμα αναγωγής*
Riot	*Στάση*
Salvage	*Επιθαλάσσια αρωγή*
Salvage operation	*Επιχείρηση επιθαλάσσιας αρωγής*
Salvor	*Πρόσωπο που παρέχει υπηρεσίες θαλάσσιας αρωγής*
Scope	*Πεδίο εφαρμογής*
Sea waybill	*Δελτίο θαλάσσιας μεταφοράς*
Seafarer	*Ναυτικός*
Seaworthiness	*Αξιοπλοΐα*
Ship	*Πλοίο*
Ship operation	*Εφοπλισμός*
Ship registry number	*Αριθμός νηολογίου*
Ship under construction	*Ναυπηγούμενο*
Shipbuilder	*Ναυπηγός*
Shipbuilding contract	*Σύμβαση ναυπήγησης*
Shipped bill of lading	*Φορτωτική φόρτωσης*
Shipper	*Φορτωτής*
Shipping agent	*Ναυτικός πράκτορας*
Shipping company	*Ναυτιλιακή εταιρεία*
Ship's articles	*Ναυτολόγιο*
Shipwreck	*Ναυάγιο*
Shipyard	*Ναυπηγείο*
Simple mortgage	*Απλή ναυτική υποθήκη*
Stationary floating structure	*Στατικό ναυπήγημα*

Storage	*Αποθήκευση*
Stores	*Εφόδια (πλοίου)*
Stowage	*Στοιβασία*
Sub-charterer	*Υποναυλωτής*
Sub-chartering	*Υποναύλωση*
Sub-freight	*Υποναύλος*
Termination without notice	*Άτακτη καταγγελία*
Territorial waters	*Χωρικά ύδατα*
Through bill of lading	*Διαφορτωτική*
Time charter	*Ναύλωση κατά χρόνο*
To order bill of lading	*Φορτωτική σε διαταγή*
Ton	*Κόρος*
Tonnage	*Χωρητικότητα*
Tonnage certificate	*Πιστοποιητικό καταμέτρησης*
Towage	*Ρυμούλκηση*
Tramp service	*Μη τακτική γραμμή*
Transfer of flag	*Αλλαγή σημαίας*
Transfer of register	*Μετανηολόγηση*
Transferee	*Αποκτών*
Transferor	*Μεταβιβάζων*
Transhipment	*Μεταφόρτωση*
Unit of account	*Μονάδα υπολογισμού*
Unjust enrichment	*Αδικαιολόγητος πλουτισμός*
Unloading	*Εκφόρτωση*
Unseaworthiness	*Αναξιοπλοΐα*
Usufruct	*Επικαρπία*
Usufructuary	*Επικαρπωτής*
Volume contract	*Σύμβαση όγκου*
Voyage	*Πλους*

www.ingramcontent.com/pod-product-compliance
Lightning Source LLC
LaVergne TN
LVHW081937200926
848484LV00009B/2450

9781838410636